Community Justice

Community Justice discusses concepts of community within the context of justice policy and programs and addresses the important relationship between the criminal justice system and the community in the USA.

Taking a bold stance in the criminal justice debate, this book argues that crime management is more effective through the use of informal (as opposed to formal) social control. It demonstrates how an increasing number of criminal justice elements are beginning to understand that developing partnerships within the community that enhance informal social control will lead to stabilization and possibly a decline in crime, especially violent crime, and make communities more livable. Borrowing from an eclectic toolbox of ideas and strategies – community organizing, environmental crime prevention, private–public partnerships, and justice initiatives – *Community Justice* puts forward a new approach to establishing safe communities and highlights the failure of the current American justice system in its lack of vision and misuse of resources.

This book is essential for undergraduate and postgraduate students of criminology, law, and sociology. It provides detailed information about how community justice fits within each area of the criminal justice system and includes relevant case studies to exemplify this philosophy in action.

John R. Hamilton, Jr. is an Associate Professor Emeritus of Criminal Justice Administration at Park University. He retired as a major from the Kansas City, Missouri, Police Department after 26½ years of service. He has extensive experience in community policing and problem-solving and volunteers with the Center for Conflict Resolution in Kansas City, Missouri.

Tamera D. Jenkins is Assistant Professor of Criminal Justice Administration at Park University. She previously worked in the Missouri Department of Corrections within the Division of Probation and Parole. She is deeply committed to advancing Restorative Justice and conflict resolution methodologies and actively engages in Peacemaking Circles and Neighborhood Accountability Boards. She also co-hosts the Park University podcast "CriminalJustUs."

Todd R. Clear is University Professor at Rutgers University in Newark, NJ, USA. He is a past president of the American Society of Criminology, the Academy of Criminal Justice Sciences, and the Association of Doctoral Programs in Criminology and Criminal Justice. He was the founding editor of the journal *Criminology & Public Policy*, published by the American Society of Criminology.

Community Justice

Third Edition

John R. Hamilton, Jr., Tamera D. Jenkins, and Todd R. Clear

NEW YORK AND LONDON

Designed cover image: zhengshun tang

Third edition published 2025
by Routledge
605 Third Avenue, New York, NY 10158

and by Routledge
4 Park Square, Milton Park, Abingdon, Oxon, OX14 4RN

Routledge is an imprint of the Taylor & Francis Group, an informa business

© 2025 John R. Hamilton, Jr., Tamera D. Jenkins, and Todd R. Clear

The right of John R. Hamilton, Jr., Tamera D. Jenkins, and Todd R. Clear to be identified as authors of this work has been asserted in accordance with sections 77 and 78 of the Copyright, Designs and Patents Act 1988.

All rights reserved. No part of this book may be reprinted or reproduced or utilised in any form or by any electronic, mechanical, or other means, now known or hereafter invented, including photocopying and recording, or in any information storage or retrieval system, without permission in writing from the publishers.

Trademark notice: Product or corporate names may be trademarks or registered trademarks and are used only for identification and explanation without intent to infringe.

First edition published by Routledge 2003
Second edition published by Routledge 2010

ISBN: 978-1-032-49436-4 (hbk)
ISBN: 978-1-032-48857-8 (pbk)
ISBN: 978-1-003-39381-8 (ebk)

DOI: 10.4324/9781003393818

Typeset in Sabon
by codeMantra

Access the Support Material: www.routledge.com/9781032488578

To Bini, Jenifer, and Jessica, your support is appreciated. Also, I thank my colleagues Greg, Eugene, Tamera, and Dianna for their encouragement and professionalism.

John R. Hamilton, Jr., Ph.D.

To Jim, Candace and Jaysen, Tony and Mariah for your love, encouragement, and support. Also to my mother Ruth who keeps telling me to write more.

Tamera D. Jenkins, Ph.D.

To the memory of Dennis Maloney, the heart of community justice.

Todd R. Clear, Ph.D.

Contents

Preface ix

1 **What Is Community Justice?** 1

  Elements of Community Justice 2
  How Does Community Justice Differ from Popular Criminal
    Justice Philosophies? 6
  Why Do Classical and Neoclassical Theories Not Seem to Be Effective? 6
  Using a Systems Approach to Identify Root Causes 8
  Elements of Systems Thinking 9
  So, What Is Community Justice? 14
  References 16

2 **Criminal Justice and the Community** 17

  Criminal Justice and Social Justice 17
  The Importance of "Place" 20
  Place-Based Strategies and Public Safety Goals 34
  Community-Oriented Strategies in Criminal Justice 34
  Evaluation of Community Justice Initiatives 38
  Community Justice Within Traditional Criminal Justice Functions 40
  Conclusion 41
  Suggested Web Sources for Readers 41
  References 41
  For Further Reading 42

3 **Policing and Community Justice** 44

  A Brief History of Community Policing 44
  Policy and the Community: A Dual-Track Rationale 45
  The Community Relations Rationale for Community Policing 46
  The Criminal Justice Rationale for Community Policing 54
  Community Policing 56
  Community Policing and Community Justice 64
  Suggested Web Sources for Readers 77

References 77
For Further Reading 79

4 The Courts and Community Justice — 81

Criminal Cases, Communities, and Courts 81
The Two Functions of Criminal Courts 82
How Courts Work Today 85
The Victims of Crime 87
The Community Court 88
Community-Oriented Court Functions 92
Courts for Specialized Communities 98
Suggested Web Sources for Readers 109
References 110
For Further Reading 111

5 Corrections and Community Justice — 113

Pillars of Traditional Correctional Services 114
Pillars of Correctional Community Justice 117
How Community Justice Changes the Traditional Correctional Functions 124
References 148
Suggested Web Sources for Readers 150

6 The Future of Community Justice — 151

The Essentials of Community Justice 151
Varieties of Community Justice 153
Four Prototypes of Community Justice Programs: The Models of Community Justice 154
Which Community Justice Model Is Best? 162
Leadership in Community Justice 162
Issues in Community Justice 165
The Future of Community Justice 169
References 171
For Further Reading 171

7 Community Justice in International Settings — 173

The Four Legal Traditions 173
Cultural Components of the Legal Traditions 175
Can Community Justice Be Effective in International Settings? 178
References 179

Appendix A: Community Justice as a Strategy: How CASES Make It Work — 181
Appendix B: Focused Deterrence — 185
Index — 187

Preface

This work is an updated version of the *Community Justice* book that was originally authored in 2003 by Todd Clear and Eric Cadora. It provides updated examples of community justice in practice and continues the belief that community justice is an effective way to build healthy, viable communities.

Community justice borrows from an eclectic toolbox of ideas and strategies: community organizing, environmental crime prevention, public–private partnerships, justice initiatives, and so forth. Each of these strategies has its own rich heritage and literature, and it is not our intention to provide a comprehensive literature review for any of them. We hope that readers will explore these topics more in depth on their own, and we have provided bibliographies at the end of each chapter that provide suggested readings to learn more about these strategies.

Recent news reports in the United States have told the stories of budgetary cutbacks in federal, state, and local government. With these cutbacks comes the realization that criminal justice agencies will suffer from a lack of funding to assist them in achieving their mission. Often times, agencies believe that they must increase staffing to meet the demands the public places upon their organizations. Community justice offers new strategies that can assist criminal justice agencies in not only achieving their mission, but also strengthening partnerships with the community that empowers them. While additional personnel are always welcome in criminal justice agencies, community justice strategies may enable these agencies to achieve more with fewer employees and better weather the effects of the economic downturn. With increased implementation of community justice practices comes more information that can assist criminal justice agencies, academics, and other stakeholders in fine-tuning and improving the delivery of services. The message of community justice is also clear about the need for the private sector and nonprofits to join the partnership to make community justice a reality. The authors believe that community justice is an exciting concept that can make criminal justice agencies more effective and efficient, but we also believe that it is the right thing to do in helping to strengthen communities hard hit by crime, poverty, and malaise. Community justice can be successful if the criminal justice system, government at all levels, the private sector, and nonprofit organizations develop partnerships to address the variety of problems that face hard-hit communities.

In this book, the reader will find examples of community justice in practice and case studies that provide more information about specific community justice efforts. In Chapter 1, the reader is introduced to the concept of community justice as well as some of the difficulties encountered by high-impact areas. Chapter 2 examines policing and community justice and how the concept is already partially in place in many police agencies. Chapter 3 provides a discussion about the role of the court system in community justice. Because of the technical nature of the court operation and the traditions that the court system is built upon, many would argue that the court system cannot be much of a player in the community justice movement. This chapter illustrates how courts have embraced this philosophy without losing their emphasis on justice being served. Chapter 4 looks at the role of the correctional system in community justice and discusses the role of community corrections in community justice. Programs in the institutional setting are also discussed, helping the reader to better understand how the entire correctional system can participate in providing community justice. Finally, Chapter 5 discusses the future of community justice and addresses some of the more common questions that are raised about the concept of community justice. At the end of selected chapters, the reader will be provided with a list of suggested readings as well as websites that more completely explain some of the concepts discussed in the chapter.

This book would not have been possible without the hard work, dedication, insight, and enthusiasm of Todd Clear, Eric Cadora, Charles Swartz, Sarah Bryer, and Joel Copperman, who authored the first version of *Community Justice* and brought forth a challenging concept for the field of community justice.

1
What Is Community Justice?

Imagine being a community education specialist at a major hospital in your city. You are asked to present to community members about strokes and their effect on a person's quality of life. You have been informed that medical personnel will attend the meeting to answer any technical medical questions that may arise during the session.

As you prepare for your presentation, you realize that this is a wonderful opportunity to share information about a new, innovative medical device the hospital has acquired that can help to reduce the debilitating effects of a stroke if treatment can begin within 30 minutes of the onset of the stroke. You can rely on the medical personnel in attendance to answer specific questions about the operation of the equipment and its success rate. While looking for additional information that might be helpful to attendees, you discover that substantial literature suggests that individuals can significantly influence stroke prevention through lifestyle changes and education about early warning signs of stroke.

At the event, you introduce the medical experts who explain in detail how the new clot-busting device can minimize the damage of the stroke if treatment begins within 30 minutes of the onset of symptoms. The doctor shares stories of success but also explains that there are times when the machine is unsuccessful. After their presentation, you return to the podium and begin discussing how many strokes can be prevented by being more attentive to diet, exercise, family history, blood pressure, and stress. You emphasize that each person has control over their health and that the medical experts prefer that people take an active role in keeping themselves healthy.

To your points about the importance of stroke prevention, you close the presentation with this comment and question:

> After this presentation, I hope you see how much of an effect you can have on your health. So, which would you prefer, watching this machine work to save your life or taking action to improve your health so you do not have to experience a stroke?

One brave participant stands and states, "I want to have a stroke to watch the machine work. It sounds like it is very effective in saving lives." One by one, everyone else in the room nods in agreement.

While this narrative may seem farfetched, consider what happens when we replace the topic of stroke treatment and prevention with that of the criminal justice system. Indeed, upon scrutinizing the operation of the criminal justice system, a similar scenario unfolds, yet its absurdity is far less easy to recognize.

DOI: 10.4324/9781003393818-1

The criminal justice system is the machine in this analogy. It's supposed to manage acute attacks of crime and disorder if applied early and often. Community members look to the machine to handle these issues and are frequently disappointed when the system has a different outcome. Community members may want, or even be encouraged to, take proactive steps to maintain public safety (i.e., Neighborhood Watch Programs). Still, sometimes, the "experts" responsible for the operation of the justice system dismiss those desires and instead emphasize the importance of letting the system run its course. It is common for the "experts" to minimize the effect of proactive efforts by the community and then pivot to seek aid from the community when emergent criminal events need to be solved.

Just like the medical machine in the story, the criminal justice system is in place to address acts that violate established laws by bringing justice to those who have been wronged and sanctions to those who are the violators. In the health care and criminal justice systems, there is no action until there has been an event and someone has been harmed. But, in both cases, potential victims can take proactive actions to lower the risk that they may be harmed, whether that harm results from a stroke or the hands of a perpetrator.

Indeed, it is understood that preventing harm entirely is not always possible. Therefore, it is essential to have formal processes in place to address any harm that has occurred. The concept of community justice emphasizes the importance of involving community members proactively. This aims to create public safety while also recognizing the importance of the criminal justice system in addressing criminal acts that might not have been preventable.

Elements of Community Justice

Community justice can be defined in many ways. Clear and Karp (1999) define community justice as "all variants of crime prevention and justice activities that explicitly include the community in their processes and set the enhancement of community life as an explicit goal" (p. 25). This definition changes the role of formal criminal justice agencies from solo actors working to address crime and disorder to partners working with communities to address quality of life issues, with crime being one of the elements that affect quality of life. While law enforcement proponents may argue that they work with communities to address quality-of-life problems, community justice emphasizes the equality of the groups as they develop actions to improve the quality of life. Furthermore, this approach broadens the scope of quality-of-life issues to include more than just criminal behavior.

In 1996, a U.S. Department of Justice Working Group developed four basic principles that laid a foundation for the development of community justice: (1) the community is the ultimate customer and the full partner of the system; (2) the primary goal is harmony among system components and the community; (3) community-based sanctions are worthy responses to the problem of crime; and (4) work efforts must focus on the underlying causes of crime rather than respond only to *criminal behavior*. These principles emphasize equitable collaboration to enhance community well-being. It is essential for the criminal justice system and communities to jointly strategize against crime and identify its underlying causes rather than solely reacting to the criminal behavior produced. The group further validated the use of community-based sanctions as viable solutions to address crime, legitimizing the use of philosophies such as restorative justice and probation in preventing future criminal behavior and rehabilitating offenders.

Much like the four fundamental principles of community justice established by the U.S. Department of Justice Working Group, Karp and Clear (2000) offer five core elements that can identify community justice. These elements include philosophies such as problem-oriented policing and community policing (Goldstein 1990; Trojanowicz & Bucerqueroux 1990) adopted by the law enforcement community in the early 1990s. The first principle is that community justice is designed to operate at the neighborhood level. For community justice, it is essential to think beyond larger territories such as states, counties, or cities and concentrate on the physical localities that define neighborhoods. Second, community justice includes problem-solving, where crime is seen as a series of problems that can be addressed to improve public safety and the quality of life in communities rather than a contest to win. Third, authority and accountability are decentralized in a community justice approach. This principle contradicts the hierarchical design of most agencies in the criminal justice system. Community justice authority and accountability *must* be decentralized so that criminal justice personnel working directly with community members are empowered to make decisions and create partnerships. Fourth, community justice goes beyond looking only at crime and prioritizes the quality of life in a community. Building the capacity of a community to become more self-governing can impact illicit behavior and create better living conditions in the neighborhood. Fifth, which may be more difficult for criminal justice agencies to accept, community justice involves citizens in the justice process. Strengthening informal social controls can effectively prevent and address illicit behavior in the neighborhoods. Criminal justice agencies provide formal social controls, which have not been as effective in controlling crime and disorderly behavior.

Nicholl (1999) expounds on the importance of informal social controls in creating law-abiding behavior. She explains that informal social controls display social disapproval and interpersonal influence through elements such as a

> frown or words of encouragement from persons you care about; close ties within a family, at work, at school, and among friends; communities that share values about responsibility, respect, and care; parents who take time to teach or play with their children; and volunteer mentors who assist those who are vulnerable in some way.
>
> (p. 14)

Nicholl argues that to establish co-production of public safety there needs to be a balance of a formal system of control with informal means of regulation and that "public safety demands a coherent, strategic plan balancing punishment (a rational choice in public alarm) with informal social controls, prevention, and problem-solving" (p. 16).

Barajas (1995) suggests that community justice involves the justice system actively working with citizens to share the goal of maintaining a peaceful community. He adds that an essential value of community justice is that universal justice and fairness are created through proactive, problem-solving practices focused on creating and maintaining safe, secure, and just communities.

In 1998, at a conference sponsored by the United States Department of Justice on "Community Justice: Transforming the System to Serve Communities," it was emphasized that the state could no longer pretend that it provided public security by itself, isolated from communities. While no attempt was made to define community justice, several key themes emerged. Those themes included community and professional *partnerships*, identifying and defining *community*, collaborative *problem-solving*, and focusing on *community safety* (Nicholl 1999, italics original). Box 1.1 lists some of the characteristics or common elements of community justice identified by Nicholl.

> **Box 1.1 Characteristics or Common Elements of Community Justice**
>
> 1. Community justice operates at a local level
> 2. The localized nature of community justice is provoking changes in the system's priorities, from focusing on the offender to thinking about public safety
> 3. Community justice is altering the role of many criminal justice practitioners and widening their focus beyond the legal response of punishment
> 4. Community justice is shifting criminal justice from a purely adversarial approach to include problem-solving methods beyond dealing with the offender
> 5. Community justice is characterized by a reduced distance between professionals and lay communities
> 6. Community justice is creating new lines of accountability
> 7. Offender accountability is moving toward accountability to the community, as distinct from paying dues to the state (e.g., fines).
> 8. Greater community engagement and partnership are emerging from community justice experiments
>
> From Nicholl, C. (1999). *Community Policing, Community Justice, and Restorative Justice: Exploring the Links for the Balance Approach to Public Safety*. Washington, D.C.: U.S. Department of Justice, Office of Community-Oriented Services.

Zehr and Mika (1998) cautioned that while community justice showed promise, there were still many characteristics similar to core elements of the criminal justice system (see Box 1.2 for a list of those characteristics). They further warned that until community justice involves the community as a meaningful partner in solving problems, progress in the implementation of community justice will be severely limited. Zehr and Mika argue that to create these meaningful partnerships, the role of professionals as sole decision-makers must be transformed into facilitators of community involvement and a resource to the community. They also emphasize the importance of informal social controls in keeping the public peace. In a bold pronouncement, they argue that no amount of police can enforce civilization where regular casual enforcement of it has broken down. In addition, they say that democracy will suffer if policing and justice continue treating the problem of crime as one requiring more, rather than less, use of a professionally run criminal justice system.

> **Box 1.2 Community Justice Characteristics That Are Similar to Core Elements of Criminal Justice**
>
> 1. Defines harms and effectiveness in the same terms, primarily in relation to the offender and what laws have been broken
> 2. Retains a conventional punishment prerogative – and, almost exclusively, a control mandate

3 Conducts overwhelmingly offender-oriented services
4 Is unable to promote an alternative vision of justice; effectiveness is measured according to traditional criteria
5 Refuses to become involved in interpersonal violence (hence, does not serve critical needs of classes of victims, such as women, minorities, poor, and youth)
6 Seeks to reduce incarceration but seldom succeeds in reducing the marginalization of offenders and victims in their own communities
7 Affects too few offenders, victims, and communities
8 Fails to address social and community problems that shape crime, i.e., may respond to crime problems but does not seek to prevent crime

From Zehr, H. & Mika, H. (1998). "Fundamental Concepts of Restorative Justice." *Contemporary Justice Review.* 1 (1).

Reprinted in Nicholl, C. (1999). *Community Policing, Community Justice, and Restorative Justice: Exploring the Links for the Balance Approach to Public Safety.* Washington, D.C.: U.S. Department of Justice, Office of Community-Oriented Services.

The previous discussion supports thinking of community justice as an umbrella under which the elements of problem-solving, community policing, restorative justice, community building, and crime prevention can be placed. Community justice emphasizes prevention as a vital part of creating public safety. Kurki (2000) opines that

> community justice is based on the idea that crime is a social problem that corrodes the quality of life in communities, and it redefines the operation of criminal justice agencies. Rather than focus solely on punishment, deterrence, or rehabilitation of individual offenders, agencies should broaden their mission to include preventing crime and solving neighborhood conflicts. Operations should be moved to local communities, and citizen involvement should be encouraged.
>
> (p. 236)

It is also essential that communities receive resources that can assist them in being more self-governing to address issues as they develop and not have to be as dependent on the criminal justice system to intercede.

Self-governance also encourages communities to seek out resources that can make them stronger and develop a voice with elected officials so their concerns can be heard. In most cases, the criminal justice system's actions are not set into motion until an offense has occurred. That means that a community member has been victimized, and the work of the criminal justice system becomes focused on apprehending the perpetrator and bringing them to justice. While restorative justice techniques have increased, in most cases, they are only implemented after an incident. However, recent research in restorative justice has facilitated a shift toward a more proactive approach in its implementation. Restorative justice practices and philosophies will be discussed in later chapters of this volume.

How Does Community Justice Differ from Popular Criminal Justice Philosophies?

From the previous discussion, it is clear that community justice differs from the traditional and popular approach of addressing criminal events. The traditional model focuses on apprehension, conviction, and incarceration as the primary methods to address criminal incidents and prevent future incidents from occurring. This approach is rooted in the theory of classical criminology and, more specifically, the work of Jeremy Bentham. Classical criminology posits that individuals have free will and are motivated by hedonism, a principle that maintains individuals work to maximize pleasure while minimizing pain. In this principle, individuals are considered rational actors who will continue maximizing pleasure until the anticipated pain outweighs the expected enjoyment or benefits (Hagen 2011; Schmalleger 2021). Classical criminological theory posits that increasing the amount of pain that might be suffered by committing a criminal act will deter the individual from choosing that path of action. Should the individual choose to chance being apprehended by continuing their illicit acts, punishment would be administered with certainty, severity, and celerity (Akers & Sellers 2012). Not only would the individual be deterred, but the consequences of their behavior could serve as an example to others that this behavior has consequences. If they acted similarly, they could expect the same consequences. This belief created the foundation for deterrence theory, a still popular approach to addressing crime in many societies. Specific deterrence refers to how actions taken against the individual will prevent her or him from reoffending, and general deterrence argues that the example of the plight of the offender can be used to convince others not to follow suit, lest they meet the same consequences.

The neoclassical school took the classical doctrine and added environmental, psychological, and other mitigating circumstances to be considered (Hagen 2011). One of the neoclassical theories proposed was the rational choice theory (Cornish & Clarke 1986). This theory posits that offenders consider criminal acts' opportunities, costs, and benefits. Rational choice theorists do not argue that offenders are purely rational in their decisions but that they do consider some costs and benefits of the actions they are considering. Neoclassical theorists support increasing the certainty and severity of punishment to make crime less rewarding, but they also recognize that crime can be a matter of situational choice (Hagen 2011). Situational crime prevention is a theory developed to increase prevention and decrease the opportunities for committing crimes. Elements of this theory include target hardening, fencing, lighting, surveillance, and locks (Clarke 1987).

It was clear that the classical and neoclassical approaches focused on the offender's actions. Except for having community members install hardware to decrease opportunities for crime, the community played little of a role in applying these theories. There also appeared to be more of a focus on property crime prevention since there was a greater likelihood that a person would be victimized by a property crime and not a violent crime. Statistically, this made sense because there were usually four to five times more property crimes than violent ones.

Why Do Classical and Neoclassical Theories Not Seem to Be Effective?

Popper (1965) discussed the topic of human rationality in a lecture entitled "Of Clocks and Clouds." He described physical systems that are highly irregular, disorderly, and unpredictable as being like clouds. On the other extreme, he used the example of a pendulum clock to represent physical systems that are regular, orderly, and highly predictable. In general, the thought is that repairing a clock-like item is not difficult because it is understood that if Part A is malfunctioning, replacing it with a new Part A will address the problem. In a "clock issue," taking specific actions will successfully address the problem, and we can move on. For example, if a light bulb burns out, we can remove the bulb and replace it with a new bulb. Cloud problems, on the other hand, are more complex, and addressing them can be complicated. Popper uses the analogy of a cluster of gnats to illustrate his point. While we can see the gnats and the clusters they form, we find it almost impossible to predict where they may go or how they may change their formation. Popper discusses that even clock problems may have some unpredictable elements and may not be as easy to solve as initially thought. Returning to our light bulb example, if we replace the bulb and the light does not come on, we may find that there may be a problem with the fixture, the wiring, or the fuse.

An in-depth analysis of Popper's discussion is beyond the scope of this book. It is, however, instructive when looking at how society has tended to look at the issue of crime. If we apply the Clocks and Clouds discussion to the Classical School, we can see that the issue of criminal behavior has been approached as a clock problem. Increase pain, decrease pleasure, and crime is eliminated. While that statement is more simplistic than the entire theory, it does guide us to understanding that in the Classical School, the approach to addressing crime seems clock-like. With the rise in violent crime in recent years, lawmakers and many members of the criminal justice system advocate for heightened penalties to discourage violent behavior, aligning with the Classical School of thought.

Popper continues his discussion to formulate his thought that humans are constantly engaged in problem-solving by trial-and-error and that responses to old and new problems are more chance-like or cloud-like, trials that are eliminated if successful. This belief does not assume humans act rationally when deciding on a course of action. Rational thinking may include a sense of right and wrong that factors into the decision, but right and wrong may have different meanings to different people. Popper tends toward a sense of survivalism that can enter the trial-and-error phase, and the ultimate decision may be affected by a sense of surviving and not knowing what is right or wrong. For example, consider the story of a man who had been laid off and had no income. He had a family and was concerned about his ability to provide for their basic needs. The man went to a local grocery store and attempted to steal food for his family but was apprehended and charged with stealing. When asked if he knew that stealing was wrong and against the law, the man responded that he was fully aware of that, but he needed to feed his family so their health did not suffer. Was the man right or wrong in his decision? Indeed, there are ethical issues involved in this example, but it also illustrates that trying to survive can often override the consideration of what may be right or wrong.

Popper's theory can lead to a clearer understanding that numerous factors can lead to the occurrence of a criminal event. If we focus solely on a single aspect of the criminal event, we might achieve a short-term impact, but achieving long-term effects is less likely. For example, suppose a police agency notes that there has been an increase in larcenies in a particular geographical area. In that case, they may increase police presence to apprehend the offenders. If they successfully apprehend the offenders, they will probably see a decrease in offenses and conclude they successfully addressed the issue. Officers will be redeployed, and the area will have less presence. After a while, the larceny problem may return, and the agency has to take action to identify and apprehend the offenders again. Eck (1993) calls this perpetrator displacement, which means that when one offender is removed, another takes her or his place. Why did the apprehension and charging of the offender not work to keep the offense from recurring? What conditions are present that encourage larcenies to occur? Why this location and not another? Who are the offenders? Do they have anything in common? Were the offenders able to bypass physical security modifications put in place to deter offenders? The list of questions can become long, and trying to answer them can become time-consuming, but asking and answering the questions can lead us to discover the root causes of the offenses. Discovering the root causes can lead to the creation of actions that may have a longer-term effect on the problem and make the area safer for residents and businesses. It is important to emphasize that this discussion is not meant to diminish the value of the criminal justice system but to ensure that the system is invoked when appropriate and not as a default for addressing all crime and disorder problems.

Using a Systems Approach to Identify Root Causes

Systems thinking can also clarify community justice and aid in finding root causes that may lead to poor public safety. Meadows (2008) describes a system as "a set of things – people, cells, molecules, or whatever – interconnected in such a way that they produce their own pattern of behavior over time" (p. 2). Systems thinking can become complex because systems can be embedded in systems, which can then be embedded in other systems (Meadows 2008). For example, a town contains a set of systems that help it operate successfully, but it combines with other towns to create counties. Each town brings its systems of operation into the county. Counties then combine to create states, and states combine to create the country. The system of each town remains in operation but becomes more deeply embedded in each larger system that is created. To avoid making the systems thinking process too complex, Meadows (2008) recommends looking for interconnections that hold the systems together. When problems are viewed through the system approach, it can reveal that the system itself can often be the source of its problems. When the elements of those problems are addressed, the system will often change its outcomes. In other words, multiple factors can affect how a larger system operates, and if the factors are addressed, the system can change.

The operation of the criminal justice system can also provide an example. The criminal justice system generally contains the elements of law enforcement, courts, corrections, and juvenile justice. Each of the four elements has its systems that contribute to the element, but all four elements contribute to the larger criminal justice system. The larger systems do not replace the individual operating systems. Still, if any of those smaller systems are not operating efficiently, the operation of the larger system will be affected. Each individual system has a relationship, or interconnectedness, with the other elements, and poor efficiency in one or more systems can affect the operations of another element. For example, suppose a law enforcement element is cracking down on criminal behavior and increasing arrests. In that case, the court system may be backlogged, and the processing of cases may be slow. That slowdown may result in more offenders remaining on the street and cause an increased workload for the law enforcement element. If members of the public observe this, they may perceive that the larger criminal justice system is inefficient and push for the system to be overhauled or "fixed." As Meadows (2008) explains, the inefficiency of the larger organization can be best addressed by examining the elements of the system and their relationships or connectedness with each other. When those factors are addressed, the larger organization can become more efficient. In the example presented, it would be necessary for the law enforcement element and the court to discuss what is occurring and develop actions that would help both operate efficiently.

Once the process of listing the elements of a system begins, Meadows (2008) says there is almost no end to the process. She recommends that instead of pursuing that approach to the extreme, it is better to start looking for the interconnections, or relationships, that hold the system together. Meadows (2008) also recommends deducing the purpose of the system by watching the system to see how it behaves. The behavior can identify the purposes, not the rhetoric or stated goals.

According to Meadows (2008), a system typically maintains its identity and changes slowly, if at all, even if all of its elements are entirely changed, as long as its interconnectedness and purposes remain intact. Meadows argues that if the interconnections change, the system may be altered, so changing interconnections in a system can change it dramatically. Changing relationships usually changes system behavior.

Elements of Systems Thinking

To understand systems thinking, it is essential to have a clear understanding of the associated terms. *Stocks* are the foundation of any system; they represent the elements of the system that you can see, feel, count, or measure at any given time. They are the "thing," so to speak. Over time, stocks can change through inflow or outflow, and understanding this dynamic of stocks and flows can create a better understanding of the operation of complex systems (Meadows 2008). In systems thinking, an example used to describe the inflow/outflow process is water in a bathtub. The stock is the amount of water in the bathtub. The inflow would be water added to the tub from the faucet, raising the stock. The outflow is the drain that removes water from the bathtub, which would decrease the stock.

Meadows (2008) explains that as long as the total of all inflows exceeds the total of all outflows, the stock level will rise; conversely, if the total of all outflows exceeds the total of all inflows, the stock level will fall. If the total of all inflows and outflows is equal, the stock level will not change and will be held in dynamic equilibrium.

In the criminal justice system, we often see this process in actions taken by law enforcement organizations. If the stock is the level of safety perceived by the community and crime increases, the perception of safety will decrease. To counter this decrease, police may increase patrols and arrests, crime may decline, and the perception of safety should rise. When officers are removed from the area, crime may likely rise, and the perception of safety will decline.

According to Meadows (2008), the human mind focuses more easily on stocks than flows. When the focus is on flows, it tends to be on inflows, not outflows. It is essential to realize that the stock level can be increased by decreasing the outflow rate and increasing the inflow rate.

Meadows (2008) explains that one often misunderstood thing is that changing the flows does not result in an immediate change. Flows take time to flow, and stocks tend to change slowly, especially if the flows are dynamic or if the stock is large. If there is a sense of stock change rates, it can become less likely that an expectation for things to happen faster than they can happen will occur. This misunderstanding can often be seen in the example discussed. Community members often expect that when police actions begin, there will be an immediate visible effect, and when that does not occur, they may become frustrated and impatient.

Meadows (2008) writes that changes in stocks set the pace of the dynamics of systems and that most institutional decisions are designed to regulate the level of stocks. She says that systems thinking involves people monitoring stocks and making decisions about actions to take to raise or lower stocks or to keep them within acceptable ranges. According to Meadows, systems thinkers see the world as a collection of stocks along with mechanisms for regulating the level of stocks by manipulating flows. So, systems thinkers see the world as a collection of "feedback processes" (Meadows 2008, p. 25).

If a stock grows swiftly, declines swiftly, or is held within a specific range no matter what is occurring around it, it usually means that there is a control mechanism at work. Meadows (2008) explains that the mechanism operates through a feedback loop and that a feedback loop is formed when changes in the stock affect the flows into or out of the stock. She defines a feedback loop as

> a closed chain of causal connections from a stock, through a set of decisions or rules or physical laws or actions that are dependent on the level of the stock, and back again through a flow to change the stock.
>
> (p. 27)

In other words, when a change in the amount of the stock is observed, it can be because there have been inflows or outflows that may have occurred. To return the level of the stocks to the established acceptable level, actions must be taken to either increase or decrease the amount of the inflows. When the stock returns to an acceptable level, it is monitored to see if additional changes may occur. If so, the process begins again.

Balancing feedback loops are goal-seeking or stability-seeking. Each loop works to keep a stock at a given value or within the accepted range of values. As Meadows (2008) explains, a balancing feedback loop opposes the direction of change imposed on the system. It can serve as a mechanism for equilibrium or goal-seeking, as a source of stability or resistance to change.

A second kind of feedback loop is amplifying, reinforcing, self-multiplying, or snowballing, according to Meadows (2008). She explains that these loops can cause healthy growth or runaway destruction. This type of loop is referred to as a reinforcing feedback loop, which enhances the direction of the change imposed on it. Meadows (2008) notes that reinforcing loops tend to be found wherever a system element can reproduce or grow as a fraction of itself. An example shared by Meadows is:

> The more prices go up, the more wages have to go up if people are to maintain their standards of living. The more wages go up, the more prices have to go up to maintain profits. This means that wages have to go up again, so prices go up again.
>
> (p. 31)

Meadows also observes that information delivered by a feedback loop can only affect future behavior because it cannot deliver the information fast enough to correct the behavior that drove the current feedback. This observation is important because it explains one of people's significant frustrations with systems. Once an action is introduced, immediate change is expected, and anger or disappointment can occur when there is no immediate change. These frustrations can be seen in many programs the criminal justice system implements to address criminal behavior. The programs are often discontinued and labeled unsuccessful when desired results are not immediately seen.

Stroh (2015) argues that conventional or linear thinking can effectively address more minor problems, but it is not well suited for complex, chronic social problems. His argument is similar to the one offered by Popper. In both arguments, there is a recognition that multiple factors can contribute to the creation of the problem that has been identified. Concentrating on one factor or element may successfully address simple problems, but it is ineffective when multiple factors are involved. Social issues, especially ones that affect the criminal justice system, are complex and do not lend themselves to a one-factor approach to ameliorating or solving the issue. For example, focusing only on the offender in a crime event may solve that specific incident. Still, it does not encourage looking at factors such as homelessness, lack of education, poverty, or family structure as possible contributors to the offender's actions. Stroh (2015) offers several other contrasts between conventional and systems thinking approaches. First, in conventional thinking, there is a connection between problems and their causes, which is apparent and easily traced, whereas in systems thinking, the relationship between problems and their causes is not direct or obvious. Second, it is believed that others, either within or outside of the organization, are to blame for the problems and must be the ones to change, while in systems thinking, it is recognized that we unknowingly create our problems and have significant control in solving them through changes in our behavior. Third, in conventional thinking, a policy designed to achieve short-term success will also ensure long-term success, while in systems thinking, most quick fixes have unintended consequences. Finally, in conventional thinking, many independent initiatives are tackled simultaneously, while in systems thinking, relationships must be improved to optimize the whole.

While the intentions of those persons addressing an identified problem may be good, Stroh observes that burdens are shifted, unexpected results surface, and other systems issues can arise from the actions taken to address the problem. He argues that for any complex problem to be solved, the individuals involved need to recognize how they unwittingly contribute to it. Once they understand their own responsibility for a problem, Stroh (2013) believes they can begin changing the part of the problem over which they have the most control, themselves. According to Stroh, systems thinking focuses on leveraging the few things that can change everything else. That, he argues, contrasts with a conventional approach that addresses many issues independently and simultaneously through attacking symptoms. Stroh cites several situations where incorporating systems thinking can be effective: (1) when a problem is chronic and has defied people's best intentions to solve it; (2) when diverse stakeholders find it difficult to align their efforts despite shared intentions; (3) when people try to optimize their part of the system without understanding its impact on the whole; (4) when stakeholders short-term efforts might actually undermine their intention to solve the problem; and, (5) when people are working on a large number of disparate initiatives at the same time (pp. 24–25). These situations can be experienced when trying to solve community issues such as violent crime.

Relationships are important in a systems process. Stroh (2015) says that to optimize the entire system's performance, people should shift from trying to optimize their part of the system to improving relationships among its constituent parts. This shift allows people to understand better how only focusing on their part of the system can limit the system as well as support it. He also cites the importance of recognizing the unintended impacts of their intentions, thoughts, and actions on others and themselves. Becoming more self-aware can help build relationships with others in the system.

Stroh (2015) sees three shifts people need to make to optimize the system. First, people need to see more of the whole system, not just their part of the system. Second, there needs to be a shift from hoping others will change to seeing how they can first change themselves. Finally, there should be a shift from focusing on individual events to understanding and redesigning the deeper system structures that cause these events. Stroh emphasizes that "one of the premises of systems thinking is that the best way to optimize the system is to improve the relationships among its parts, not to optimize each part separately" (p. 35). Community justice emphasizes the need for partnerships and relationship-building to create safer communities and requires continual dialogue between the different working groups. That dialogue is vital in creating open and honest relationships that allow inefficiencies and tensions to be identified and addressed.

Archetypes in Systems Thinking

In systems thinking, familiar patterns of behavior often repeat in diverse settings. These patterns are called archetypes and can help identify structures that drive systems. While twelve archetypes have been identified, two appear to be quite common in community justice: Fixes That Backfire and Shifting the Burden.

In Fixes That Backfire, the main story is about unintended consequences. The process begins with identifying a problem, symptom, or pressure. After the issue is identified, a solution is developed that works in the short run but does not address the root causes of the problem. After a while, the issue recurs, and the short-term fix is implemented again, often with an escalation of intensity, and once again, no root causes are researched. This process becomes a vicious cycle that becomes hard to break and, in many cases, less effective as time goes on. While this cycle is operating, unintended consequences often worsen the issue. Stroh (2015) says that some of the typical keys for overcoming Fixes That Backfire include questioning the wisdom of the quick fix, identifying possible alternate responses, or mitigating the negative consequences of the fix if no alternative can be developed.

One example of Fixes That Backfire can be seen in how municipalities address the issue of homelessness. As the number of homeless people increases, municipal governments receive complaints from constituents who feel uncomfortable around homeless persons who may beg for money or are unkempt. Litter, discarded drug paraphernalia, and "dumpster diving" also appear more prevalent, especially around encampments established by homeless people. Responses created involve criminalizing the behavior of being homeless and using law enforcement or other city entities to demolish homeless encampments. The problem seems to diminish until new encampments are established, often in new locations, and behaviors perceived as troublesome return and, in some cases, increase in intensity. Once again, city services implement actions, usually the same ones, and law enforcement officers may begin to make arrests to deter future encampments. This cycle can continue for a long time, with governmental activities intensifying each time the cycle repeats; however, the issue does not appear to be solved. In the meantime, law enforcement officers may see calls for service for homeless persons continue to increase, placing a strain on the delivery of law enforcement services to the community.

In most cases, the people arrested cannot post bond, so they tax the capacity of the city or county jails. Courts also see increased cases on the docket due to increased arrests, and their resources become strained. With jail and court capacity strained, those arrested are often released on their recognizance, putting them back on the streets with no place to go for shelter. Those released will likely not return on their assigned court date, resulting in warrants being issued. Law enforcement officers will encounter these people on the street and arrest them for warrant violations, thus starting another vicious cycle. Although not intended, the original actions to solve the issue have created at least three additional problems.

The second archetype often seen in Community Justice is "Shifting the Burden." Two balancing processes try to adjust or control the same problem in this archetype. The two processes are symptomatic solutions (short-term fixes) and fundamental solutions (long-term fixes). Senge (1990) suggests that choosing symptomatic solutions can gradually atrophy the ability to focus on fundamental solutions and further increase reliance on symptomatic solutions. He also observes that strengthening fundamental responses almost always requires an orientation that is long-term and paired with a sense of shared vision. Senge's points can be seen in communities where formal social control mechanisms have brought more symptomatic approaches to addressing crime problems while fundamental responses that address root causes have decreased. Dependence on formal mechanisms may have damaged the ability of communities to diagnose and address the issues of crime and disorder.

Senge (1990) says there are three clues to discovering if a Shifting the Burden structure may exist. First, a problem gradually worsens, although it may ebb and flow periodically; second, the system's overall health slowly worsens; and third, a growing fear of helplessness appears. In addition, he recommends looking for situations of dependency in which there is a sense that the real or more profound issues need to be addressed more effectively.

Senge also identifies four actions to identify a Shifting the Burden structure. It is essential to identify the problem symptom, which, as Senge suggests, could manifest as the attention-demanding "squeaky wheel." Next, identify a fundamental solution that would lead to a meaningful improvement. After identifying a fundamental solution, identify one or more symptomatic solutions that might improve the symptoms for a while. Finally, identify the possible side effects of implementing the symptomatic solutions.

An example of Shifting the Burden can be seen in how the criminal justice system handles violent crime. When violent crime incidents occur, the focus is usually placed on the offender who committed the crime. Apprehending and prosecuting the offender becomes the highest priority, as it should. Once the offender is arrested, the public and elected officials often push to revise or create new laws or statutes that would increase the punishment for persons who commit violent acts. Those actions tend to be based on the philosophy of classical criminology that relies heavily on the "pain-pleasure" principle. That thought is that if the pain of committing the act is greater than the pleasure or benefit, the individual will choose not to commit the act. Classical criminology also posits that the person can consider the costs/benefits of the act rationally. Law enforcement increases its focus on persons and areas where violent crime is prevalent, and new laws increase the punishment. Often, for a while, there is a decrease in violent crime, which is usually credited to the crackdown on violent offenders. When violent crimes begin to increase again, the response cycle repeats itself but is escalated with the thought that "what we did before worked, so if we do more this time, it should work again." Since the actions in most cases do not involve working to find root causes that may contribute to creating the violence, no long-term solutions are developed, and a side effect is that new violent offenders are created, and a violent subculture becomes stronger.

Differences Between Fixes That Backfire and Shifting the Burden. Stroh (2015) notes that while implementing a quick fix is present in both structures and creates similar behavior patterns, there are important differences between the two archetypes. First, in Shifting the Burden, people generally know the more fundamental solutions but need help generating the motivation and investments to implement them. In contrast, there is no clear fundamental solution to the problem symptom in Fixes That Backfire, so the quick fix is the only possible response.

The second difference lies in the effectiveness of the quick fix, which is typically the most obvious and easier of the two alternatives. This quick fix creates a temporary improvement in the system, but it weakens people's motivation to develop and implement more fundamental solutions.

Thirdly, implementing a quick fix produces unintended consequences that can undermine the ability of persons to implement fundamental solutions even if they want to do so. Stroh says that one common way the ability is reduced is that the quick fix consumes the resources that would otherwise be available to solve the problem more permanently. Those resources can include people, time, and money.

Finally, Stroh argues that people depend more and more on quick fixes over time and invest less in developing core solutions to the symptoms of the problem. He says that the growing dependence on the quick fix can be called an addiction, and even though people may know better, they become addicted to the quick fix.

Stroh opines that the keys to overcoming the tendency toward Shifting the Burden include asking questions about the quick fix, challenging assumptions that may discourage investing in the fundamental solution, and creating a long-term vision that motivates implementing fundamental solutions.

So, What Is Community Justice?

Community justice is an idea that addresses how criminal justice operations ought to be carried out in places where public safety is a significant problem, and criminal justice is a prominent aspect of daily life. These locations are called high-impact areas due to the concentrated presence of crime and corresponding criminal justice responses. Community justice offers a way of rethinking how traditional criminal justice approaches to public safety can be reformulated to help make those high-impact locations better places to live and work.

Two assumptions are inherent in the idea of community justice. First, it assumes significant variations exist between communities within established jurisdictions, such as states or large cities. These differences suggest that criminal justice strategies must be tailored to fit those differences. The same criminal law applies to everyone living in, say, California, but criminal justice strategies, if they are to be successful, will need to take different forms in locations as divergent as the crowded and impoverished Watts section of central Los Angeles and the pristine, wealthy neighborhoods of La Jolla. The second assumption is that formal systems of social control, such as the criminal justice system, are not the main mechanisms of public safety. Instead, informal social controls – families, neighbors, social organizations, and friendship relations – form the most important foundation for public safety. Community justice, therefore, builds varying formal social control strategies depending on the local area's specific problems. One of its main aims is to strengthen the capacity of informal social control within that location.

High-impact areas are the logical targets of community justice initiatives because the formal and traditional criminal justice methods have proven inadequate in these locations. The criminal justice system identifies offenders, apprehends them, and imposes criminal sanctions on them; however, in high-impact areas, this focus on processing individual criminal cases through the justice system does not consider the cumulative impact of these individual decisions when they disproportionately concentrate in specific places. In some high-impact areas, for example, more than 10% of adult males are arrested, convicted, and incarcerated in any given year (Cadora & Swartz 2000). However, the impact of removing these active offenders is blunted by the fact that an equivalent number of males re-enter this same neighborhood each year from prisons or jails. The collective impact of all these arrests, convictions, incarcerations, and returns can be a significant destabilizing force in the neighborhood, exacerbating the effects of poverty, broken families, unsupervised youth, and unemployment. Without tackling these critical aspects of community life in high-impact areas, traditional criminal justice is little more than a debilitating revolving door. This process is explained well in the Systems Theory discussion earlier in the chapter. When factors contributing to criminal behavior are not addressed, the possibility of improving life in high-impact areas is greatly diminished.

Community justice targets high-impact areas for another reason: these areas are where the problems are and where any progress made by community justice has the most payoff. A 10% reduction in crime in a neighborhood with ten crimes a year will barely be felt, but a similar impact in a high-crime location with, say, 1,000 crimes yearly will significantly improve the community's life. This is why these areas are called high impact – the potential for impact by purposefully tailored strategies is much higher in these locations than in other areas where problems are less severe.

Thus, community justice can be thought of as a broad strategy that includes the following priorities:

1 Community justice selects high-impact locations with a concentration of crime and criminal justice activity for unique strategies designed to improve the quality of community life, especially by promoting public safety.
2 Community justice approaches its tasks in these areas by strengthening the capacity of informal systems of social control: families, neighborhood groups, friends, and social supports. This means that instead of adopting the usual reactive strategy of merely responding to criminal cases as they occur, community justice undertakes a proactive strategy designed to work in partnership with these informal social control sources to strengthen the foundation for public safety.
3 To strengthen community capacity, community justice initiatives develop partnerships with residents, businesses, and other social services to coordinate the way public safety problems are addressed.

Community justice, therefore, is both a strategy and a philosophy. As a strategy, community justice broadens the responsibility of traditional criminal justice agencies to make room for partnerships with various citizen groups and other service providers so that a more comprehensive level of activity is sustained in the high-impact areas. Strategies of community justice are directed to deal with criminal events and to address the informal social control deficits that make crime possible. As a philosophy, community justice seeks to be evaluated for how it responds to criminal events or public safety problems. It also accepts responsibility for helping to improve the quality of life and building social capital in the locations where community justice is most needed. Community justice brings important notions of social justice to the criminal justice agenda.

A broader view of community justice also addresses economic conditions in high-impact areas. Ensuring that minority-owned businesses are created and provided the opportunity to thrive is essential in creating employment and stability in high-impact areas. While economic issues are important and will be mentioned, this book focuses on crime and how the criminal justice system can better address the issues of crime and disorder that affect high-impact areas.

References

Akers, R.L., & Sellers, C.S. (2012). *Criminological theories: Introduction, evaluation, and application*, 6th ed. Oxford University Press.

Barajas, E. (1995). Moving toward community justice. *Topics in community corrections*. Annual Issue, U.S. Department of Justice, National Institute of Corrections.

Cadora, E., & Swartz, C. (2000). *Community justice atlas*. Center for Alternative Sentencing and Employment Services (CASES). Unpublished report.

Clarke, R.V. (Ed.). (1987). *Situational crime prevention: Successful case studies*, 2nd ed. Harrow and Heston.

Clear, T., & Karp, D. (1999). *The community justice ideal: Preventing crime and achieving justice*. Westview Press.

Cornish, D., & Clarke, R.V. (1986). *The reasoning criminal: Rational choice perspective on offending*. Springer-Verlag.

Eck, J. (1993). The threat of crime displacement. *Problem Solving Quarterly*, 6(3), Police Executive Research Forum, p. 2.

Goldstein, H. (1990). *Problem-oriented policing*. McGraw-Hill.

Hagen, F.E. (2011). *Introduction to criminology: Theories, methods, and criminal behavior*, 6th ed., Sage.

Karp, D., & Clear, T.R. (2000). Community justice: A conceptual framework. In *Boundaries changes in criminal justice organizations, vol. 2, Criminal Justice 2000* (pp. 323–369). National Institute of Justice.

Kurki, L. (2000). Restorative and community justice in the United States. *Crime and Justice*, 27, 235–303.

Meadows, D. (2008). *Thinking in systems: A primer*. Chelsea Green Publishing.

Nicholl, C. (1999). *Community policing, community justice, and restorative justice: Exploring the links for the delivery of a balanced approach to public safety*. U.S. Department of Justice, Office of Community-Oriented Services.

Popper, K. (1965). *Of clocks and clouds: An approach to the problem of rationality and the freedom of man*. The Arthur Holly Compton Memorial Lecture, Washington University, April 21, 1965.

Schmalleger, F. (2021). *Criminology*, 5th ed. Pearson.

Senge, P. (1990). *The fifth discipline: The art and practice of the learning organization*. Doubleday.

Stroh, P. (2015). *Systems thinking for social change*. Chelsea Green Publishing.

Trojanowicz, R.C., & Bucqueroux, B. (1990). *Community policing: A contemporary perspective*. Anderson Publishing Company.

Zehr, H., & Mika, H. (1998). Principles of restorative justice. *Contemporary Justice Review*, 1, 47–55.

2
Criminal Justice and the Community

Criminal Justice and Social Justice

Modern philosophers make an important distinction between criminal justice and social justice. Because both involve notions of justice, they are each based on the existence of a fair set of rules for how people treat each other and how citizens are treated by their government. Criminal justice is a type of "negative" justice. It concerns how a society allocates undesirable experiences to its members. The study of criminal justice is the study of the rules, procedures, and practices under which citizens experience the application of a criminal label and the imposition of a criminal sanction. Criminal labels and criminal sanctions are considered just when they are imposed upon the guilty, but only when imposed within the rules of substantive and procedural due process.

By contrast, social justice is concerned with the distribution of "good" things within a society: opportunities for advancement, personal wealth, and other assets such as health care, housing, and basic goods of life. In a socially just society, these benefits are provided by a fair set of rules and are applied to everyone equally.

Criminal justice and social justice, then, are both concerned with what people "deserve." Criminal justice is a set of institutions and procedures for determining which people deserve to be sanctioned because of their wrongdoing and what kind of sanctions they deserve to receive. Social justice is the set of rules by which people get the good things they deserve as a consequence of their talents and by the fruits of their efforts.

To a degree, criminal justice and social justice can be seen as flip sides of the same coin. When a person does something wrong, criminal justice ensures that the person gets the kind of punishment that goes with wrongful behavior. When a person's actions are meritorious – working hard and contributing to society – social justice requires that the person enjoy the benefits of having lived that way. We say that criminal justice is flawed when a person can break the law without suffering the consequences. Yet we also recognize that social justice is lacking when people are unable to get ahead, no matter how hard they might work or how much they might "play by the rules," because the cards are stacked against them.

Although perfect criminal and social justice is a laudable desire, we live in a society with well-known flaws in its criminal and social justice systems. Regarding criminal justice, we are troubled that sometimes innocent people are convicted of crimes and the guilty go free. In terms of social justice, some groups face unfair disadvantages that make it hard to succeed because of an uneven playing field. Both types of injustice make us ask hard questions about the fairness of criminal and social justice. We have a very strong cultural expectation

DOI: 10.4324/9781003393818-2

that people should realize the consequences of their actions so that both those who break the rules and those who work hard and play by the rules get what they deserve.

Recently, we have come to see that criminal justice and social justice are related. The most obvious relationship is that places where people face the toughest odds against living out the American Dream are also the places where there is the most criminality. Crime and disadvantage are mutually reinforcing aspects of community life. The existence of disadvantage, in the form of an inadequate labor market, failing schools, and impoverished households, creates the foundation for drug markets and other criminal enterprises. At the same time, the existence of criminal activity makes neighborhoods less desirable places for people to live and for businesses to flourish, with the result that disadvantage becomes even more ingrained in these areas, and the people who try to live and work in these places find it harder to build successful lives.

The fact that social injustice and crime reinforce one another in high-impact areas has provided one of the main incentives for the development of community justice strategies with an objective of reducing crime, as well as the social injustices that accompany high rates of crime. Community justice brings together the two concepts of criminal justice and social justice to build a response to crime that takes both ideas into account. Community justice is a strategy of criminal justice because it is concerned with the problems that contribute to and result from crime. Yet the essence of community justice as a strategy is to strengthen the capacity of places that are hard-hit by crime; in that sense, community justice has a concern for broader matters of social justice.

The marriage of criminal justice and social justice is most evident in the way community justice approaches local areas with an eye toward building social capital. The aim of community justice is not merely to process criminal cases but to restore order, strengthen community cohesion, repair the damage from crime, and build partnerships that nurture a more beneficial community life. Taken together, these capacities represent social capital, which enables communities to act in defense of their interests and to pursue collective goals. The marriage of criminal justice and social justice is most evident in the way community justice approaches local areas with an eye toward building social capital. The aim of community justice is not merely to process criminal cases but to restore order, strengthen community cohesion, repair the damage from crime, and build partnerships that nurture a more beneficial community life.

Social capital refers to the social networks that persons establish to solve common problems. These networks involve the development of trust and reciprocal relationships to achieve the attainment of goals. Putnam (2000) discusses the collective value of these networks, which involves getting to know persons of influence. Also important in these networks is the idea of norms of reciprocity, which means that persons do things for each other with the understanding that the favor will be returned sometime in the future, possibly by a different person or group. These acts create a connectedness that creates a bond and ensures that necessary acts are done to move the relationship in a positive direction.

Putnam (2000) also proposes two other important concepts in social capital networks: bonding social capital and bridging social capital. Bonding social capital binds people who are similar closer together and reinforces the norms of reciprocity and solidarity. Bridging social capital is a bit trickier because it closes the gap between groups that are not alike. It involves groups learning about the differences that separate them from other groups and making a concerted effort to find common ground that can build trust. Once trust is established, norms of reciprocity and networks with collective value can be developed.

Putnam argues that "bonding social capital constitutes a kind of sociological superglue, whereas bridging social capital provides a sociological WD-40" (2000, p. 23). Certainly, while bonding social capital is important in strengthening like groups living in high-impact areas, the development of bridging social capital will be the means by which meaningful resources and assistance may be brought to communities.

In more recent research on immigrant integration, Putnam (2007) discovered that the more diverse the community, the less its members trust each other or the government, and the less they participate in collective life or believe in their ability to change their plight. A surprising finding was that more diverse communities are less trusting, less cohesive, and less participative places to live. Putnam (2007, p. 149) said that in these locations, people tend to "hunker down" and become less trusting not only of person who are not like them but also of people who are like them. While this research addresses the issue of immigration, there are still potential lessons to be learned in examining current high-impact communities. Putnam's finding indicates that persons in their 20s are as likely as persons in their 40s to be less trusting of others. As these communities grow and evolve, diversity will more than likely be one of their defining characteristics. The implication here is that as new generations become the dominant population in communities, caution must be taken to insure that isolation within the communities does not occur. Also, it cannot be assumed that younger persons will be more open toward tolerance of those who differ from them. Putnam's belief is that isolation can be prevented by helping people better understand that ethnic diversity can occur while people still identify themselves as Americans and part of the greater society. Such information can be helpful for external groups that provide services or resources to high-impact areas. This would let them know that there may still be some standoffishness and they might not be welcomed with open arms.

Another lesson that may be taken from this research is that it is conceivable that those who may be different may be offenders and former offenders who return to the community. When those who are labeled as offenders come into contact with law-abiding citizens, the result is often the "hunkering down" that Putnam describes in the area of immigration. This hunkering down results in isolation and a lack of support for offenders who are trying to rebuild their lives. Opportunities in employment, education, and the acquisition of necessary social skills dry up when the perception is that former offenders are the individuals looking for those resources. Using the prescriptions provided by Putnam to ease tensions in communities regarding immigration may be just as applicable for communities facing the return of offenders from prison or those placed on probation or parole.

Another philosophy that may apply toward addressing the building of social capital and relationships in communities is *communitarianism*. Communitarianism holds that there are some moral duties that we are required to do, even if there is no immediate benefit realized. This belief is founded on the belief that it is vital that members of a community behave in ways that benefit the greater good and not in ways that benefit only the individual. Communitarians argue that having a community is vital for free individuals because it "backs them up against encroachment by the state and sustains morality by drawing on the gentle prodding of kin, friends, neighbors, and other community members, rather than building on government controls or fear of authorities" (Etzioni, 1993, p. 15). This philosophy dovetails well with the idea that informal social control is the most effective methods of crime prevention. Communitarianism appears to provide one roadmap for implementation of informal social control.

This philosophy encourages the development of behavioral standards that are morally grounded and based on the public interest. One concern often raised when discussing morality is who sets the moral standards. Many communities fear that those in powerful positions would push their morality and cultural standards on the less powerful. Communitarians argue that these standards must be developed by members of the community and should be agreed upon by most of the people living in the community. After these standards are communicated to members of the community, it is vital that most of the people abide by the standards most of the time in order to preserve the values. For these standards to take root and become part of the fabric of the neighborhood, reinforcing actions must occur. Communities can not only encourage moral behavior, but they can also help those who struggle find their way back onto the path. The moral principles can be important because they not only censure the unacceptable behavior but also sanction behaviors that help achieve the common good.

Communitarians realize that in many communities less emphasis has been placed on developing moral values and individualism has taken over as the guiding principle. They also realize that if members of a community begin to dialog more with each other they would tend to find many items of acceptable behavior on which they agree. Encouraging members of the community to abide by these agreed-upon principles would diminish the need for formal control mechanisms to control unacceptable behavior. This type of behavior would also contribute to the building of social networks that develop the ability to self-govern.

It is obvious that some communities are capable of developing a moral compass and implementing informal social controls to reinforce acceptable behaviors, and some communities are not. Communities lacking the cohesion or structure to help themselves must receive a helping hand from elements of society that can bring resources to help make the change happen. These elements can include governmental agencies, nonprofit agencies, and even criminal justice agencies. Adopting a communitarian approach can still allow for individual identity, but behaviors become less self-serving and more oriented toward strengthening the common good.

Community justice, therefore, is not simply about a desire to increase public safety. It is also concerned with the quality of public life and the efficacy of collective community action. Using crime as a fulcrum for leveraging social capital, community justice seeks to improve the community's life by attacking the problems surrounding public safety and ultimately undermining the capacity of entire social groups in a place to effect their well-being. Criminal justice strategies are typically individual and negative: they remove residents, one by one, from their everyday lives and impose negative, undesirable sanctions upon each. Community justice pays attention to social justice in that it is not merely negative and individual in its orientation. It seeks a positive, collective outcome as a response to crime: better communities. Community justice is a vehicle of social justice because these aims are sought in the most disadvantaged areas of a specific jurisdiction.

The Importance of "Place"

Community justice begins with an essential insight about contemporary life: places matter. In our modern society, with its technological infrastructure, it is easy to think that space has constricted in size and that everything today is global. It is true that the advent of such everyday technologies as the telephone, television, and especially the Internet has reduced the importance of distance as a constraint on daily living. Today, a person can talk to someone living thousands of miles away, see events happening halfway around the globe, and chat by email with someone sitting at home on the other side of the country. Distance is no longer the all-encompassing limitation it was a century ago.

Recognizing that space is no longer so impassable does not mean local environments are unimportant. Where a person lives is one of the most important aspects of that person's life. This is true in developing countries, where a person is born into a community that may become that person's environment for an entire lifetime, but it is just as accurate in a thoroughly modern society such as the United States. In this country, people commonly move from place to place precisely because where a person lives has so much to do with what a person's life is like. America, one of the wealthiest nations in history, is highly segregated in the layout of its living areas – its neighborhoods. The poor, especially impoverished people of color, live in ghetto-like conditions where almost everyone shares a common dialect, dark skin, and poverty. Those with means move out to middle-class neighborhoods, where schools are better and expectations for life are more optimistic. The affluent live in places where privilege dramatically expands the array of choices about how to spend their time and resources.

The place where a person lives significantly affects the schools that a person's children attend, the leisure-time activities used to occupy time, the places the person eats, and so on. There are other constraints for people experiencing poverty, who often need more easy access to transportation. The neighborhood is the place that provides work opportunities (however meager) and is home to the friends that a person will have. Whatever is available in the form of recreation – and in poor areas, this is often very limited – will form the field of choices for spending free time. Shopping for groceries, clothes, and other amenities will be dominated by selections within walking distance. All this can be easier in city settings, which is one reason that rural poor often migrate into dilapidated city areas.

Therefore, even though we live in the era of cell phones and Web searches, place matters. It sets the stage for how a person lives much of daily life and is especially important for those who lack the resources to easily leave their surroundings.

What Is Community?

In this book, we will commonly use the terms *community* and *neighborhood*. What do these words mean? Are they interchangeable? Do they have specific meanings we should keep in mind?

Much has been written to define *community*, and there are numerous interpretations of the word *neighborhood*. In this book, we will often use the terms interchangeably. However, these terms are not strictly the same, and it is helpful to make some distinctions in the meanings as applied to the idea of community justice.

The term *neighborhood* almost always refers to a particular geographic area within a larger jurisdictional entity. Neighborhoods of this type develop a reputation and an identity, and residents say, "I live in so-and-so." But the boundaries for these sorts of neighborhoods are only sometimes concrete. People sometimes have differing views about where one particular neighborhood ends and another begins. Over time, the boundaries of neighborhoods are fluid, and areas that were thought to be inside one area come to be thought of as belonging to another. Despite this definitional murkiness and spatial fuzziness – the idea of the geographical neighborhood is one of the more standard and traditional ways we understand the places where we live and work: downtown, the north side, the Heights, the west side, Maple Hills, the valley, Riverside, and so on – we learn to designate meaningful areas within larger jurisdictions, name them, and understand them as coherent neighborhoods, even though locating the actual boundaries of those places can be problematic. For the most part, when we say "neighborhood," we mean a coherent area within a larger jurisdiction that most people see as different in some meaningful way from the surrounding areas.

The term *community* can indicate a neighborhood, but it usually has more personal significance. Community refers to people more than places. Even when the community is a neighborhood, the term connotes people who live there, as in the Elm Avenue or West Atlantic communities. When we hear these phrases, we think not only of location but also of the people who live (or work) in those places. When we say "community," we can mean more than just a location. Sometimes, the term refers to a group of people who share a common personal identity, regardless of where they live: the Ukrainian community or the African-American community. In this way, the term community designates a collection of people who see themselves as belonging because of their backgrounds rather than their addresses. Another broader use of the term refers to a group of people who share a common goal or set of interests. In this case, the student community, or the business community, has shared interests that, despite other differences, link them in the pursuit of collective goals.

Persons lacking connections with other persons who share common interests may be unable to pursue their established goals. *Life chances* often affect people's ability to connect with others who share their interests. The concept of life chances is discussed in the next section of this chapter, but it can be an important factor in whether or not some persons can connect socially with groups outside of their physical environment. Life chances play an important role in battling a sense of hopelessness that may pervade communities whose residents do not see a way out of the cycle of poverty. The inability of persons to connect with others who share a common goal or interest may cause them to "fall between the cracks" when it comes to accessing needed services. These types of communities provide not only social support for members, but also advocate for their needs to those who may have the resources needed.

A vivid example of persons falling between the cracks in the United States occurred during Hurricane Katrina in 2005. As the storm's effects inundated the city of New Orleans, government officials began implementing an evaluation plan intended to take residents to safe places in and around the city. News reports from the scene showed that many residents living in the poorer sections of New Orleans were struggling to find their way to the locations where they could access the public transportation that was to take them to the designated safe places. It became obvious from watching televised news reports that a large number of persons had medical, physical, or transportation issues that prevented them from moving from their residences to designated pick-up points. While one can only speculate, if more people living in these areas had been able to connect with external communities that shared common concerns, there might have been more information available to the rescuers. Such information might have guided those in charge to modify rescue plans to accommodate the large numbers of persons who struggled to escape the hurricane's fury. More importantly, the information possessed by social communities could have been used in authoring the rescue plan as it was written, alleviating much of the panic during evacuation efforts. Sadly, the actual need of high-impact communities is often not recognized until such a disaster occurs and emergency crews are already at work.

Community and neighborhood are related in America because people with common backgrounds or collective purposes often live near each other. Patterns of immigration have led to areas of cities dominated by people of like ethnicity: Little Italy and Chinatown are good examples. People who immigrated to the United States may have found it easier and more comfortable to live in areas where others from their country had already settled and where their native language was widely understood and spoken. Alternatively, they may have been victims of discrimination, and these areas were the only places they were allowed to live. Whatever the reason, ethnic enclaves typically developed in the urban centers because of waves of immigration.

This has also been true of internal migration patterns, especially concerning African-Americans migrating northward from the South. These formerly enslaved people and offspring of formerly enslaved people came to America's northern cities to find better work and to escape racism in the South. When they arrived, they moved into areas populated by other urban African-Americans. Again, this resulted from the dual pressures of housing discrimination and cultural comfort zones. Today, in the Southwest, this pattern is repeating itself concerning Spanish-speaking immigrants, legal and undocumented. Within cities, areas are coming to be dominated by those of Mexican descent, and these locations have the qualities of being both a neighborhood and a community.

It is important to stress that the neighborhood experiences of the last two centuries waves of immigrants – Germans, Irish, Italians, Jews, and so on – emigrating here from Europe have not been the same as those of Blacks and Hispanics in the United States. Although many European immigrants have kept their identity as a community, they have been able to leave restrictive neighborhoods in a pattern of economic upward mobility. Over time, those whose parents were born outside the United States assimilated into neighborhoods where everyone's family did not hail from the exact original location. Ethnic integration and intermarriage have occurred, a process called the melting pot. However, people of color have not had the same experience. Many areas that were dominated by people of African descent nearly a century ago are still places where African-Americans outnumber others by 20 or more to 1. This concentration of poor, economically immobile Black families has been referred to as "the Urban Underclass" (Wilson 1980). It has not been broken down by the usual form of integration and assimilation that other ethnic groups experienced. Instead, it has experienced multiple generations of racial isolation from the mainstream and concentration in urban ghettos, without a reasonable expectation of any different circumstances. In the Southwest, the experience has not continued long enough to be determined the same, but there are troubling signs of a similar spatial concentration of Spanish-speaking poor in certain locations.

At the same time, communities of common interests, such as students or business owners, likewise suffer the effects of poverty, economic immobility, and social stigma. In socially isolated and economically disadvantaged districts, students endure run-down facilities, limited pedagogical resources, and an often disorderly and sometimes violent school environment. Similarly, local business owners experience fewer paying customers and lowered revenues and are unable to maintain their stores or provide quality products. When social isolation is coupled with economic disinvestments, we face a growing problem of concentrations of poor members of certain communities in certain neighborhoods, with little prospect of change.

How Do Neighborhoods Affect Community Life?

This is a problem of deep significance to community justice. For people who find themselves born into these areas, place really does matter. There is diminished social mobility, economic viability, and personal possibility. Community justice, because of its concern for broader social justice, considers this aspect of poor places to be one of the most important issues that officials of justice must understand and confront. The place a person calls home affects the way a person lives.

Place and Life Chances. The most important way that a person's residence affects quality of life is through the way location influences later life chances. The term *life chances* refers to the possibilities people encounter in their lives and the likelihood that a person will be able to achieve personal and social goals. Being born to two college-educated parents increases one's life chances, as does living in a wealthy family. On the other hand, being born into an impoverished, single-parent family or having a drug-addicted parent reduces one's life chances.

The idea of life chances is one way to keep the popular image of the American Dream honest. In this country, it is true that people who are born into deprived circumstances are free to work hard, apply themselves, and "make it." Some do. But people who start out with significant disadvantages find it hard to rise above them, and for most, there is little prospect of success in the upper ranges. The concept of life chances holds that most of the pivotal experiences of one's social and economic life – from getting into a college to landing a good first job; from developing social skills to meeting people who can help along the way – are established by the circumstances of one's birth.

One of these important circumstances is the place a person lives. "Bad" neighborhoods typically have a dearth of good choices: schools are usually below standard or worse, job prospects are limited, and positive youth activities are few. A short distance away, a "good" neighborhood will offer a youngster born there a good education, plenty of structured and safe leisure activities, and when the time is right, a convenient chance to make a little money while finishing an education. In the former area, kids, especially young males, find it easy to get involved in a gang, easy to start down the road of drugs and alcohol abuse, and easy to meet others who are involved in serious criminal activity; they find it hard to get reinforcement for keeping up in school, hard to envision a realistic road to a conventional life of success, and hard to develop the life skills that help a person succeed. In the good neighborhood, almost the exact reverse is true.

The way a person's place of residence influences that person's life chances challenges our sense of social justice. It does not seem fair that so much of a person's life is determined by the circumstances of birth, because where a person is born is a complete accident. Someone who happens to have a billionaire for a father will likely be wildly wealthy one day, but how can we say that this person's extreme wealth is deserved? Similarly, a child of a crack-addicted mother who grows up in homeless shelters will likely encounter the criminal justice system as a youth or even as a young adult; and even though we might all think that a criminal act requires a criminal justice response, it is hard to see how anyone could come from such circumstances unscathed.

Thus, place matters in life. It sets up a series of social circumstances that play out over time as a major part of a person's life story. If you disagree, try this exercise: Tell your life story to date. Make sure you try to do it in a way that helps explain why you are where you are and what is important about your life today. Then, notice that the significance of the role played by the circumstances of one's birth, including where you grew up and how you grew up there, is as determinative for everyone else as it is for you.

The Concentration of Crime and Criminal Justice. Neighborhoods differ dramatically in the degree to which they experience crime and criminal justice. This is part of what makes the concept of community justice so important, because each neighborhood will face a series of different issues regarding crime and justice. A one-size-fits-all style of criminal justice may work in some places but will probably not be effective everywhere.

To understand how crime and criminal justice concentrate, we can use geographical analyses that show spatial distribution of each. For example, when we compare crime rates among police precincts in Brooklyn to incarceration rates among police precincts, the variations are remarkable. The police precinct with the highest crime in Brooklyn has three times the amount of crime as the lowest. The difference in criminal justice activity is even more dramatic: the precinct with the highest incarceration rate has nine times more people per capita going to and from prison than the precinct with the lowest rate. These numbers tell a powerful story of what it must be like to live in these places. In the 73rd precinct, for example, crime is common, and a large proportion of residents – one in eight adult males – is removed for incarceration. By contrast, both crime and criminal justice are comparatively rare in other locations only a few blocks away. In the former, crime and criminal justice are an everyday part of life; elsewhere, crime and justice are remote concerns (Cadora & Swartz 2000).

Place and Public Safety. Recent scholarship has uncovered the importance of place as an element of public safety. This is most commonly understood through the idea of hot spots. For example, Lawrence Sherman (Sherman et al. 1989) showed that in the places he had studied, the majority of crimes were committed in concentration in very specific locations – for example, street corners, blocks, or addresses – which he called hot spots. Crime is far more likely to occur in hot spots than in the immediate surrounding areas. Later researchers have found that the pattern uncovered by Sherman is the norm. A small number of specific locations account for a disproportionate number of police calls for assistance and reports of criminal events.

What are hot spots like, and how do they become problem locations? The answer is complicated because there is not a particular formula for a place becoming a hot spot. Often, but not always, there is a late-night tavern nearby; usually, there are dark streets or hidden alleyways. A couple of abandoned buildings or a secluded empty lot can also become a hot spot. What almost all hot spots have in common is not so much their physical attributes but the fact that they are configured to allow criminals to engage in crime with relative ease, and they exist in locations or neighborhoods where crime is generally higher than elsewhere.

The discovery of the existence of hot spots has had an enormous impact on strategies of policing, as we describe in this chapter. The effective police administrator can target policing strategies surrounding these hot spots in order to cool them down or curtail criminal activity altogether. The first step is to use crime mapping to identify the hot spot; second, an analysis is made of what makes crime occur at the location; and third, a strategy is developed to overcome the factors in those locations that lead to crime.

Crime mapping is traditionally seen as a tool utilized by the criminal justice system to track incidences of crime and disorder. New technology, such as geographic information system (GIS), has allowed criminal justice agencies the ability to track "hot spots" of crime and plan how to address those crime issues. It is important to realize that mapping and spatial analysis can be used to assist governmental and social service agencies, as well, in tracking important demographic information which can be used to guide the administration of support programs in communities. The discussion about place cited the importance of this concept. Because those living in a certain location may experience poor schools, high unemployment, minimal transportation options, and poorly developed social networks, the need for diagnosing these problems gains more importance. GIS can provide a valuable tool for examining the health of communities.

For GIS to be successful and meaningful, spatial data is needed. In other words, it is necessary that the data are tied to something that may serve as a physical marker for tracking purposes. Roads, school districts, city council districts, and buildings are just a few examples of spatial locations that could serve the purpose. Data collected by municipal or social service agencies can be overlaid onto maps of communities. The data selected for analysis is limited only by the creativity of the person conducting the analysis. Any data that can be related to a spatial location can be mapped, and a vivid picture of the infrastructure of the community can be developed. Advancements in newer GIS software have provided agencies with the ability to provide meaningful visual images to accompany written documents or statistical analyses. For information to be used properly, it must be in a form that is understandable and GIS allows even those not formally educated in evaluation principles to more closely understand the problem.

Instead of looking solely at crime or offenders' residences, analysts can use non-crime data to paint a more accurate picture of the health and needs of a particular community. For example, mapping data about home ownership can tell a person if there is stability and resident investment in the community. Traditionally, persons living in rental housing do not become actively involved in neighborhoods because they have no tangible investment in the neighborhood. Neighborhood associations do not usually give attention to renters because they are not seen as having an investment in the neighborhood, and there is a general opinion that should things in the neighborhood get worse, those who rent will just move instead of pitching in to help address the problem. Knowing the specific locations of rental properties and the demographics of the renters could assist neighborhood in reaching out to these residents. Many of the renters may bring social connections or knowledge to the neighborhood that could be tapped if they were invited to participate in the neighborhood operations.

Public works data could also be helpful for governmental and nonprofit agencies in determining where basic services are lacking or absent. When residents of a community are lacking basic services, they are forced to spend their time and energy in obtaining those services. This leaves little time for networking with other neighbors or building social capital. When basic services can be provided to a community, residents are more likely to experience feelings of self-worth, and increases in self-esteem should logically follow. Residents of high-impact areas tend toward feelings of hopelessness because they see few ways to get out of the situation they are in. Overlaying public work data on crime and disorder data may provide a thorough insight into the relationships between these elements. If the relationship shows a correlation, actions other than intervention by the criminal justice system could move a community toward developing the ability to establish stronger informal social controls and strengthen the fabric of the neighborhood.

Having a wider array of information about a community would allow governmental and nonprofit entities to better focus resources and interventions on where they are needed most. If the ultimate goal is to make communities more self-sufficient and to strengthen informal social controls, a focused approach makes sense. Many in the field of criminal justice argue that this type of diagnosis is not part of the charge that society gives to the criminal justice system. The common wisdom is that the criminal justice system was created to address those who, for whatever reason, choose to violate the statutory laws. Implicit in this wisdom is that the role of criminal justice professionals is to apprehend criminals, investigate crimes, determine guilt or innocence, and incarcerate or otherwise supervise those found guilty of a violation of the law, nothing more. Such comments show the need for a change in thinking regarding the relationship between criminal justice professionals and communities, as well as a reexamination of the role of criminal justice professions in the practice of crime prevention.

From a criminal justice perspective, the idea that crime concentrates in certain locations has led to new thinking about how to overcome crime there. Today, there are three main schools of thought about how to overcome problems of public safety that concentrate in certain areas: disorder, disorganization, and inadequate informal social control. These each make assumptions about the sources of crime and the circumstances that are thought to promote it. Although these models share some common themes, they are worth discussing separately in order to understand their core tenets.

Disorder Models: Broken Windows The "broken windows" theory is one of the most popular ideas about the way crime comes about in urban settings. First enunciated by James Q. Wilson and George Kelling (1982) in an article in the *Atlantic Monthly*, the broken windows argument sees a link between urban disorder and crime that involves a process of deterioration in those areas. Disorder, in the form of trash, unsupervised groups of young men and boys, noise, and the broken windows that gave the theory its name, creates an atmosphere that makes people think a place is not being "taken care of." It becomes a distasteful environment, so the tendency is for people to stay away from an area where disorder predominates by avoiding it, moving to a new area, or simply staying indoors. This urban disorder also sends a signal to those inclined to engage in crime that such an area will not be cared for, so deviant or even criminal activity will not be stopped or otherwise hindered.

These two impressions of disorderly public space combine to make crime much more likely. Law-abiding citizens feel uncomfortable in disordered areas and do not remain there long. Offenders, however, feel empowered in these locations, and when they engage in minor deviance that seems to be allowed without formal controls, they interpret this as encouragement. Their deviance escalates from minor activity to ever more major crime. At least one study (Skogan 1992) of the relationship between disorder and crime has supported this pattern.

Advocates of the broken windows idea should be and are the most interested in the repair of urban disorder. William Bratton was one of the first practitioners of the broken windows idea. When he became commissioner of the New York City subway system in 1990, he decided to keep the subway cars clean of graffiti and quickly stopped any other disorder in the subway. His strategy proved very successful, and the New York subways vastly improved.

Surprisingly, however, the broken windows idea has led to a different emphasis among law enforcement officials: arresting and jailing minor offenders. Their reasoning is that these are the people who break the windows in the first place; these are the people who create disorder and whose minor deviance in public space leads, inevitably, to an escalation of deviance and more serious crime. Many New Yorkers believe that the aggressive arrest policies of the New York City Police Department under Commissioner Howard Safir have played a major role in the dropping crime rates, although many citizens have been troubled by aggressive police tactics that affect young men of color more than other groups. Studies of crime in New York suggest that this strategy may have had less to do with the drop in crime than did new police practices targeting problem locations (Silverman 1999) and changes in the socioeconomics and demographics of the city (Karmen 2001).

Disorganization Models: Systemic Theory The first important theory of crime and place, called social disorganization theory, was developed in the 1940s by Clifford Shaw and Henry McKay (Shaw & McKay 1942). Shaw and McKay were concerned with explaining why certain neighborhoods in Chicago seemed to produce the most juvenile delinquents, year in and year out. They theorized that something about those places made it more likely for kids to become delinquent. Their analysis highlighted three sociological characteristics that seemed to matter most: poverty, ethnic heterogeneity, and mobility. When these attributes are present, the society in these places becomes "disorganized," and young people fail to become adequately socialized.

It is easy to see why these characteristics might matter. Poverty has always been a foundation for crime, one reason being that poor people have less stake in the status quo. Shaw and McKay argued that ethnic heterogeneity led to a situation in which there was less acceptance and agreement about the norms of conduct in the neighborhood, because different groups would have different values. Mobility out of the neighborhood meant that there are more people entering and soon leaving a place than there are long-term residents; consequently, people did not stay long enough to form attachments to others and thus help build the strong sense of social interdependence that made crime less desirable among neighbors who knew one another.

Recent studies assessing the usefulness of the Shaw and McKay approach have found evidence that cuts both ways: not only have poverty and mobility contributed to crime, but reciprocally, crime itself has come to perpetuate poverty and mobility. Poverty continues to be such an important cause of crime that some scholars (see Wilson 1980) have described an entrenched, inner-city poor so alienated from dominant economic and social forces that they form an urban underclass in which criminal activity becomes passed along intergenerationally and little hope exists for joining the economic mainstream. Ethnic heterogeneity is no longer thought to be as important as racial composition: areas, where nearly 100% of the residents are African-Americans living in multigenerational poverty, are typically areas with very high crime rates. These are places where most people find it hard to gather the resources to leave, so mobility tends not to be the issue it was in 1940. Recent work on coercive mobility (Clear & Rose 1999) suggests that the prison and jail system removes from and returns so many people to these areas that it has become the primary source of a high rate of mobility in high-crime areas.

Social disorganization theorists seek strategies that "organize" neighborhoods by building social groups and creating political capacity. The idea is that an organized community can counter the forces of poverty, ethnic conflict, and outward mobility, which serve to promote disorganization in an area. Many studies have been conducted on community organization strategies (Moynihan 1969), including the famous Back of the Yards Project of Saul Alkinsky, designed to overcome the problems Shaw and McKay identified. So many community organization projects have been tried that it is impossible to summarize them in a few sentences. However, many of the community organization approaches fail or attract strong resistance from city government, and getting the poorest communities to organize on their behalf is very difficult.

Informal Social Control Models: Collective Efficacy. Collective efficacy is an idea that borrows from the disorder tradition and the social disorganization tradition. Again, this work is based on studies in Chicago by Robert Sampson and his colleagues (Sampson et al. 1997), but it takes a different view of how demographic forces work at the neighborhood level. The thesis of the collective efficacy idea is that crime is reduced when there are strong forces of informal social control at work in the neighborhood.

Informal social control comes from two sources: from families and other loved ones who exert controlling influences on the young people near them and from social groups and friendship networks that serve a similar function in addition to or instead of families. Some neighborhoods have strong families or wide bonds of social relationships among adults and youth, which leads to less criminal involvement by those youth. Other places have weak or "broken" families that exert inadequate control over the youth and residents who neither know one another nor form social networks that have the capacity to support one another.

Thus, social networks – interpersonal relationships that people value and sustain – provide the ability for people to be collectively effective at producing control in the places they live. There can be little collective efficacy when social networks are weak or thin. Research supports this view, finding that crime is lower regardless of poverty or racial composition in neighborhoods where people know their neighbors and help each other (Sampson et al. 1997). Moreover, these studies find that disorder plays an insignificant role compared to collective efficacy.

Advocates of collective efficacy try to prevent crime by building social relationships in problem neighborhoods. They try to develop neighborhood organizations and centers that engage residents with one another, helping to develop social networks and strengthen social bonds. Unlike the externally directed community organizing under the social disorganization model, which was aimed at organizing to get money and resources from the city government, collective efficacy strategies try to build strength from within by forming groups that attend to neighborhood matters.

Box 2.1 describes two case studies where the goal was the revitalization of communities. The case studies show different approaches to how revitalization might occur. In the Ivanhoe Neighborhood (n.d.) case study, the project was generated by a federal program, and the neighborhood was selected due to its high violent crime rates. The approach involved the police targeting violent crime and identifying and arresting perpetrators. One lesson learned was that the funding supported the actions of the police but provided little funding to strengthen the self-sufficiency of the neighborhood. In the Point Neighborhood case study, the revitalization was initiated by non-criminal justice groups, and the focus became more on improving the physical needs of the neighborhood as well as improving the image of the neighborhood. While crime was an issue, it was not the driving force for the project. Lessons learned for the project are included in Box 2.1.

Box 2.1 Ivanhoe and Point Neighborhood Case Studies

Ivanhoe Neighborhood

In early 1992, the Kansas City, Missouri, Police Department received a "Weed and Seed" grant from the United States Department of Justice. The Weed and Seed program is best described as follows:

> The U.S. Department of Justice's Weed and Seed program was developed to demonstrate an innovative and comprehensive approach to law enforcement and

community revitalization, and to prevent and control violent crime, drug abuse, and gang activity in target areas. The program, initiated in 1991, attempts to weed out violent crime, gang activity, and drug use and trafficking in target areas, and then seed the target area by restoring the neighborhood through social and economic revitalization. Weed and Seed has three objectives: (1) develop a comprehensive, multi-agency strategy to control and prevent violent crime, drug trafficking, and drug-related crime in target neighborhoods; (2) coordinate and integrate existing and new initiatives to concentrate resources and maximize their impact on reducing and preventing violent crime, drug trafficking, and gang activity; and (3) mobilize community residents in the target areas to assist law enforcement in identifying and removing violent offenders and drug traffickers from the community and to assist other human service agencies in identifying and responding to service needs of the target area. To achieve these goals, Weed and Seed integrates law enforcement, community policing, prevention, intervention, treatment, and neighborhood restoration efforts.

(National Weed and Seed Program, U.S. Department of Justice, Executive Office for Weed and Seed 1998)

After careful consideration of locations to implement the program, the Ivanhoe Neighborhood, located within the Central Patrol Division (CPD), was selected. The one problem with the selection was that only one-half of the Ivanhoe neighborhood was physically located within the boundaries of the CPD. The southern portion was located within the boundaries of the Metro Patrol Division (MPD), and the grant parameters were specific to the northern half of the neighborhood only. While the MPD portion of the neighborhood was upset with not being part of the program, it was decided to move ahead because the northern portion best met the criteria for selection and, from an internal communications standpoint, it would be difficult for officers from different divisions to collaborate on the program.

The northern portion of Ivanhoe was entirely contained within patrol beat 144, and the crime statistics for that area showed a neighborhood racked by violent crime and drug dealing. There were large numbers of abandoned houses, and the majority of the residents did not own the houses in which they lived. Drive-by shootings were a problem with – having occurred in 1991. Other violent crimes also flourished in beat 144 as well. Since Weed and Seed had just been launched, only three sites were awarded the initial grants: New York City, Kansas City, and Seattle. Each location was free to design their own program based on the problems occurring in the target areas selected. In Kansas City, it was determined that to achieve a better long-term effect, the program should be built upon the philosophy of Problem-Oriented Policing (POP). Lawrence Sherman of the University of Maryland was chosen to be the evaluator for the Kansas City program, and he brought many resources from the university, including a full-time graduate assistant, to the program.

Because violent crime was such a problem in Beat 144, the program team decided to target gun crime as the major focus of the program. Special patrols were sent out to try to get guns off of the street and the program because of what was later known as the Kansas City Gun Experiment (Sherman, Shaw, & Rogan 1995). Police patrols were intensified with the "weeding" money, and violent crime was lowered due to the effort.

The Ivanhoe Neighborhood Association was in place at the time the program began, but it was struggling because resident involvement was lacking. Many who live in the neighborhood were concerned, but they were frightened of the drug dealers and others who were involved in violent crime. During the duration of the program in beat 144, many stories of courageous residents standing up to the violent offenders emerged. Unfortunately, the funding for the program contained an abundance of "weed" money and almost nothing in "seed" money. The neighborhood leaders were unable to attract many interested investors, and commercial development in the area was progressing very slowly. There was little money for low-interest loans for those who wished to improve their property, and so the majority of the activity in the neighborhood was law enforcement related. At one point during the early stages of the program, President George H.W. Bush visited the neighborhood and had a meeting with a few of the longtime residents of the neighborhood. His visit was welcomed and highly publicized in the local media, but it did not translate into any immediate "seed" money from the government.

The program did have positive results in the area of reduction of violent crime in beat 144. A portion of the program that did not show results immediately was the strengthening of the neighborhood association. There were committed residents who continued working to build a social network within the neighborhood and encourage economic development. In 1997, the neighborhood took an upward turn and began to build momentum with the creation of a governing council that began to steer the neighborhood in a positive direction. Around that time, the police department extended the boundaries of CPD to Emmanuel Cleaver II Boulevard, making the neighborhood part of only one patrol division.

Today, the Ivanhoe Neighborhood Council is a thriving body that is very much self-governing. They established working committees in the areas of crime and safety, beautification, housing, and youth. Volunteers are utilized to operate the committees, and the neighborhood is very much in control of their future. The neighborhood currently operates several programs for residents including youth sports, scouting, music, and restorative justice. The council is also active in economic development and job creation for residents. In addition, the council established a website that provides information for residents (www.incthrives.org) Accessed 8/7/2024.

In 2001, the Kauffman Foundation provided funding to hire staff, open an office, and begin the creation of a strategic plan. The neighborhood has continued and strengthened its partnership with the police department, and a large number of drug houses have been closed. Approximately 200 lots that were placed in land trusts have been returned to the neighborhood for rehabilitation, and cleanliness campaigns have reduced the number of illegal dumping sites. The council now boasts a long list of partnership that include banks, law firms, Legal Aid of Western Missouri, government offices, religious foundations, and the University of Missouri-Kansas City. In the Fall of 2009, the council became a working partner in the Green Zone project that will rehabilitate homes to make them energy efficient using labor hired from within the neighborhood.

Revitalization of the Point Neighborhood in Salem, Massachusetts

The Point neighborhood (also known as El Punto) is in Salem, Massachusetts, about 15 miles north of Boston. This neighborhood has been a settlement destination for new immigrants and has faced a stigma of crime and poverty. Because of that stigma, an invisible division between the neighborhood and the rest of Salem developed. A collaborative community-wide planning effort led by the North Shore Community Development Coalition (NSCDC) for the Point neighborhood started in 2012. The NSCDC renovated and modernized 35 buildings and 247 apartments from 2012 to 2022, with another 7 buildings with 157 apartments in progress for 2023.

The neighborhood has a long and rich history. Before colonization, Indigenous people inhabited the region. The neighborhood was also devastated by a fire in 1914 that destroyed over 1,300 buildings, left more than 18,000 people homeless, and caused an estimated $15 million in damage. The local government created a new fire code that required any building three stories or taller to be masonry. The resulting buildings established a distinctive style, which became an important aspect of Salem's architectural history. Architects and builders rebuilt the Point neighborhood with styles popular during the period before 1940, including colonial, classical, and Renaissance revival.

The Point continued to face a stigma of crime and poverty, which created a division between the neighborhood and the rest of Salem. Some of the challenges faced by the neighborhood have included high rates of unemployment, drug addiction, and violence.

Demographics

In 2012, the population density of the Point neighborhood was nearly triple that of the rest of Salem. Green space and open space were limited to a few small urban parks. Parts of the neighborhood had relatively small walkable blocks, while others were oversized and difficult to navigate by foot.

As of the 2010 census, the Point neighborhood's population was 63% non-white, compared to the population of Salem as a whole, which was 75% white. A majority of Salem's foreign-born population resides in the Point, and the country of origin for most Latino immigrants was the Dominican Republic. Other immigrants came from Haiti and other African countries. At the start of the project in 2012, 20% of the neighborhood residents met federal poverty guidelines, compared with 11% for Salem as a whole.

The Planning Process

To develop the Action Plan, the NSCDC met with a broad group of neighborhood residents, including senior citizens, teenagers, small business owners, and community leaders. They held nine focus group sessions in both English and Spanish.

During the meetings, attendees shared that there was a lack of meaningful opportunities for young people. The primary challenge identified was the lack of opportunities for young adults who could not find living-wage jobs after leaving high school.

Another issue identified was the deep prejudice against the neighborhood related to perceptions of poverty, violence, and crime. It appeared that the perception was that poverty equals crime. Persons who lived in the neighborhood believed it was a friendly place with a strong sense of community, so the plan incorporated a goal to address the stigma and communicate positive stories.

The Action Plan

The Action Plan carefully recognized existing assets and resources and proposed creative ways to use and improve them. The Plan identified several goals:

- Improve public safety for residents and visitors.
- Cultivate neighborhood pride and civic engagement.
- Provide resources and connections for job training and placement.
- Expand open space and offer quality recreational options for people of all ages.
- Increase affordable housing and economic development opportunities in the neighborhood.
- Develop sustainable infrastructure and transportation modes.

One of the most significant pieces of the revitalization effort was creating the Innovative Punto Urban Art Museum (PUAM). The goals of PUAM are:

- To create a beautiful, uplifting environment for Point residents, particularly children.
- To celebrate the immigrant community and support the neighborhood's residents.
- To break down the inevitable divide between the Point neighborhood and the rest of Salem
- To attract visitors to the Point to experience world-class art.

PUAM's educational programming used the neighborhood as a platform to address topics such as racism, inequality, the history of redlining, and the immigrant experience. Since 2017, more than 5,000 students and 3,000 visitors have participated in the educational tours.

Below are some observations and lessons learned from the project.

1 Make a conscious commitment to community stability.
2 Develop community resilience.
3 Engage surrounding communities.
4 Deploy the arts to serve community revitalization.
5 Elevate historic preservation.
6 Replicate successful models.
7 Pursue continued advocacy and dialogue.

From "Revitalization of the Point Neighborhood in Salem, Massachusetts. ULI Case Studies, October 2023.
The entire, detailed report on the project can be found at www.uli.org.

Place-Based Strategies and Public Safety Goals

This discussion of theories of community life and community safety leads us to a discussion of action strategies to produce more significant public safety at the neighborhood level. We discuss two general types of strategies: community-oriented criminal justice strategies and community change strategies.

Community-Oriented Strategies in Criminal Justice

Because this book is devoted to the idea of community justice as a criminal justice approach, the following chapters discuss criminal justice strategies of public safety directed at the community level. However, it is essential to recognize how these community-oriented criminal justice strategies for public safety are different from the traditional criminal justice approach, and we discuss five such ways. The following chapters will develop and elaborate the themes we list here.

Places, Not Just Cases. The most important way that criminal justice changes its strategic approach in a community justice orientation is by focusing more on the attributes and circumstances of places than on cases. Because various aspects of places – neighborhoods and communities – are so important to forming and maintaining public safety, it makes sense to focus on places in order to produce safety. This focus means that physical aspects of areas afflicted with high crime are studied and, when necessary, altered: vacant lots are renovated into small parks or playgrounds, dark streets are lighted up at night, vacant buildings are torn down, streets that house open-air drug markets are closed off, and so forth. A concern for places also considers the importance of the people who live there. Residents are mobilized into action groups to provide support for one another and help reclaim public space. Child-care programs are created for unsupervised children. Job creation and placement programs are established for residents who need work. This, then, is a dual-track strategy: clean up the broken windows aspects of the neighborhood that tend to encourage criminal activity and organize residents so that more effective services can be provided to improve their prospects.

It is not easy or natural for criminal justice to change its level of focus from cases to places. Criminal events and the people involved in them are inherent and, traditionally, the only level to which the criminal justice system has attended. Police arrest suspects, prosecutors charge them, judges sentence them, and correctional officials supervise them. The expectation that all criminal justice action flows from criminal events and concerns itself with those events is deeply ingrained in traditional thinking. A concern for community-level issues does not replace the case-level action of criminal justice. After all, how individual criminal complaints are handled ultimately forms an important basis on which we evaluate criminal justice, even with a community focus. The concern for places, however, provides an additional target for criminal justice activity: to make neighborhoods and communities better places to live, work, and raise children.

Proactive, Not Reactive. By adding a concern for places, community-oriented criminal justice begins by becoming proactive rather than simply reactive. By proactive, we mean that community-oriented criminal justice tries to head off problems before they occur, particularly by identifying the causes of public safety problems and overcoming them.

A case-level orientation is reactive by nature. Nothing can be done about a criminal complaint until a crime has occurred (or is alleged to have occurred). However, community-level problems, especially cyclical ones, can be dealt with *before* they happen. That is one priority of a community safety agenda, which seeks both to handle events that damage public safety after they have occurred and to prevent their occurrence in the first place.

Just as the focus on places does not replace a focus on cases, the concern for proactive strategies does not eliminate the need for effective ways of reacting to criminal events that occur despite the proactive work. Criminal justice will always be evaluated, at least partly, on how well it responds to crimes that have occurred. The advent of community justice has meant that criminal justice is also evaluated on the extent to which it has been able to build strategies that prevent crime from occurring in the first place. This is especially true for both individual-level and community-level strategies.

Problem Solving, Not Just Blaming. Traditional criminal justice has been described as a "blaming" and "sanctioning" institution. Legal philosopher Andrew von Hirsch (1993) has pointed out that a criminal conviction requires both a finding of personal culpability and a finding of blameworthiness. In finding a person guilty of a crime, we hold that the person did the crime (culpability) and that the person was wrong to have done it (blameworthiness). From this perspective, the "problem" of a crime is that a person appears to have committed one, and the "solution" is that the person needs to be punished.

Community-oriented criminal justice recognizes that a broader view of the crime problem is needed. How the crime affects the victim and the community is a potential problem that needs to be addressed; how the sanction might affect the offender and those close to that offender also matters. Just as significant is the need to understand the problems that may have given rise to the crime and then to try to address those as part of the prevention agenda for public safety.

Under a community-oriented criminal justice philosophy, it is reasonable to expect wrongdoers to be found culpable and blamed for what they have done. It is also expected that the problems the crime has created for the community and the victim will be addressed, and the problems that a sanction will impose on those connected to the offender will be considered in determining how to sanction the offender. Another objective of the community justice orientation is to identify the problems in the community that make crime more likely to occur and to try to reduce their impact on community life. Thus, public safety is seen as a challenge to the system's problem-solving capacity at several levels.

Decentralization, Not Hierarchy. Because criminal justice so often places a premium on the use of authority in response to crime, there is a tendency for criminal justice organizations to have a hierarchical, authoritarian style: a chief district attorney to whom everyone else is an assistant and a chief probation officer to whom everyone else is a deputy. The same hierarchical structure is typical in law enforcement and institutional corrections, with a chain of command, operations manuals, and standard rules and procedures. In this kind of organization, authority is concentrated at the top, and discretion is limited at the bottom.

Community-oriented criminal justice strategies cannot operate within a rigid, hierarchical organizational culture. There are several reasons for this, but two are prominent. First, because these strategies tend to be oriented to specific places – neighborhoods – within larger legal jurisdictions, it is necessary to decentralize leadership to those sub-jurisdictional levels. Criminal justice officials responsible for services delivered in specific neighborhoods must have a certain autonomy to work there. This autonomy is made necessary by the second reason for decentralization: neighborhoods are not all alike, so a degree of flexibility is needed to tailor the activity to fit the particulars of the given neighborhood. Even though the law must give all citizens equal protection, the justice official working in a particular neighborhood must form relationships with residents and businesses there, develop problem-solving strategies that meet neighborhood needs, and prioritize the most critical issues in that neighborhood. A command structure where every decision emanates from the very top of the organization does not fit this service delivery philosophy at the neighborhood level.

Fluid Organizational Boundaries, Not Fragmented Organizational Accountability. Traditional criminal justice organizations have a sense of their "turf" and work hard to protect it. Police do not like meddling by courts, prosecutors, or correctional officials; prosecutors are not concerned with how their work affects other parts of the system, and so forth. In classic organization theory, criminal justice organizations work hard to protect their boundaries from incursion by other organizations, even sister organizations serving the same constituency.

Community-oriented approaches form partnerships at the neighborhood level, and protecting organizational boundaries takes a backseat to the need to form and sustain cross-organizational strategies that produce public safety. Police and probation officers start to work together, and court services intermingle with traditional social services to provide a more comprehensive response to the problems arising from crime that are faced by victims, offenders, and other citizens. A premium is placed on effective coordination and cooperation, not effective separation.

Comprehensive Community Change Initiatives

Some neighborhoods face problems besides public safety, including housing, employment, child care, and health. Each of these problems is difficult, but together, they can create a daunting situation for those who want to improve the neighborhood's prospects. These issues are challenging to deal with because they are interconnected. People with poor health find it difficult to obtain or maintain good jobs, for example, and single mothers can only easily work with child care.

In recent years, a new strategy for addressing the multidimensional aspects of poor communities has emerged, called comprehensive community change (CCC). CCCs are systematic ways to confront the most entrenched problems communities face. They work by establishing a local development corporation that operates under legal authority to build approaches that confront the communities' most pressing problems. CCCs that form neighborhood development corporations composed of resident staff and volunteers are referred to as local intermediaries. They are local in that they do not address problems outside the specific neighborhood boundaries within which they work. They are intermediaries in that they build partnerships among businesses, services, and institutions operating inside the neighborhood, and they seek grants and other funds to establish new services or augment existing services for the neighborhood area. Sometimes, they provide the services themselves, but other times, they help bring together organizations and individuals who are in a position to provide the services themselves.

The starting place for CCCs, and their most successful work area, has been housing. Working in neighborhoods where affordable housing was a real need, CCCs brought together investors, builders, and community groups to take advantage of federal tax credits and create a climate in which the renovation and construction of housing were more likely to succeed, both financially and socially. With a history of success in developing housing, CCCs have recently turned their attention to creating jobs and improving services for children, especially health care for infants and expectant mothers.

Some people believe that a natural next step in this work is to address public safety concerns. This seems to be an obvious expansion of the CCC idea because the lessons learned by focusing on housing, employment, and youth fit well into the problems surrounding public safety. Three examples follow.

Political Empowerment. Most people think of community organizing as a process by which residents band together and march on City Hall to demand new services, more resources, and attention for their political leadership. However, one of the most important new lessons of the CCI movement has been that this form of confrontational organizing often does not work in the face of more insidious contemporary responses. As with any power-based confrontation, there is the ever-present prospect of confronting a more powerful opponent. City Hall can overcome this sort of pressure in many ways: build a counter-pressure bloc, pit one neighborhood against another, or even buy off some of the leaders of the complaining group. The approach can even backfire if the neighborhood comes to be seen as a political problem and no political actors want to be associated with it. City Hall may dig in its heels to teach the organizing group a lesson or avoid facing similar claims from other sources. Although sometimes unavoidable, confrontational strategies rarely work out as intended and usually lead to a series of countermoves by opposing political forces.

Therefore, CCCs have developed a new understanding in recent years of what it means to be empowered and what empowerment requires. In these cases, rather than try to become powerful "against" some group, neighborhoods try to find a way to align themselves with strong interests, redirect the efforts of those interests toward mutually beneficial outcomes, and gain power through the coalition of interest groups. For example, a neighborhood that wants to renovate its schools will find that rather than march on City Hall, it will have more success by building a cooperative relationship with a firm that does renovation, a bank that wants to invest in improving the community, and a citizens' group willing to volunteer time working on the project. Rather than start a public outcry for more police protection – which, even if responded to positively, may not address the core issues and may produce other unintended consequences – the neighborhood will have more success by developing relationships among a local parents' group, the police precinct leadership, and some of the local faith leaders. Today, grassroots approaches to organizing are increasingly employing more sophisticated ways to create power by bringing together groups who share a common interest in solving the underlying problem.

Economic Development. Economic development is one of the best areas where mutual interests can lead to empowerment. Investors know that places where employment is low, people are poor, and businesses are few – as in most high-crime areas – are places where it takes much work to establish a profitable business. At the same time, these locations represent untapped markets because there is such a dearth of business that the competition is slim. Suppose a few of the problems these places face can be alleviated. In that case, they will become wide open as potential markets for new businesses, especially businesses that provide essential goods and services to residents.

Seeing these areas as opportunities for economic development rather than as economic disasters opens up an entirely new conversation about them. Instead of avoiding them, businesses should be encouraged to form partnerships to help cultivate these changes. For example, construction firms that renovate existing structures benefit as partners when investors open up new businesses in these areas, and employers benefit when housing improvements lead to a more stable residential population. For all parties, providing an environment with fewer public safety problems is an essential foundation for economic expansion.

Therefore, CCC initiatives have started fashioning a workable partnership among investors, housing interests, and renovators that can create a basis for economic improvement. Here again, the act of forging partnerships among those whose interests align creates the empowerment needed to establish economic improvements.

Service Sector Improvements. In most areas, services are provided by separate agencies operating in a fragmented manner. In multiproblem areas, residents often contact more than one service provider at a time: it is not uncommon for a single family to have different members involved with welfare, housing support, child care, and health care. Again, this is an area where forging coalitions of organizations whose interests align can help solve problems. In a one-stop-service-center model in these communities, local organizations have been facilitating the creation of service consortiums that work together in the same building, enabling them to coordinate and strengthen their services to those in need. CCC initiatives often provide office space to these entities and channel residents to those comprehensive service centers.

Public safety organizations have observed these CCC-based strategies and have begun to see how these approaches can be adapted to the public safety agenda. They see, for example, the profound empowerment that occurs when private and public interests combine to create solutions to the problems that make public safety a priority. They can see how economic development and public safety go hand in hand, and making headway on one necessitates improvements in the other. They can also see how creating effective partnerships among justice service providers can increase the impact of those services. Therefore, the CCC model has lessons for those seeking to promote community justice.

Evaluation of Community Justice Initiatives

As criminal justice agencies begin to work more closely with communities to build informal social networks and human capital, methods and standards for evaluation will be needed. Evaluation must be completed to know if projects or programs are having the desired effects. Knowing if goals and objectives are being met allows the participants to modify or continue a program depending on the results obtained during the evaluation.

Currently, criminal justice agencies utilize qualitative methods to determine effectiveness, but these standards will not work in this new type of relationship development. Pure numbers will not properly assess the work being done and governmental entities must be prepared to utilize broader, non-numerical evaluation methods. One reason that numerically based evaluation has been so heavily utilized in criminal justice program evaluation is that it is easily done. The collection of numerically based data can be completed quickly, and the results can be reported succinctly to the governing bodies that fund the criminal justice agencies. These funders may be local, state, or federal governments relying heavily on numerically based evaluations. Funding for criminal justice projects may also come from external funding entities such as foundations or nonprofit organizations. Reporting results to these funders in a numerically based evaluation is quick and usually can be done through in-house criminal justice agency elements. What criminal justice agencies may struggle with is the acceptance that community justice evaluation will best be completed with a combination of quantitative and qualitative methods, which will necessitate evaluating criminal justice agencies' performance differently than it has been in the past.

The evaluation methods utilized will affect entities outside of the criminal justice system as well, and it would be prudent to consult with these various groups prior to developing evaluation standards. As discussed earlier, a cookie-cutter approach to evaluation would be problematic because each community will have different needs and objectives. While criminal justice agencies may have the most difficulty adjusting to new evaluation criteria, there may also be discomfort with other participants, especially those who may commit to funding programs or projects.

In most evaluations, evaluators examine outputs, outcomes, impacts, and processes. Outputs are the goods or services produced by the program or project. They are usually easily measured but do not address the effect of the program or project. Outcomes are the effects of the interventions and can be measured. Measurements can provide the evaluator with information about what events or actions resulted from implementing the program or project. Impacts are longer-term effects that address broader issues beyond the specific program or project. Because impact evaluation depends more on longitudinal methods, they do not tend to provide the immediate feedback that outcome and impact evaluation can provide. Processes are the methods or mechanics used to implement and carry out the program or project. Evaluation of processes focuses on efficiency issues relating to the program or project. In order to obtain a comprehensive evaluation of a program or project, all four evaluation methods should be utilized.

Thurman et al. (2001) discuss several approaches to conducting evaluation. While their work primarily focuses on community policing, it provides some possible approaches for developing evaluation in the area of community justice where more stakeholders will be involved in the interventions. The approaches are:

1 **Intuitive versus Scientific.** Intuitive approaches depend upon the beliefs and perceptions of those evaluated. Often, there is no systematic method for collecting this data, and it relies on perceptions from those who may not have all the information necessary to draw an informed conclusion.
2 **Passive versus Active.** Passive approaches rely on unsolicited information provided by the participant. While it is not wise to discard all unsolicited input, those receiving it must be aware that emotion or other personal agendas may drive the sharing of the information; therefore, it is imperative that this information be carefully scrutinized. Active approaches are initiated by the evaluator and involve systematic data collection. Such approaches usually contain more objective data that can be analyzed and generalized.
3 **Narrow versus Broad.** Narrow approaches may only focus on one or two aspects of the program and exclude vital information needed for a proper program evaluation. Broad approaches tend to be more comprehensive and allow more information to be learned about the program.
4 **Summative versus Formative.** Summative evaluations are concerned with the effectiveness of a program as it relates to specific program objectives. These evaluations will advise the evaluator if the program meets specific goals. Formative approaches focus on gathering information that allows needed changes or modifications to the program. Information gathered from this approach will provide the evaluator with data about how to change or modify the program to meet the stated goals.
5 **Insiders versus Outsiders.** Inside approaches utilize people working in or with the program to gather data and determine the findings. Outside approaches utilize independent persons to carry out data collection and analysis.

The Police Executive Research Forum recommends five perspectives on implementing the philosophy of community policing. These approaches appear appropriate for implementing community justice as well and could be modified to meet the needs of involved constituents.

The perspectives are deployment, community revitalization, problem-solving, customer, and legitimacy.

The *deployment* perspective addresses how resources are moved into the community. In community policing, this involves how officers are deployed to increase positive contact with citizens. From a community justice approach, this perspective would explain how necessary resources are deployed into a high-impact area. Because community justice involves more entities than criminal justice agencies, these resources should include governmental, nonprofit organizations, and private sector workers. By developing a deployment plan, the resources needed can be identified more accurately, and the deployment can be completed in an organized and efficient manner.

The *community revitalization* perspective focuses on neighborhood decay and eliminating the fear of crime. This perspective appears to be custom-designed for a community justice approach since much of the work in high-impact areas entails addressing physical infrastructure problems, reducing opportunities for crime, and lowering the fear of crime. In a community justice approach, it could also involve the strengthening of social networks to build social capital.

The *problem-solving* perspective involves a focused approach to crime and disorder problems that involves both the police and the community in identifying a problem, analyzing its scope, developing a response, and assessing the effect of the response. Such a structured approach to problem-solving in community justice could ensure that all constituents are working together to solve identified problems. Problem solving in community justice involves solving problems in issues outside of crime such as education, employment, transportation, and the physical infrastructure.

The *customer* perspective emphasizes the importance of listening to the needs of the citizens. This perspective is vital because for community justice to succeed, those in high-impact areas must become part of identifying and solving problems affecting their lives. The paternalistic approach of telling citizens in high-impact areas what their problem is and how an outside element will fix it will not empower the residents to take charge of their community. The community justice efforts cannot be seen as something that is being done *to* residents but something that is done *with* residents.

The *legitimacy* perspective involves establishing the credibility of the police as a fair and equitable public service organization that works with all aspects of the community without favoring one element over another. In community justice, such a perspective expands the earning of credibility to elements outside the criminal justice system. Governmental agencies, businesses, and nonprofits must ensure their actions show that their resources are dispensed equally. One prominent place where this credibility could be shown is in the area of economic development projects in high-impact areas. Economic development requires not only private sector investment but also government and nonprofit support.

The above perspectives could be used to establish goals and objectives in implementing community justice initiatives. Data could be collected via direct observation, focus groups, surveys, official records, and social and physical disorder inventories (Thurman et al. 2001).

Community Justice Within Traditional Criminal Justice Functions

Community justice ideas are not new to the criminal justice system. The leading criminal justice organizations – police, courts, and corrections – have been exploring various ways to improve community relevance with new programs and strategies, and these have formed the basis for a more comprehensive understanding of the possibility of community justice more broadly realized. The following three chapters discuss how some criminal justice agencies have approached community-oriented activity.

Conclusion

It is important to remember that community justice is still an emerging set of experiments that range widely in scope and practice. Policymakers and practitioners are inventing new applications every day. In some cases, these applications will be rooted in the broken windows theory of neighborhood disorder. In others, they will seek to address community weaknesses ascribed by social disorganization theories. Moreover, in still others, they will look to strengthen informal social control and build social capital in a neighborhood, which is crucial to public safety in theories of collective efficacy. What holds these differing initiatives together as community justice and distinguishes them from other criminal justice innovations is that they are rooted in two basic assumptions: (1) there are critically important differences between communities – as between rich and poor – that suggest the need to tailor criminal justice strategies to the particular problems and priorities of each and (2) the influence of stable families, good neighbors, effective social organizations, positive peers, and other informal networks of social control are the most critical foundation for public safety.

The result is that regardless of their scope or the particular form that they take, community justice strategies will be characterized by a unique set of common concerns. They will focus on the circumstances of specific places, not just on individuals. They will be proactive in that they will head off problems before they occur rather than respond to them only after they have become critical. They will be enacted through collaborations within the criminal justice system that cross agency boundaries and collaborations outside the system with new community partners, such as community development corporations. In so doing, community justice will adopt new priorities associated with community well-being that are not strictly limited to immediate public safety concerns but also include factors contributing to the underlying causes of crime. In neighborhoods entrenched in poverty, improved employment prospects, health care, and housing all become the shared concern of community actors and the criminal justice system.

Because community justice is as concerned with social justice as with traditional criminal justice, it will measure its success in new terms. Whether the operations of the police, courts, or corrections are being considered, community justice will seek to answer this question: Have justice activities improved the community's well-being and the capacity of its residents to affect the quality of safety in their neighborhood?

Suggested Web Sources for Readers

Social Capital – www.bettertogether.org
The Urban League – www.nul.org
Housing and Urban Development – www.hud.gov Accessed 8/7/2024
CommunityTool Box from the University of Kansas – http://communityhealth.ku.edu/ctb/about_the_ctb.shtml

References

Cadora, E. & Swartz, C. (2000). Community Justice Atlas, Center for Alternative Sentencing and Employment Services (CASES). Unpublished report.

Cear, T.R., & Rose, D. (1999). *When neighbors go to jail: Impact on attitudes about formal and informal social control*. National Institute of Justice Research in Brief (July).

Ivanhoe Neighborhood Council. (n.d.). *Welcome Ivanhoe: A thriving community*. Retrieved 2/11/2024 http://www.incthrives.org

Karmen, A. (2001). *New York Murder Mystery: The true story behind the crime crash of the 1990s*. New York University Press.

Moynihan, D.P. (1969). *Maximum feasible misunderstanding: Community action in the war on poverty*. Free Press.

Putnam, R.D. (2000). *Bowling alone: The collapse of American community*. Simon and Schuster.

Putnam, R.D. (2007). E Pluribus Unum: Diversity and Community in the Twenty-first Century- the 2006 Johan Skytte Prize Lecture. *Scandinavian Political Studies, 30*(2). https://doi.org/10.1111/j.1467-9477.2007.00176.x

Sampson, R.J., Raudenbush S.W., & Earls, F. (1997). "Neighborhoods and violent crime: A multilevel study of collective efficacy." *Science* (August), 277 (5328), 918–924. DOI: 10.1126/science.277.5328.918.

Sherman, L.W., Gartin, P.R., & Buerger, M.E. (1989). Hot spots of predatory crime: Routine activities and the criminology of place. *Criminology, 27*, 15–27.

Shaw, C.R. & McKay, H.D. (1942). *Juvenile delinquency in urban areas*. University of Chicago Press.

Silverman, E. (1999). *NYPD battles crime: Innovative strategies in policing*. Northeastern University Press.

Skogan, W.G. (1992). *Disorder and decline: Crime and the spiral of decay in American neighborhoods*. University of California Press.

Thurman, Q., Zhao, J., & Giacomazzi, A. (2001). *Community policing in a community era: An introduction and exploration*. Roxbury Publishing Company.

U.S. Department of Justice (1999). National evaluation of weed and seed. *National Institute of Justice: Research in Brief*. NCJ 175685, June 1999. https://www.ojp.usdoj.gov/nij

Von Hirsch, A. (1993). *Censure and sanctions*. Clarendon Press.

Wilson, J.Q., & Kelling, G.L. (1982). Broken windows. *Atlantic Monthly, 249*(3), 29–38.

Wilson, W. (1980). *The declining significance of race: Blacks and changing American institutions*, 2nd ed. University of Chicago Press.

For Further Reading

Social Justice

Barber, B. (1984). *Strong democracy: Participatory politics for a new age*. University of California Press. A description of a civic democratic model of politics.

Braithwaite, J. (1979). *Inequality, crime, and public policy*. Routledge. A theory of the impact of social inequality on crime.

Pettit, P. (1997). *Republicanism: A theory of freedom and government*. Oxford University Press. An explication of the "republican theory" of just governance.

Rawls, J. (1971). *A theory of justice*. Harvard University Press. This is the classic description of a democratic theory of a just society.

The Concept of "Place."

Anderson, E. (1991). *Streetwise: Race, class, and change in an urban community*. University of Chicago Press. A description of how living in impoverished inner cities affects social capability and social life.

Bursick, R.J., & Grasmick, H.G. (1993). *Neighborhoods and crime: The dimensions of effective social control*. Lexington Books. A summary of the literature on social disorganization theory and an integration of that theory with systemic social control theory.

Logan, J. R., & Molotch, H.L. (1987). *Urban fortunes: The political economy of place*. University of California Press. A description of the analytical framework for thinking about "place."

Community

Etzioni, A. (1993). *The spirit of community: Rights, responsibilities, and the communitarian agenda*. Crown. An explanation and advocacy of the philosophy of communitarianism.

Gottdeiner, M. (1994). *The social production of urban space*, 2nd ed. University of Texas Press. How cities and local areas create space, and how space affects social life.

Broken Windows Theory

Kelling, G.L., & Coles, C.M. (1996). *Fixing broken windows: Restoring order and reducing crime in our communities*. New Simon & Schuster. Description of broken windows theory and studies of broken windows policing in action.

Skogan, W. (1992). *Disorder and decline: Crime and the spiral of decay in American neighborhoods*. Free Press. A study of the impact of disorder on crime in Chicago.

Taylor, R.B. (2001). *Breaking away from broken windows: Baltimore neighborhoods and the nationwide fight against crime, fear, and decline*. Westview. A critical assessment of broken windows theory in Baltimore.

3
Policing and Community Justice

The police were, in large part, the first criminal justice agency to embrace the concepts of community justice. So, it is appropriate that we begin our discussion of criminal justice functions with the police. The most apparent way police exemplify community justice is in the deeply embedded community-oriented policing movement that swept across America in the 1980s and 1990s. We will discuss this movement in more detail, but it is worth noting that community justice as a concept owes much of its momentum to the abundant success of community policing.

It is an understatement to say that community policing has swept the profession. Although the roots of community policing go back to at least the 1940s (Carter & Radelet 1998), a groundswell of support for the idea materialized in the 1980s, and by the turn of the twenty-first century, most urban (and many suburban and rural) police departments in the United States openly described themselves as using community-oriented principles which is still true today. This shift to the community level represents an attempt to bring the police closer to the public they serve. Instead of simply responding to crimes, the community police officer builds relationships and partnerships with local businesses, organizations, residents, and social service agencies; the officer uses these relationships to understand the community's needs better, address local problems, and share information more efficiently.

However, the community policing movement, vital as it has been, is not the same as the community justice movement. The latter has derived several of its most important lessons from the former, but their differences are essential to bear in mind. Community policing is both a comprehensive strategy of policing and a philosophy of law enforcement. On the other hand, community justice is a strategy and a philosophy of criminal justice. Recent police innovation experiences in the United States have tested many of the most critical community justice concepts in the police setting and illustrated why community justice has become a popular idea.

In this chapter, we describe the police as an agency of community justice. We begin with a review of some of the issues that face modern police, and we show why community-oriented policing seemed such a valuable way to deal with those issues. We then provide a detailed description of the community- and problem-oriented policing approaches and assess their effectiveness. We conclude with a discussion of the current agenda for community policing advocates.

A Brief History of Community Policing

In the late 1800s and early 1900s, the police were under the control of those with political power – the police helped those who had power and punished those who opposed these powerful individuals. During this time, the public saw the police as corrupt and lawless. Eventually, after much public outcry, the reformers of the 1920s managed to separate the police from political influence and created a professional, military-like administration system. To solve many of the problems of the past and to appear more professional, the police became more distant from the public (Greene 2000; Kelling & Moore 1988).

Technological innovations also increased the rift between officers and the community. Automobiles severely decreased the number of neighborhood beat cops, and the widespread use of telephones and radios allowed residents to quickly and easily contact the police for assistance. The ease with which the police could be contacted significantly increased the number of calls for service, reducing the time officers could spend on crime prevention and relationship building (to ensure public safety, police departments must respond to almost every call). Using computers further increased the gap between officers and the community by increasing the importance of performance statistics and highlighting inferior policing, high-crime areas, crime trends, and response times. Instead of listening to public concerns, officers and managers became slaves to crime statistics (Bureau of Justice Assistance 1994).

The distance between residents and police officers culminated in the social and political unrest of the 1960s when members of both the civil rights movement and the antiwar movement actively participated in civil unrest (Palmiotto & Donahue 1995). During this time, the police were severely criticized for their brutal behavior toward nonviolent protesters and blamed for instigating major riots through their aggressive, uncontrolled actions. These violent incidents, in addition to the well-publicized hostile relationship between minority communities and the police, sparked another set of reforms to improve the relationship between communities and police officers. After a few attempts to establish community policing had failed, the concept evolved and took root in the mid-1980s (Greene 2000). These topics will be expanded upon later in this chapter.

Policy and the Community: A Dual-Track Rationale

Community-oriented policing has two justifications that also apply to community justice in law enforcement. The two aims of community-oriented policing are better community relations and better crime prevention.

Better community relations are needed because police rely on the public to do their jobs, but there are several important impediments to good community relations. Some have to do with different public images of the police: citizens with advantaged social classes tend to see the police positively; people who suffer significant social disadvantages do not have that same positive view. The problem is that the police mission is much more reliant upon the ability to sustain the latter's confidence than the former, and therein lies a challenge: how to obtain and maintain positive interaction with citizens who may be predisposed to be suspicious of the police. But the problem is not only in the attitudes of citizens. Aspects of police culture, the police ethic, and police operations management also interfere with a capacity for positive relations – for example, when police develop cynicism about citizen groups and become pessimistic about their work and when the culture of the "thin blue line" prevents police from having confidence in citizens. Thus far in the 2000s, we have seen community members pay more attention to the tactics and interpersonal skills used by the police when they interact with members of the community. This focus has been more intense in communities of color because more police–community interactions tend to occur in these areas and the concern has grown over recent fatal encounters by police against persons of color during the interactions. Incidents such as the fatal shootings of Michael Brown, Brianna Taylor, Akai Gurley, Tamir Rice, Philando Castile, Stephon Clark, Botham Jean, and Atatiana Jefferson, as well as the deaths of Eric Garner, Freddie Gray, and George Floyd, have created a movement to address police conduct and find ways to fund other social service activities that may help prevent these violent incidents from recurring (*ABC News* 2020).

Better crime prevention relies on community-based practice. As we saw in the previous chapter, street crime concentrates in some locations more than others, and police are more active in these areas. However, if the policing approach is simply to be more active in response to crime – more investigations and more arrests – then the police will always be playing catch-up. If, on the other hand, the solution to high crime levels is to take a proactive approach, there are more possibilities for public safety results. To do this, the police must change how they act in the communities where the most significant police presence is called for.

The Community Relations Rationale for Community Policing

To understand the need for a different orientation to policing, we must begin by reviewing the main issues interfering with police effectiveness. We might be tempted to say offhand that the problem with police effectiveness is too many criminals. There is some truth to the idea that the sheer volume of criminal behavior makes police work a difficult assignment, but that discounts a profound and important truth: Police work faces a series of built-in problems that tend to frustrate police capacity to do their jobs well. This has to do with the nature of the problem and the police themselves, at least in their traditional form.

We begin with a discussion of what we might call "the way things are," that is, certain factors in the job of policing serve to limit the way police can do their work. These are neither criticisms of the police nor complaints about the community. They are merely facts that set the stage for understanding the complexity of the public safety task. This discussion begins with a call for improved community relations as an essential first step in an improved police force, not simply as a desirable but less important goal. The nature of the policing job explains the importance of prioritizing community relations.

The Police: Essential Services Ensnared in Quandary

In most places in the United States, the police and the hospital emergency room are the only public service organizations available 24 hours a day, seven days a week, for citizens in crisis. Hospitals help us when we are sick or have a medical emergency; the police deal with us for almost everything else – and they often get involved in medical emergencies as well. Although we see police around us routinely, we encounter them only when our lives are not routine, such as when we are stopped for a traffic violation, experience some form of victimization, or face an emergency that requires an immediate response from someone in authority.

The fact that police are a full-time community service and that their work almost always comes into play when people are in trouble provides an essential foundation for understanding the police as a part of community justice. In a democracy, where citizens have personal rights and the police exercise carefully limited powers, it is impossible to understand the police and the community without acknowledging a quandary. The most important services provided by police usually take place in the context of somebody being in trouble or in some crisis, so it is quite natural to expect the police to arrive with special powers to intercede. Yet the powers of the police to act are carefully circumscribed by democratic law and tradition, so the immediacy of the predicament is always tempered by the limitations placed on police authority. This often leads to disappointment because the police will often feel constrained in their actions, and citizens will often fail to grasp those constraints. In police–citizen encounters, the reverse problem can also occur. A police officer may interpret the facts of a situation as calling for serious or even urgent action. At the same time, the citizen feels intensely that her or his rights ought to constrain the actions taken by the police.

Small wonder that police often feel in that classic double bind, "damned-if-I-do, and damned-if-I-don't." In this situation, it is easy for police to become cynical, believing nothing can be done to satisfy the public. It is equally likely that the public can become indignant, either objecting to an overreach of authority or disputing a seemingly lackadaisical approach. The significant incidents previously cited have increased the emotions in the community and police agencies. Those in the communities want change to occur immediately, and those in the police service believe that the processes they have in place are necessary and driven by unlawful behavior by members of the community. In conversations between police organizations and the community about these and other use-of-force issues involving the police, there appears to be a sense that some change needs to occur, with both sides struggling with how the change should occur. As the struggle continues, both sides become more entrenched in their beliefs and perceptions, and there can be a tendency to see the other side as unwilling to understand the needs and desires of the other side. This has created polarities, a sense of either-or thinking, and it seems neither side is able or willing to see the positives in the thoughts and feelings of the other. Not having a good structure or process to address these polarities creates frustration and can encourage each side to retreat deeper into the tenets they hold fast.

This predicament of police–citizen encounters provides a powerful backdrop to our understanding of contemporary policing. It helps explain why the topic of policing receives such strong, often opposing, opinions: some people seem to despise the police, while others hold them in extremely high regard. A major defining characteristic for how people feel about the police can be race and age: people of color have lower opinions of the police than do Whites, and young people (especially those of color) have lower opinions than do older people, regardless of race (Pew Research 2022; Sampson & Bartusch 1999). This makes sense, as these are the people most likely to be stopped by the police. But it would be easy to exaggerate this problem when the reality is more complex. In the past, police consistently received a more upbeat performance appraisal than other criminal justice system sectors, even with all these built-in problems (Bureau of Justice Statistics 2000). In a 2022 Gallup poll conducted on confidence in U.S. institutions, confidence in the police was still higher than confidence in the criminal justice system. Interestingly, the confidence level for police dropped from 51% in 2021 to 45% in 2022, and the confidence level for the criminal justice system dropped from 20% in 2021 to 14% in 2022 (Gallup 2022). These results indicate that there is still much work to be done to raise these institutions' legitimacy in the public's eyes.

How can it be that police are simultaneously so heavily criticized and so deeply respected? The answer to this important question lies in an understanding of three aspects of contemporary policing. The police may be simultaneously thought of as a symbol of modern culture, a function of the legal system, and a function of power in society.

Police as a Symbol of Modern Culture

The police represent social control, and they stand for social order. As the main coercive arm of the state, they also represent the power of the government. Consequently, the police generate strong feelings among the public.

Many see the police as the symbol of a safe and secure society. This view holds that all law-abiding citizens share a common interest in safe streets, and the police are one of the primary sources of safety. When police face constraints on their powers, those who see the police as the mechanism of social control often fear that disorder and criminality will follow. Those who hold the symbolic vision of the police as the agency of social control typically support a strong police presence, and they object to "civil liberties" views of the police that emphasize citizens' rights. When police are viewed in this fashion, it is easy to think of society as composed of "good guys" and "bad guys" – the police come from the former group and are asked to control the latter group.

Yet the police also symbolize the raw power of the state, and in a democracy, such power is uncomfortable to citizens. It is disconcerting to members of minority groups who receive more attention from the police: African-Americans, Latinos, and the poor. To those who see the police as a symbol of power, the problem is not public safety but the way to place meaningful reins on that power. These people worry about police authority run amok and police action without control. Because the most disadvantaged in our society are also the most likely to encounter police power used against them, this concern often arises along the lines of social class and social status. People of color, especially young men, are very likely to be suspicious of police and less likely to accept their authority as legitimately exercised. There is a tendency to view the police as treating them and their neighborhoods differently than other people and locations. After the murder of George Floyd in 2020 by a member of the Minneapolis Police Department, a movement was generated that wanted police agencies to be defunded and the money diverted to social service agencies that serve minority communities. The movement gained favor throughout the United States. Still, there was no concrete plan as to how money would be diverted from police agencies and how it would be allocated to social service agencies. In communities where the police were seen as an essential part of social control, the movement to defund police agencies began to lose momentum and support.

It is easy to see how the symbolic importance of police carries community significance. The United States is a residentially segregated society today. Those who live in the residential areas occupied by dominant majorities see the police far more positively than those who live in poor, minority areas. Some of this opinion relates to how the police treat people in those areas. In high-crime locations, suspects are numerous, and suspicious situations are routine; police often tend to take an aggressive stance, and the result is that many citizens feel deeply disrespected on account of the color of their skin. In the low-activity areas, police are less vigilant about crime, and citizens feel under less scrutiny.

Thus, part of what determines the way citizens react to the police is how the police define the citizenry. When police see citizens as potential problems, those citizens often respond by seeing the police as a potentially unwelcome power in their lives. When police see citizens as "residents," those residents will see the police as a support system. How police attitudes toward the public tend to create a public reaction was one of the original sources of the movement toward community policing.

Police as a Function of the Legal System

No matter what the police symbolize, they are, first and foremost, the initial stage of the criminal justice process. They take reports of criminal events, investigate suspicious situations, and make arrests. Few cases enter the criminal justice system without first encountering the police.

For this reason, police work must be assessed on three different criteria: How do police actions affect the willingness of citizens to report crimes? How do these actions encourage citizen cooperation with criminal investigations? And how effective are these strategies in identifying suspects accurately?

We would think that most law-abiding citizens would be anxious to cooperate with the police. However, studies of police–citizen relations find that citizens who have had negative experiences with the police often become reluctant to assist the police in their investigations or report crimes to the police in the first place – even when they are the victims (Clear & Rose 1999). Indeed, in places where police–community relations are poor, citizens show a marked reluctance to report crimes and a strong hesitation to trust the police response to problems.

For police, this lack of cooperation has two sides. Any police officer who has worked in a poor neighborhood, especially a poor minority area, knows the level of mistrust and even antagonism that can permeate the attempt to do the work. It is frustrating because police officers' point of view is that they are only trying to protect the law-abiding citizens from the "bad guys," and the lack of cooperation makes the work that much harder. Then again, not everyone is uncooperative. Some residents have an unabashed enthusiasm for the police to do their work, and this positive response by many highlights the problematic behavior of the others. It is easy for the police to view all the residents who express suspicion as somehow being aligned with "the bad element."

Nonetheless, when folks are reluctant to report crimes, and those surrounded by crime are disinclined to assist the police, the job of law enforcement, difficult enough without citizen recalcitrance, becomes more untenable. After a while, some police can develop an attitude toward the residents of these areas: "Since they don't care, why should I?" Under these circumstances, the fundamental work of policing becomes more and more difficult. To protect themselves from an all-too-often unfriendly public, police adopt a first-choice style of indifference. When a victim or a citizen shows an appreciation for a police officer's effort, this can energize activity on behalf of that citizen. Still, others may come to see this as a kind of favoritism. Ultimately, the credibility of the criminal justice system suffers as citizens lose confidence in it, and the police become more cynical about their work.

Police as a Function of Power in Society

The critical distinction between authority and power can become blurred in this context. *Authority* is the legitimate capacity to require compliance imbued in a role by law, standards, or custom. It is housed in the idea that some consensus exists that the person occupying a specific role ought to have a level of obedience to his or her directives so long as they flow from the legitimate exercise of duties within that role. Judges have authority in the courtroom, teachers in the classroom, supervisors in the workplace, etc. So long as the person with authority is acting consistent with the expectations of the role, we expect voluntary compliance with the directives that emanate from the legitimate performance of that role. All of us have a specific expectation that people will *willingly* comply with the valid directives of a person with the authority to give those directives.

On the other hand, *power* is the raw ability to compel compliance, regardless of the person's willingness to comply. When a person has power concerning specific actions, it means that person can make others do what is wanted through some implied or actual coercive capacity. The ultimate source of power is the force of might – one who is stronger than another might be able to make that person do something, whether that person wants to or not – but power can also derive from the force of law or group solidarity. For example, a police officer stops a person to ask a few questions, using authority, but then decides to detain that person, using the power of arrest.

The distinction between power and authority is critical to bear in mind. Authority is a far more efficient means of getting a person to do something since it works without any direct threat. Someone with the authority to ask does so, and based on that recognized authority, the requested behavior follows. Power, by contrast, requires implied or demonstrated threat: we all know the implications of the statement "You are under arrest." Few of us will doubt the meaning of the order "Stop, or I'll shoot," but pulling out the handcuffs or revolver communicates the statement's meaning.

There is a significant irony here. To work, authority relies on voluntary cooperation, whereas power can be exercised regardless of the other person's willingness to comply. *Authority is given* to the person exercising it by the person who has decided to comply, while *power is taken* by the person giving orders. Power, then, typically comes into play when authority is absent. Yet authority is absent not because of something missing from the police officer's role but because of something missing in the citizen's response to that role. Authority exists because people voluntarily accept the dictates of the police.

Sometimes, power and authority flow together, as when a judge oversees a courtroom, but usually, there are important distinctions between them. In truth, teachers who hope to have broad authority in the classroom have limited power there. Police, who appreciate having broad authority over citizen conduct, exercise power only in ways carefully constrained by law.

Thus, a police officer frustrated by a lack of authority cannot get authority by obtaining more power, even though this may seem to be the way to go. Authority is obtained by coming to be seen as legitimate in the eyes of the citizen, but obtaining power has almost nothing to do with the eyes of the citizen. Indeed, some might say that the more a person turns to power to compel others' compliance, the less everyone would expect that person to have (or even eventually obtain) authority. Often, the exercise of power comes at the expense of authority.

This is one reason why *the police culture* is such an important force in the work world of the police. The police culture is a set of informal standards and norms that develop among police officers and influence how they approach the job (Crank 2004). Volumes have been written about the origins and effects of police culture. The most common descriptions include our points: police learn to approach the public with distrust and suspicion, expect that the public will not understand the job of policing, and view everyone as a potential problem (even dangerous). This cynical stance regarding the public is repeated when it comes to the criminal justice system when the dominant view is some version of "the cops keep doing their job, but everyone else – from judges to probation officers – is soft on crime."

Three points must be emphasized here regarding the police culture. First, the police culture develops in response to the pressures of the job and the department's traditions. Any problem with the police culture is much less an issue of "bad cops" than a human response to the difficulties inherent in police work. Second, police culture is not uniform across all departments and all divisions within departments. Important differences exist that make departments vary from deeply cynical and pessimistic orientations to ones that are much less so. These differences can even exist between, say, plainclothes detective units and the uniformed officers. Third, the police culture is not solely adverse in its effects. By adopting the informal norms of the police culture, newly hired police learn to support each other, avoid common mistakes, and deal with job pressures.

But the police culture can, and often does, get in the way. Because it is typically cynical in its orientation, it tends to discount the value of authority and exalt the importance of power. Indeed, it is common for police to confuse the two, seeking an increase in formal power because of the weak potency of their authority. Most importantly, the dominant police culture puts the police officer at odds with the public. In high-activity areas, where public suspicions often match those of the officers, this is a recipe for alienation. Both the police and the citizens can come to feel that the officers in blue constitute an occupying army from an alien force, all parties at odds with one another and little stake in common. What is often seen is a standoff.

Two very strong values in the police culture are *control* and *dominion*. Control is a term that has unfavorable connotations. In police culture, control refers more to the ability of the officer to ensure that the responsibilities he or she is assigned are carried out in an orderly and effective manner. Officers must secure crime scenes and direct those not cooperating with the officer in discharging required duties. Control assists the officer in order maintenance within the assigned district or patrol area. Much of the emphasis on control comes from the basic academy training received by the recruit officer. Recruits are taught that they must take charge of all situations and that any sign of compromise or inaction can be seen as a sign of weakness, which will be capitalized upon by lawbreakers and disorderly persons. Officers are taught that they must take control first and ask questions later.

One difficulty that arises is that this behavior style is reinforced because the officers encounter more confrontational situations than regular interactive situations. Officers become accustomed to acting this way and find it hard to adjust their controlling behavior in less threatening situations. This can be illustrated by a story once told by an elderly lady attending a community meeting. She said that an officer had arrived at her residence to take a report on a burglary that had occurred, and during the interview, he insisted that she be seated while he stood up to gather the information. The lady noted that the officer stood about 15 feet from her at about a 45-degree angle. The officer also had his feet at a 45-degree angle with his gun side away from her. In relating the story to a commander attending the community meeting, the lady said that she felt the officer's questions were terse and that it was obvious that the officer had no compassion for her victimization. For one familiar with police training, it is clear that the officer was in a "power stance." This stance allows the officer to respond to any threat quickly and sends a message that he or she is ready should an aggressive move be made. The disheartening elements of this story are that the officer while doing nothing wrong, sent a message that he was in clear control of a situation where no threat was present. On the street, the officer's posture would probably not have been noticed; however, in a non-threatening, non-confrontational situation, his posture sent a clear message that he was in charge and the communication was strained.

Dominion is a more passionate part of policing. Crank (2004) uses this term to describe what many would describe as territoriality. While people are somewhat territorial, dominion takes the territoriality one step further. When a person is territorial, they are attentive to the property they own and ensure that others do not damage or take their property. What is often missing in territoriality is the intensity of knowing tiny details about the property or feeling a moral relationship to protect the property. Crank's term dominion refers to the belief of that officer that she or he has personal ownership over the area of assignment. In dominion, the officer knows as many physical details about the area as possible and is very attentive to the comings and goings of persons there. This type of behavior is often perceived unfavorably by residents living in the area, and the behavior can lead to feelings that the police are an occupying force that rules their lives. On the other hand, officers see dominion as a moral responsibility toward protecting the area and the people who reside there. These differences in perception often lead to friction in the relationship between the police and the community, especially where the population is mainly African-American or Hispanic.

While the degree of control an officer uses may be able to be moderated through the changing of training methods, dominion is something more profound. Because dominion is based to a degree on a relationship with the area to which the officer is assigned, it might be possible to modify its exercise into behavior that may be more constructive. If the officer can work with community members to encourage them to be as passionate about their community, social networks could lead a community toward more self-governance. One downside may be the creation of communities that infringe upon other people's rights, but if the passion was implemented in a spirit such as Communitarianism, results could be positive. In any event, community details would be left to the residents, which would positively strengthen community networking.

O'Hara (2012) argues that police effectiveness in communities can also be attributed to law enforcement agencies themselves. He notes several factors that can damage police effectiveness, but four appear to be ones that could negatively affect the relationship of the police and the community and lead to police acting to increase their power over the community as they perform their duties. Structural failure, oversight failure, cultural deviation, and institutionalization are the factors he cites.

Structural failure occurs when the operations, procedures, and processes that are functioning as designed lead to failure. In other words, while the organization may be following their established procedures with good intent, the procedures might actually be causing unintended damage. When police organizations do not recognize this problem, corrections cannot be made to modify or eliminate the procedure. In some cases, "shadow structures" may dilute the authority of the formal structure by not buying into the goals, practices, and norms of the organization and, thusly, counter corrective work being done by the management personnel. Besides the "shadow structures," O'Hara (2012) cites other factors such as inadequate resources, task overload, conflicting mandates, hierarchical dysfunction, and flawed communication systems. An example of a shadow structure in policing could be the informal rogue policing tactics that officers might employ to gain citizen compliance. While the actions may be in opposition to the stated policies of the agency, the working group accepts the behaviors and ensures that through informal processes, the actions are not discovered by management. Officers in these shadow structures often feel that allegiance to each other is more important than allegiance to the organization's policies.

Oversight refers to the monitoring of the integrity of the organizational systems to identify and correct abnormal behaviors that damage morale or the reputation of the organization. When oversight in this area fails, deviant employees may be retained, and their destructive behavior continues unchecked. There have been multiple examples in American policing where an officer has committed an egregious crime, and after investigation, the organization learns the officer was known by other officers for actions outside of accepted practices. Most often, this failure occurs when officers who receive numerous citizen complaints do not receive training or disciplinary actions to correct the behaviors.

Closely connected to the oversight problem is the issue of cultural deviation. According to O'Hara (2012),

> cultural deviation occurs when a group of employees operate in disregard of organizational rules and official norms as a matter of daily process and moral value. When the condition is acute, culturally deviant elements of an organization operate largely unto themselves and for themselves.
>
> (p. 139)

While police culture run amok can be included in the discussion of cultural deviation, it should be recognized that police managers often contribute to this problem by how they handle officers who have misbehaved. Police organizations very often transfer problem officers to different assignments, usually in patrol functions, rather than confront and correct the behavior. This practice can lead to the creation of units or shifts where disgruntled or problematic officers are put into direct contact with community members. A police commander in a patrol function shared with one of the authors that his superiors once informed him that a detective was being transferred from a detective assignment to an assignment under his command due to the detective conducting personal business on duty. The job performance of the detective was well above average, and the infraction had no effect on his work or integrity, but because his commanding officer did not want to implement a disciplinary process to address the infraction, he transferred him. The patrol commander shared that when the officer arrived at the new assignment he was bitter and angry because he enjoyed detective work and felt embarrassed by the transfer. He acknowledged his transgression but became rude to community members on calls for service, creating a new issue that had to be addressed by the patrol commander.

According to O'Hara (2012), institutionalization failure can also contain many symptoms associated with structural failure, oversight failure, and cultural deviance. He describes the condition of institutionalization as one "which incorporates a range of problematic practices to create an organization that is at once pathology-prone and change-resistant" (p. 181). In institutionalization, the organization believes itself to be so important that it becomes arrogant and narcissistic. If the organization is powerful enough, it can get away with these behaviors and ignore the preferences of others. Frequently, these organizations tend to discourage outsiders, including those with legal authority or those directly impacted by their actions, from involvement in their affairs. Moreover, they often demonize those advocating for change or offering suggestions for improvement. Law enforcement organizations can be susceptible to institutionalization when they adopt an attitude of "the public does not like or understand us" or "the public has no idea what we do, and we are the trained experts." In an institutionalized organization, the organization prioritizes maintaining its processes, ways of behaving, and each other. As a result, the organization does not show interest in searching for better practices. According to O'Hara (2012), it ignores the views of communities, opinion-makers, and elected officials about how the agency should or should not conduct business.

Community members often express concern that officers' decisions also create strained relationships with the community. One method to improve officer decision-making processes is problem-based learning (PBL). It is a style of learning developed in medical schools, but recently, it has been incorporated into police training. The goal of PBL is to assist the student in solving unstructured problems. Educators have discovered that students may learn concepts well in the classroom, but when they encounter a problem that does not conform to their technical knowledge base, they are unsure how to address it. Since many problems that police officers encounter are messy and unstructured, PBL provides a method of helping officers pull together knowledge learned in training with experience on the job to address better the problems they confront. Proponents of PBL believe that critical thinking skills and problem-solving improve when learning is based on this model. For police officers, a curriculum based on PBL would involve examining case studies, participating in role-playing, and having open dialogue about unstructured problems. Such training could be very helpful to officers assigned to communities where they encounter daily problems that are not handled effectively through traditional policing methods.

The community-oriented policing movement was an antidote to this sense of a police–citizen standoff. Leadership in policing saw the considerable negatives facing the police: problems with citizen relations, especially in the most disadvantaged communities most needing an effective police presence; difficulties with authority; and concerns about the impact of the police culture on police practices. All of this came together to suggest a need for change. Almost nobody was happy with the way that many communities regarded the police, and there was increasing criticism of the way the police regarded the communities they served. But even with this widespread and growing distress about the relationship between the police and the public, it took an unforeseen development to usher in the police–community era: a string of studies suggesting that the traditional approach was not working.

The Criminal Justice Rationale for Community Policing

Improving police–community relations may be a central objective in building a better police force. Still, other equally important reasons exist to change the relationship between the police and the community. Studies have shown that without good police–community relations, the police face extreme difficulties in carrying out their work. These studies were concerned with various topics in policing, but they led to a consistent general conclusion: the traditional manner of business in police work was not producing good results.

To understand this line of studies, it is important to summarize the traditional policing model. In this approach, police see themselves as professional crime fighters concerned with the problem of serious felonies. This model has two important elements. Concerning citizens, police are expected to be detached and impartial, working "beat assignments," not communities or neighborhoods. Concerning crime, police are reactive and investigative, responding to criminal events based on their seriousness and building the evidence for criminal cases after crimes have been reported.

This professional model was the dominant policing model from the early 1900s until the late 1960s. For most of this time, there was little questioning of the importance of the professional model, and police reforms took consistent patterns: more training, an emphasis on investigation technologies and crime-prevention hardware, and the adoption of paramilitary thinking about command, police deployment, and accountability. The idea was to downgrade the importance of duties that had little to do with crime (traffic, emergency services), allocate the most resources to the most serious crime, focus on rapid responses to criminal events, and maintain a visible deterrent presence on the streets.

The first signs that this orientation might be in trouble came with the 1967 President's Commission on Law Enforcement and the Administration of Justice, which pointed with concern to the increasing problem of urban unrest, often taking the form of riots that began in the wake of some violent encounter between the police and a young person of color. The commission pointed out the urgent need for improvements in the way police dealt with the public, and it called for a reassessment of the way the police defined their responsibilities and provided services to the community.

There was also a serious concern about police performance. Crime and fear of crime were both increasing, while clearance rates for crimes and public confidence in the police were decreasing. Although this context was becoming less hospitable to the traditional policing model, a series of studies led some to conclude that the old emphasis on command policing did not provide adequate results.

The first and most important such study was the Kansas City Preventive Patrol Study (Walker 1992). This study employed a randomized field experiment to compare the effectiveness of standard policing patrol to proactive methods, in which two to three times as many police patrolled the streets, and reactive methods, in which there was no police patrol, and officers only responded to explicit calls for service. After these very different levels of police work had been compared for one year, the crime rates in the areas were compared. The surprising result found no significant difference in the rates of serious crime, fear of crime, attitudes toward the police, or even police response time.

This study threw contemporary police thinking for a loop. The study not only failed to confirm all the usual arguments about the need for more police but also questioned the very assumptions underlying those arguments. Traditional police thinking received a further jolt when studies of police response time – the amount of time it took the police to get to the scene of a crime after a citizen called for help – had little relationship to the probability of apprehending a suspect and was unrelated to citizen satisfaction with the police response. What really mattered was how long it took the police to get to the scene compared to what the citizens thought should happen (Carter & Radelet 1998).

Two other studies caused police to begin to rethink their strategies. A comparison of one-officer and two-officer patrol cars in San Diego tended to favor the use of single officers, both in terms of costs and citizen interactions. In addition, a series of studies of 911 calls for service found that by carefully explaining to citizens the priorities for calls and by helping citizens know how their case was going to be handled, the ascendancy of the 911 system over centrally managed priorities for services could be stemmed (Carter & Radelet 1998).

This string of studies, together with the continuing rise in crime and increasing widespread alarm about public safety, led to a rethinking of what should be the best philosophy of policing. Foot patrol studies heavily influenced rethinking in Flint, Michigan, Newark, New Jersey, and fear-of-crime studies in Newark, New Jersey, and Houston, Texas. The foot patrol studies supported the idea that face-to-face interaction with citizens was an important part of citizen satisfaction with police. The closer cooperation between citizens and police also contributed to safer streets. The fear-of-crime studies found that citizen/police interaction resulting from foot patrols helped reduce the overall level of fear. Together, these and other studies of the emerging idea of community-oriented police work began to call attention to the possibilities of change in policing. An example of an early effort at establishing community policing can be seen in Box 3.1.

> **Box 3.1 Community Policing in Brooklyn**
>
> In 1984, the NYPD created a demonstration project named CPOP (Community Patrol Officer Program) in the 72nd precinct of Brooklyn. Through this program, ten community patrol officers (CPOs) were assigned areas ranging from 16 to 60 square blocks. The CPOs set their own patrol times to maximize their effectiveness, and they were exempt from responding to 911 calls for service. In addition, each CPO kept a "beat book" with information on local issues and problems, strategies for solving the problems, and lists of community organizations. A plan for addressing neighborhood problems was outlined each month (Pate & Shtull 1994).
>
> In 1990, the 72nd precinct was chosen to be a model precinct to test the feasibility of instigating a citywide community policing initiative. The following goals of the model precinct project were stated (Pate & Shtull 1994, pp. 387–389):
>
> - Develop an organizational structure that facilitates the transition to community policing (increase staff, consolidate units, establish neighborhood beats).
> - Develop an operational system that promotes and encourages the practice of community policing (improve communication among officers and develop monthly work plans).
> - Develop an information system that would support community- and problem-oriented policing (analyze crime "hot spots"; create daily calls-for-service reports).
> - Develop a system that would allocate the calls-for-service workload between foot patrol and motor patrol officers (low-priority calls will be routed to foot patrol officers whenever possible).
> - Work with other departments to develop a comprehensive community policing model (detectives would be required to attend community meetings; introduce a fully staffed narcotics unit to the precinct that will work with foot officers).
> - Develop a training program for all precinct personnel (teach concepts of community policing and problem-oriented policing).
>
> Officers enjoyed the flexible hours and the opportunity to do something different and interact with community members. Interactions with residents in nonemergency situations made the job more interesting and more pleasant. Some officers did not want to join the unit because of the challenges of working outside in all types of weather, the feelings of being vulnerable without a partner, problems with responding to emergencies without a vehicle, the perceived lack of excitement, the lack of a clear reward structure, and uncertainties about the possibility of promotion (Pate & Shtull 1994).

Community Policing

Community policing has three main sources of intellectual development. Robert C. Trojanowicz of Michigan State University was one of the more prominent scholars to write about the idea (Trojanowicz & Bucqueroux 1990). He founded the National Center for Community Policing, which advanced the ideas of the community-based (sometimes called neighborhood-based) model. According to Trojanowicz, community policing is a full-service policing model where the same officer regularly patrols the same area and forms partnerships with residents to solve problems. Mark Moore of Harvard's Kennedy School of Government initiated a series of Police Executive Seminars in the 1980s that clarified the theoretical and practical basis of community-oriented policing and helped spread the innovation nationwide. The most significant source of the change was the U.S. Department of Justice Community-Oriented Policing Office, which worked closely with the Police Executive Research Forum (PERF) to conduct workshops, studies, and seminars while publishing numerous reports on the concept.

Police scholars have identified three types of community-oriented policing: community-building strategies, which attempt to strengthen community capacity; problem-oriented strategies, which deal with the causes of crime; and broken windows strategies, which focus on minor crimes and physical disorder. We discuss the status of community policing using these main approaches as guides (Mastrofski et al. 1995) and have added a discussion on evidence-based policing (EBP) as a possible fourth type of community policing. EBP has elements from all three strategies, which makes it somewhat of a hybrid approach.

Community-Building Strategies

The most common form of community policing includes a range of tactics that help strengthen the community's ability to reduce crime. Some of these are mundane and have proven to be of limited value, such as Neighborhood Watch or neighborhood meetings (Skogan 1992). Others are of more durable impact, such as victim-assistance programs, police–minority relation initiatives, and the long-standing Police Athletic League. Various strategies are theorized to improve crime-prevention effectiveness in three ways.

First, the effect of increased day-to-day interaction between community residents and beat officers is thought to promote community-based "intelligence." The more police talk to local businesses and other neighborhood residents, the more information they can obtain about crime and criminals in the area. Second, the same contacts are thought to provide another way to reduce crime when the flow of information is reversed. That is, when police publicize information about trouble spots or crime events, residents are more informed and able to act to protect themselves. Third, and perhaps most broad, is the belief that "police legitimacy" within the neighborhood is crucial to effective local crime prevention because citizens are more forthcoming with crime information, and some residents act in more law-abiding ways (Sherman et al. 1996).

These strategies have in common their attempt to improve some aspect of community life by increasing interaction among residents or creating a standing relationship between the community and the police. Community building is an intuitively attractive idea, as the communities hardest hit by crime are also the ones that most need development. However, attempts to develop these communities also meet significant obstacles. Skogan's studies of community policing in Chicago show that it is difficult to sustain community interest in developmental activity, and even police who are enthusiastic about the idea sometimes find themselves like fish out of water when it comes to community organizing (Skogan & Hartnett 1997).

These obstacles derive in part from the very premise of their goals. Hard-hit communities are the ones that struggle the most to make more time to meet after hours and increase their everyday obligations. Strategies that focus on building relationships with effective community networks suffer when those networks are weak or need to be developed. Thus, the communities most in need of assistance are also the least able to take advantage of this approach.

Criminal justice agencies must change from the law enforcement approach to working more with communities. It is often difficult to convince police officers that their job entails more than just arresting offenders and putting them in jail. When discussion about forming relationships with members of the community is raised, the responses of police officers vary, but it is not uncommon for one response to be, "I'm not a social worker; I'm a cop."

One approach that has been raised in helping officers better police their areas of assignment and form relationships is the medical model of policing. This approach combines the analytical, relational, and enforcement approaches that allow officers to be varied in their work.

Harpold (1996, 2000) identifies six types of neighborhoods: (1) Integral – have high levels of pride; (2) Parochial – have homogeneous values and cultures; (3) Diffuse – residents have much in common but rarely interact; (4) Stepping-stone – starter homes where residents begin their home-owning experience; (5) Transitory – residents move frequently or have little in common with other residents, which causes a lack of consensus and cohesion; and (6) Anomic – residents have accepted criminal victimization as a way of life. By identifying these neighborhoods, Harpold helps police officers see more clearly how neighborhoods differ and why they cannot be policed with a cookie-cutter approach. In proposing the medical model of policing, Harpold argues, "Just as doctors can detect cancer early and prevent it from spreading, police can work in communities to influence the variables that threaten community pride and self-esteem. Early treatment can help the community from becoming ill" (Harpold 2000, p. 24). He sees the police as diagnosticians who can work with the residents to establish a course of treatment that addresses neighborhoods' specific problems.

In the medical model, the police officer is charged with learning about the neighborhood just like a physician would learn about a patient. For police officers, this can be done by using sociodemographic data, comparative crime analysis, and community surveys and interviews. After gathering the necessary data about the neighborhood, the officers, just like physicians, may find that traditional and non-traditional methods are needed to combat the problems. Harpold believes that just as physicians may be required to use aggressive methods of treatment such as surgery or chemotherapy, the police may have to use aggressive methods such as arrest and search and seizure. He cautions that the police officer must be careful not to treat the symptoms and not the disease. Such a mistake can be avoided by becoming intimately familiar with the neighborhood being treated.

Just as in medicine, Harpold (1996, 2000) uses some of the same terminology in discussing the implementation of the model. In *Intensive Care*, there is a need for the intense application of services from governmental, public, and private entities. In *Preventive Medicine*, crime prevention practices such as Crime Prevention through Environmental Design (CPTED) and neighborhood watch are used to strengthen immunity to crime. In *Health Education*, the officer helps residents share responsibility for their own health and define boundaries for accepted behavior by residents. While the previously listed items pertain to the neighborhood, *Bedside Manner* pertains to the police. Just as the relationship between a patient and a physician is essential, the relationship between the residents of a neighborhood and the police is equally important because for residents to follow the plan established, a relationship with the police based on mutual respect must be established. For police, this means that everyone must be treated with courtesy and respect unless they show they will not reciprocate. To help officers implement this thinking, they should ask themselves, "How would I like to be treated?" From an organizational perspective, police managers may need to intentionally select officers who have a service-oriented approach to their job to participate in this type of policing. The final point, *Physician Heal Thyself*, addresses the need for police agencies to be healthy before treating neighborhoods. Harpold says this organizational health can be achieved through pride, self-esteem, quality leadership, and comprehensive training.

The medical model concept is not flawless, but it can help police agencies understand the need to be more holistic in policing neighborhoods. It may also help police agencies that have resisted community policing strategies fell more comfortable in adopting more progressive policing techniques. Community policing has taken a rap from police because of the perception that it is soft on crime and counter to the law enforcement mission of policing. The medical model includes traditional policing methods when necessary but also interactive approaches that address long-term problem solving. Many times, police officers become frustrated because they attend neighborhood meetings where only a small number of residents attend. In these situations, it is easy for officers, especially younger ones, to believe that working with the neighborhood is not worth their efforts if the neighborhood does not help itself. With that conviction, it is easy for officers to revert to traditional law enforcement tactics to address crime and other problems. Connell et al. (2008) examined an officer-initiated community policing program in a suburban police department and found a significant reduction in violent and property crimes in the targeted area. The study noted two interesting factors that might account for the project's success. The first is that the officers selected to work on the project had been selected based on their desire to participate in the initiative. The second is that the community policing model was not implemented department-wide, only in a single unit. These findings appear to be in concert with the ideas from the medical model, which proposes a careful selection of officers who will participate with the neighborhood in developing a prescription to address the problems facing the neighborhood.

Problem-Oriented Strategies

Developed by Herman Goldstein (1991), problem-oriented policing (POP) strategies are based on the idea that crime emanates from particular, persistent circumstances that can be identified, documented, and then overcome through systematic action, and that police should be more thoughtful and innovative when dealing with neighborhood issues. The POP approach is very focused in its method, and although several problem-oriented techniques have been proposed, the SARA (Scan, Analyze, Respond, Assess) method is the most popular. Using SARA, the officer scans the community for problems, analyzes each problem systematically, designs a specific response to each problem, and then assesses the usefulness and success rate of the response (Greene 2000).

For example, an officer might scan the community and identify drug dealing as the main problem. The officer then analyzes the locations of drug-related activities, the times of day these activities take place, the opinions and feelings of community residents and businesses, and the capacity of neighborhood organizations, social services, and religious institutions to aid in developing a solution. After careful thought and planning, the officer might decide that the best response is increased foot patrols by officers and citizen groups in specific locations, along with improved street lighting in these areas. The officer might also decide to contact the landlords of the buildings where the drug dealers live or work and attempt to get the offenders evicted or arrange to have surveillance cameras installed. Once the response has been implemented, the officer assesses the change in drug dealing and any changes in resident perceptions to see if the initiative worked.

One of the more successful problem-oriented strategies has been hot spot policing. This style of strategic policing is derived from the fact that a tiny percentage of addresses in a jurisdiction account for a significantly disproportionate number of criminal events. These locations can be identified by mapping crimes, and strategies can be designed to ameliorate the problems that make these places more criminally involved. For example, a check-cashing store between two bars can become problematic, or a liquor store on a dark corner can invite crime. The hot spots model is also closely related to a school of crime prevention called situational crime prevention (Brantingham & Brantingham 1990), which is based on the idea that crimes occur when situations exist that make crime possible. Situational crime-prevention methods study the distribution of crime across time and space to identify why these two factors coincide so frequently. Cornish and Clarke (2003) developed 25 techniques for implementing situational crime prevention. The techniques are divided into five specific groups: Increasing the Effort, Increasing the Risk, Reducing the Rewards, Reducing Provocations, and Removing Excuses.

Problem-solving methods seek intelligence-based policing tactics. One of the first versions of intelligence-based policing is New York City's CompStat (comparative statistics) meetings. Credited by many as a significant contributing factor in New York City's drop in crime (Silverman 1999), the CompStat process involves the spatial analysis and mapping of crime at the precinct level (precincts are approximately the size of a neighborhood) and a report on any increases in criminal activity and the ways the local precinct will deal with these increases.

The meetings are an important facet of a comprehensive interactive management strategy emphasizing accountability while providing local commanders with considerable discretion and the resources necessary to manage their commands properly. It ensures they remain current on crime and quality of life conditions within their areas of responsibility. The meetings serve as a forum in which precinct and other operational unit commanders communicate the problems they face to the agency's top executives while sharing successful crime reduction tactics with other commanders. The process allows top executives to carefully monitor issues and activities within precincts and operational units better in order to evaluate the skills and effectiveness of middle managers and more effectively allocate the resources necessary to reduce crime and improve police performance..

It should be noted that the CompStat process and any use of computer mapping to locate crime hot spots do not, by themselves, represent community policing. This technique must be used in conjunction with community partnerships and community-level problem-solving to form a complete community policing initiative. Also, any current community policing initiative could significantly improve its crime-fighting capabilities using spatial analysis – knowing where crimes occur is one of the most critical pieces of information for police departments. Over the past few years, interest by police agencies in implementing CompStat-style approaches to fighting crime may have declined, but the Bureau of Justice Assistance (BJA) and the PERF note that there are a wide variety of CompStat-type programs still in place (2013). They found that many police agencies have adjusted the model to meet their agency's specific needs. Both BJA and PERF emphasize that it is important that agencies looking to implement CompStat-type programs focus on the four CompStat principles: timely and accurate information or intelligence, rapid deployment of resources, effective tactics, and relentless follow-up. They also found that departments are examining how CompStat can be used to track other important measures such as the use of force, public opinion about police, complaints against officers, and metrics used to assess community policing effectiveness. These additional foci could bring community members into the CompStat process and strengthen partnerships.

Crime mapping has become an important tool for intelligence-led approaches to problem solving. The ability to input data into a program that can create a visual depiction of the issue being examined has been beneficial not only for law enforcement practitioners but also to community members working with a law enforcement partner.

More recent advancements in crime mapping have included risk terrain modeling (RTM). RTM provides a statistically valid way to identify areas that may be crime-prone at the micro level. The analysis is based on the spatial influence of many landscape features, such as bars, parks, schools, foreclosures, and fast-food restaurants (Caplan et al. 2017). The risk values in an RTM do not suggest that crime is inevitable; instead, they identify locations where, if the conditions are right, the risk of illegal behavior will be higher.

Once underlying spatial factors that create risks at high-crime places are diagnosed, police agencies can design interventions that suppress crime in the short term and make them less attractive to criminals in the long run, according to Caplan, Kennedy, and Piza. They explain that the environmental risk factors are selected based on empirical research evidence and knowledge from officers who can provide experience-based justification for choosing some of the factors.

Caplan et al. (2017) note that one or more features of the physical environment can elevate the crime risk. They cite multiple benefits in using RTM, such as enabling intervention activities to focus on places, not just people, which can positively affect public perception and community relations. In addition, RTM is a sustainable technique because past crime data are not needed to continue to make valid forecasts. This allows the police to rely less on traditional law enforcement actions such as stops, arrests, and citations and instead focus efforts on mitigating the spatial influences of risky features, with the goal being to reduce risk factors in post-intervention RTMs or suppress them completely and remove them from the post model altogether.

Broken Windows Strategies

Another influential idea in policing was the broken windows thesis (Wilson & Kelling 1982). We have described this thesis in detail elsewhere, but here, we consider the concept's implications for police practices. A detailed description of the broken windows philosophy of policing has been provided by one of its originators, George Kelling, along with Catherine Coles (1996). They describe the experiences of broken window strategies in various locations of New York City, San Francisco, and elsewhere. In these locations, the idea of broken windows has been credited with reducing crime and increasing public order.

Because the broken window thesis holds that crime results from public disorder, the solution to crime is to use the police to create order. In this assumption, the strategies are directed at people whose public behavior causes the general public to believe that order has disappeared: homeless are required to go to shelters or they are arrested; drunks are arrested and placed in jail; disorderly people – those playing loud music, drinking alcohol in public, or otherwise disturbing the peace – are required to stop or are arrested. In short, the power of arrest is used to enforce public order, especially by requiring these people to abide by public expectations for conduct. In some places, the emphasis on widespread "stop-and-frisk" tactics has led to accusations of racial profiling. In these accounts, it is not behavior alone that leads to police inquiry and action, but a combination of behavior and racial characteristics, which are said to fit a profile of prospective criminal offenders. The problems associated with accusations of racial profiling represent some of the civil rights limitations to crime-prevention techniques that depend too heavily on police intervention in the absence of citizen partnerships.

Another controversial form of community policing is evinced in broken windows policing, as it was implemented in New York City's "zero-tolerance" policing practices. The zero-tolerance method uses arrests of minor offenders – jaywalkers and those holding opened beer cans in public – as a means of quelling public disorder. While stopping a person for a public order violation, the police search and question the violator. Proponents claim that this routine questioning of public nuisance cases has resulted in large numbers of illegal weapons being seized and leads to the arrest of parolees who have absconded and others who are wanted on arrest warrants and that the processing of these cases leads to a significant reduction in crime. Critics of zero tolerance say that the rate of apprehension of serious offenders is very low (Karmen 2001), and so most of the stops turn out to be a form of harassment. Many observers credit zero-tolerance policies in New York City for the tragically deteriorating relationships between minority youth (especially males, who are the most likely to be stopped) and the police. Another population that has been affected by zero-tolerance policies has been the homeless. Some cities and counties have passed ordinances directed toward criminalizing homelessness and establishing penalties for those groups that have chosen to provide meals and clothing to homeless persons. This approach targets the symptoms of the problem but does not look to discover root causes that might be targeted to reduce the problem. Making it a crime to provide aid to homeless persons has served to alienate churches and other volunteers from the police and city government officials.

It can be important to remember that the basic philosophy of broken windows is that if those looking to commit illegal acts perceive that residents in a neighborhood have no genuine interest in the conditions of the neighborhood, they may stand a better chance of getting away with their illegal acts. The primary issue with the broken windows philosophy may be more with the techniques developed to improve neighborhoods than the philosophy itself. Helping residents of a neighborhood become more involved in improving the condition of the neighborhood may be achieved through problem-solving and other community-building exercises.

Evidence-Based Policing Strategies

There are many lenses through which the profession of policing can be examined. Policing has been viewed as a blue-collar occupation where all that is necessary to perform well on the job is rudimentary training. Policing has also been seen as a male-oriented profession where being tough and having brawn is important for enforcing the law. Another perspective views policing as a craft where officers hone their skills through experience and the sharing of anecdotal stories and organizational culture. Both perspectives focus more on processes and less on outcomes. Goldstein (1979) cited and addressed these concerns when he developed the concept of problem-oriented policing.

Problem-oriented policing more fully developed in the 1990s and, eventually, was merged with the concept of community policing by practitioners and some academics. As the concept became more developed, the need for officers to develop skills in data gathering became important in analyzing identified problems and developing responses to address them. Many academics who studied policing felt that problem-oriented policing did not utilize established data-gathering and scientific processes, limiting the effectiveness of the outcomes developed in the problem-oriented policing process. They looked to other disciplines to better understand the processes they used to ensure better outcomes in addressing identified problems. Ratcliffe (2023) shares that two important disciplines that were examined were medicine and aviation. These disciplines dealt with problems that could be a matter of life or death, underscoring the importance of high-quality outcomes in problem-solving. Both disciplines rely heavily on gathering data, analyzing it, and using the results to guide policy and ensure that actions taken are supported by scientific evidence, not anecdotal evidence. Those evidence-supported actions have led to higher-quality outcomes and established a process of continual improvement. He notes that aviation safety also introduced the process of using checklists and that many police agencies have adopted the PANDA crime reduction model to provide a structured path for officers working on problems. The five steps of the PANDA model are problem scanning, analyzing a problem, nominating strategy, deploying strategy, and assessing outcomes.

According to Ratcliffe (2023), there is evidence that the standard policing model does not result in safer outcomes or improvements in the trust and confidence people place in the police. He explains that EBP is designed to reduce reliance on experiences, anecdotal stories, and blind hope that strategies will be effective. EBP can provide an evidentiary foundation that can be used to evaluate any approach used in policing, according to Ratcliffe. He emphasizes that it is designed not to conflict with the standard or more innovative policing methods but to provide a mechanism to test their effectiveness.

EBP relies on evidence developed through the scientific method of gathering and analyzing the results of selected actions taken by a police organization. The availability of this evidence can be helpful to policymakers as they review policy choices. Ratliffe (2023) explains that in an EBP approach, "police officers and staff create, review, and use the best available evidence to inform and challenge policies, practices, and decisions" (p. 10).

Ratcliffe identifies seven steps in the scientific method: identifying a problem, conducting background research, developing a hypothesis and research question, undertaking a study or experiment, analyzing results and drawing conclusions, peer review and publishing findings, and replicating or expanding the research. The process is circular, so the final step may lead to the first step, causing the process to repeat. The process would be familiar to those in the academic or research field but not as much to police practitioners. Developing a partnership between academics and practitioners would appear to be the most effective way to implement the process and ensure that useful information is developed for policymakers' consideration.

While EBP has many strengths, Sparrow (2016) shares concerns about the length of time the scientific process may take to gather, process, and analyze information. He says that police agencies are often pushed to achieve results, and waiting for an extended period of time for useful information can worsen a problem since limited action is being taken to address it. Sparrow does not dismiss the value of EBP but argues that problem-oriented policing can effectively address problems that may need more immediate attention. In problem-oriented policing, the standard model used is the SARA model, which is an acronym for Scanning, Analysis, Response, and Assessment. It is very similar to the PANDA method used in EBP. It relies on properly identifying a problem and gathering specific information about the problem before developing a response. After implementing the response, it should be assessed to determine if it effectively addressed the problem. Sparrow understands that the data gathered may not be as robust as in the scientific method, but in many problems encountered by the police, there is a need for quick action to avoid the growth of the problem. Sparrow also observes that the process of scanning, or problem identification, is prominent and guided in problem-oriented policing but not in EBP. While he sees the benefit of evidence-based work, he notes that the problem must be properly identified before that work begins. According to Sparrow, EBP does not provide guidance on how to identify problems.

Community Policing and Community Justice

Community-oriented policing services (COPS) have played a central role in the community justice movement. But community policing is not the same as community justice. The COPS movement in policing is particular primarily to the traditional functions of law enforcement: investigation and arrest. Although some of the more elaborate community policing methods move out of traditional police functions in attempting to prevent crime, community justice is a broad concept that applies not just to crime but to the quality of life in the community. It also embraces the nonpolice functions of adjudication, sanctioning, and correcting – discussions we attend to in the following two chapters.

Thus, although we may think of community policing as the bellwether for change that has set the stage for community justice, integration of community policing into the broader community justice agenda will still require more change in how the police do their business, even within a community-oriented philosophy.

The formal training of police officers provides them with the rudimentary skills necessary to enforce the law and maintain order. Highly emphasized during the training is the need for officers to take control of the situations they encounter and establish a course of action that resolves any problems contained in the encounter. This often causes the officer to become an arbitrator, providing resolutions that may be less than acceptable to the parties involved in the issue. Little skill development occurs in negotiating and mediating with persons involved in a conflict.

Understanding the differences between arbitration and mediation is essential because the terms are often used interchangeably. Arbitration is a process by which a neutral third party intervenes in a dispute, listens to both sides, and then, through a reasoned process, decides what action should be taken to resolve the issue. On the other hand, mediation is a process where a neutral third party becomes a facilitator in resolving the dispute. The mediator allows each side to present their concerns, and then she or he assists the disputants in developing their solution. The clear difference between the two methods is that the role of the neutral third party is consultative in mediation and authoritative in arbitration. Neither method will work in all situations, so the neutral third party needs to be able to diagnose the situation and determine the appropriate methods to address the problem at hand.

Police officers serving as mediators have become more accepted over the past decade, although it is still seen as being on the fringe of acceptable traditional police practice. One prominent argument against the practice is that it is too time-consuming for patrol officers and causes calls for service to be delayed while officers attempt to mediate disputes. Rarely is mediation seen as a practice that will save time in the long run by possibly eliminating repeat calls for service and improving the cooperation between police officers and the citizens they serve. Cooper (1999) argues that neutrality by the patrol officer during mediation is not impossible. The officer is required to be an objective professional during the process if it is to be successful. Cooper believes that disputes appropriate for patrol officers to mediate include property, vendor–customer, landlord–tenant, and boyfriend–girlfriend disputes where no physical actions have occurred. Patrol officers have also found mediation to be helpful in disputes involving residents in a neighborhood. Officers can often mediate neighborhood disagreements involving shared driveways, unruly children, and noisy residents. Officers who utilize mediation often report that the basic practices of mediation have made them better police officers overall because they listen more intently and ask more probing questions during interactions with citizens. They also report that those interactions are usually more favorable because the citizens feel that the officers are engaged in helping them and not just going through the motions of handling a call for service. It is also possible that mediators can be non-sworn personnel and called to the scene if officers are needed on more serious calls.

As can be seen, mediation and its concomitant skills improve the performance of police officers in many aspects of their job. It is also important to recognize that using mediation improves community members' skills. Community members who participate in mediation sessions learn how to listen more intently to each other when divergent viewpoints are presented. Cooper (1990) notes that disputes sometimes have two layers: latent and manifest. The latent, or underlying, dispute is often unspoken and must be teased during conversation. To do so takes time, patience, and good listening skills. Often, disputants see the manifest or obvious dispute and fail to resolve the disagreement because they only address the surface behavior. Persons who have participated in or been trained in mediation skills know to look for the underlying issue that may be the real issue. After participating in mediation, they learn that dialogue can solve disputes and that force is unnecessary. The listening skills developed also help residents better understand the other residents' concerns, and interpersonal skills are learned or fine-tuned. The development of these skills moves the individual into establishing social networks, which can result in acquiring resources and services.

Restorative Policing

Restorative policing is a style of policing that encourages the police to actively support victims, offenders, and the community. It incorporates the philosophy of problem-oriented policing and meshes it with the principle of restorative justice. The goal of restorative policing is to reduce harmful wrongdoings and conflicts through the positive engagement of community and government resources (McCold 2016).

Police agencies that choose to adopt restorative policing are expected to include basic tenets of restorative justice, such as integrity, openness, respect, and fair process (Lofty 2002). Including these basic tenets can be helpful to police agencies trying to move from a "force" to a "service" ethos, according to Lofty. McLeod (2003) argues that implementing a restorative policing approach can lead to police organizations shifting from being rules and regulations oriented to focusing more on results and outcomes. She also sees this approach as one that can encourage police organizations to become a "learning organization" committed to continual education, innovation, flexibility, and collaboration. She observes that

> a restorative system is value-driven, as opposed to program-driven, and committed to a process of innovation, problem solving, deliberation, and risk-taking in order to

effectively respond to issues internal and external to the organization and those of interest to stakeholders.

(p. 368)

Clamp and Patterson (2017) discuss two prominent models of restorative policing: the New Zealand Model and the Wagga Wagga Model. The New Zealand Model operates on a statutory basis where welfare practitioners generally facilitate conferences, and no script is used to guide the meeting between victims, offenders, and their supporters. The Wagga Wagga Model, on the other hand, is a purely diversionary approach for dealing with less serious offenders. The police facilitate the process, and they use a script to guide the discussion that takes place between all stakeholders involved in the issue. Clamp and Patterson note that this model has been used in Australia, the United States, Canada, and the United Kingdom. This model can be implemented using a specialized group of officers who have been trained in the philosophy and the process, alleviating the need for officers on patrol to divert time and resources away from answering calls for service. The purpose of this model is not only to foster empathy between the stakeholders but also to address the triggers that cause the offenders' behavior and the harm caused by that behavior. This leads to the effective reintegration of the offender and follows the philosophy of reintegrative shaming as discussed by Braithwaite (1989).

In this model, the victim is asked what they want to get from the conference, and when consensus is reached with the rest of the parties involved, it is formalized in a contract that everyone signs after the conference. After the conference is completed, informal interaction is encouraged to help foster relationships among the stakeholders. Offenders and their families are required to participate in completion of an activity booklet dealing with crime and its consequences. They then attend a two-hour session run by local community members, which emphasizes remedial skills that can be of help to them in making behavioral changes.

Clamp and Patterson (2017) note that in sites where formal evaluation was completed, the Wagga Wagga model reduced the number of cases processed by the courts by 50%, and 93% of the offenders fulfilled the agreements established. Evaluation results also showed high satisfaction with the process for victims and officers who participated. Offenders reported higher levels of being treated fairly and with respect, more opportunities to repair the harm caused, and an increase in respect for both the police and the law than those offenders who went to court. This positive result is related to the use of procedural justice during the conferencing process. Results of evaluations conducted at sites in the United States, Canada, and the United Kingdom showed that officers could facilitate conferences consistent with due process and restorative justice principles where ongoing training and support were offered. Canada encountered some difficulties in implementing the model due to organizational apathy, resistance, and skepticism. Much of the organizational resistance can be attributed to the reluctance of the police to see community policing as "real policing," and they continued to utilize traditional methods in their work. Eventually, some officers became involved in conferences on the street, but those issues deemed more serious were referred to community volunteers for disposition.

The Thames Valley approach, involving restorative cautions and restorative conferences, was developed in England and Wales. Restorative cautions included only the offenders and their supporters, while restorative conferences also had victims and their supporters present. In 2010, 33 out of 44 police forces around England and Wales used restorative disposals during various stages of the criminal justice process. The Thames Model has three levels: Level 1, "instant" or "on the street" disposal; Level 2, restorative conferences; and Level 3, conferences for the prolific and persistent offenders. In Level 1, response officers, or police–community support officers, discuss the causes and consequences of the anti-social behavior directly with the offender. Level 2 is used when Level 1 cannot be used or for more significant or ongoing offenses, and the offender, victim, and community members participate in the conference. Level 3 is usually used after the offender receives a sentence, emphasizing the offender's rehabilitation. Clamp and Patterson (2017) share that according to guidelines established by the Association of Chief Police Officers in 2011, to be considered restorative, the following must occur: the offender must acknowledge responsibility, the affected stakeholders must be involved, a meeting must occur to discuss what happened and what consequences occurred, and there must be efforts undertaken to repair the harm caused. Clamp and Patterson (2017) explain that "while restorative justice has traditionally been thought of and promoted as a mechanism through which to deprofessionalize justice, restorative policing relies on professionals – the police – rather than external and independent agencies to facilitate the process" (p. 69).

Clamp and Patterson (2017) identify some arguments for and against police officer involvement in restorative conferencing. One concern is the challenge of the police culture. Officers are often seen as crime fighters or law enforcement professionals, not conflict resolution professionals. Another concern pertains to cultural relevance and institutional racism. Restorative justice is often seen as a process of colonizing indigenous practices as a way of securing hegemony over justice and re-legitimating the criminal justice system in the eyes of those it has previously disenfranchised, according to Clamp and Patterson. Finally, there is the challenge of the operational policing environment. Officers emphasize crime control and do not attend to the underlying causes as to why particular events have occurred. Two major arguments are offered for police involvement. First, there are benefits for victims, offenders, and the police. Restorative justice processes help to establish a pattern of fairness through the use of procedural justice. Second, there is a potential for the transformation of police culture. Using restorative justice techniques can help officers learn the value of resolving conflict and not having to use force or make repeat calls for service.

Focused Deterrence

Within the past decade, more law enforcement agencies have looked to a process of focused deterrence to address criminal behavior, especially criminal behavior involving violence. The strategy is most often seen as a law enforcement strategy, but to be effective, it is necessary to have all elements of the criminal justice system, community members, nonprofit organizations, and the private sector engaged in the process. Because there are more participants than law enforcement organizations involved in focused deterrence, this strategy is explained in Appendix B.

Mediation in Addressing Citizen Complaints

Some police departments have incorporated mediation into the citizen complaint process. Community members who may feel the police have treated them inappropriately can elect to have their complaint mediated, and a resolution acceptable to both the citizen and the officer can be crafted. The Office of Community Complaints for the Kansas City, Missouri Police Department implemented a complaint mediation program in 2000, and the feedback from both citizens and officers has been positive. One benefit of mediation is that the complaint is addressed, and a resolution is developed. In many complaint investigations, more evidence is needed to determine if the officer's actions were inappropriate, and the complaint is unsubstantiated. Such a determination leaves the citizens feeling unvalued, and the officer feels as if he or she has been unjustly accused. Resolution to the dispute in a timely and constructive manner can be beneficial for the police and community in building solid, trusting relationships. Again, the citizen can experience expressing a concern, being heard, and engaging in a meaningful dialogue to address the concern. This type of process also makes the police more accountable to the citizens they serve, and this accountability has been lacking in high-impact locations. Trust between the police and citizens can only be developed if respect is on both sides, and mediation provides a mechanism to build some of that trust.

Polarity Management

In a community policing model, it is important that the community play a meaningful role in identifying and addressing identified problems. As discussed earlier, it can be easy for a police agency to take the lead in identifying problems and developing a course of action to address them. One reason that this scenario occurs often is that the police have become used to taking the lead in at-risk communities because they have experienced little interest by community members in investing time and effort into being partners in solving the problems. By taking the lead, the police often overlook resources the community can bring to the table to solve identified public safety problems. In many cases, the police do not realize that they have ignored community members and the result can be hurt feelings, lack of respect, and ineffective problem solving.

How could the police know they have overused their expertise and created relationship issues with the community? Unless the community speaks up and brings it to the attention of the police, there is an excellent chance that the overuse will continue. One tool that the police and the community could use to alleviate this problem is Polarity Management.

Polarities are situations where two seemingly opposite yet interdependent states must coexist over time for success to occur (Emerson & Lewis 2019). When polarities are identified and not appropriately managed, they will continue to surface and create new issues that must be addressed. Unfortunately, the polarities often surface at inopportune times and create more serious problems that must be addressed immediately, or they can become destructive.

Johnson (2014) notes that sometimes polarities are identified as problems, and the tendency is to handle them in an either/or right/wrong manner. He shares that problems to solve have a solution that can be an endpoint in a process. Once a decision is made between the options available, the problem has been solved. For example, a police agency may be acquiring new vehicles, and there is a need to identify the color scheme of the cars. The colors available are blue, white, or black and white. Once the agency gathers and analyzes information, a decision is made, and the vehicles are ordered. The problem is solved with that decision, and the agency can move on to other business. There is little chance that once the decision is made, there will be any further consequences regarding the vehicle color that will need to be addressed. The problem is solved. In this example, an either/or process was used to arrive at the decision and was appropriate based on the situation being considered.

Either/or thinking has garnered a negative connotation because it implies rigid application. It is not a wrong process because only some issues encountered are a polarity, and issues identified as problems need to be approached using this process. Johnson (2014) argues that two questions can be applied to the issue to determine whether it is a problem or a polarity. "Question 1: Is the difficulty ongoing? Question 2: Are there two poles that are interdependent?" (p. 80). If the answer is yes to both questions, the issue may involve polarities and be a problem. He notes that in polarities, two poles of any interdependent pair are continuously pulling in what appears to be opposite directions, creating an ongoing tension. In other words, polarities continue to act upon each other even if a definitive decision is made about a course of action.

Sensemaking is essential to people, and if they do not have a way to make sense of the polarity, they will tend to approach it as an either/or situation, and they will tend to place more value on one pole over the other. Johnson calls this process "prefacing" and explains that the pole selected is usually the pole in which they are working or feel comfortable, even though they might know both poles have value and are important. Without the use of some sensemaking tool, Johnson argues that people do not have an idea about how to obtain information about and try to understand the elements of the other pole. He makes the point that using a tool such as the polarity map can help people understand that this issue is not solvable; therefore, it does not qualify as a problem that can be solved. The map can help them understand that an issue containing interdependent pairs can only be navigated over time and that there will not be one right solution that can be put into place and then forgotten about. It can also help them understand that the tension is ongoing, and they can consciously manage it so it turns out creative or it will continue to manage them and become destructive.

In polarity management, the poles tend to operate predictably. Johnson (2014) writes that focusing on one pole will provide many good things and benefits in the short run. Still, if we ignore the other pole and continue to concentrate our attention on the pole on which we are focused, we begin to overuse that pole, and that can lead to the benefits becoming bad. He says that to address this concern, we tend to look at the logical solution, which tends to be to reach out to the benefits of the other pole. A caution to this is that if we move our focus to that pole, the same overuse process can occur, and we find ourselves swinging from one pole to another. It is this swinging back and forth that should be avoided.

There is a process to identify the benefits and overuses of each pole, which can help those in each pole understand the benefits of each. After identifying the benefits and overuses, Rohr (2016) recommends developing what he calls the "Third Way." In this process, the focus is on the benefits of each pole, and there is an effort to create balance between the poles. If developed properly, the Third Way provides an action that automatically balances the poles without great conscious effort. For those unfamiliar with polarity management, it can be helpful to think of The Third Way as something that helps keep the positive aspects of each pole balanced without having to take continual actions to balance the poles. Johnson (2014) uses the example of breathing to illustrate this concept. It is beneficial to inhale to bring fresh oxygen into the body, which is needed for essential bodily functions and other benefits. Still, it is also vital to exhale to remove harmful toxins and carbon dioxide from the system and provide benefits as well. If the concentration is only on inhaling, the body cannot function well because there is no way to expel the waste that needs to be eliminated from the body. So, as the process unfolds, the preferred solution to the problem is to reach toward the benefits of the other pole, exhaling. If the concentration is only on exhalation, the body will soon find out it needs oxygen to function, and it will move to the benefits of inhalation. Thus begins the cycle of the polarities. In the Third Way, an action is developed that concentrates on the benefits of both poles and prevents overuse by either pole. The Third Way binds the two poles' positive aspects together to become a more continual joint approach to meeting the greater purpose statement that has been agreed upon. In the inhale–exhale example, breathing becomes the Third Way because it takes the benefits from each pole and helps balance the use of each pole. Breathing is an action that is done without much conscious effort and is regulated by the need of the body to have the right balance of oxygen and carbon dioxide to keep the body functioning well. It prevents overuse by either pole by sounding the alarm when the benefits of either pole are becoming overused. Another way to think about the process of the Third Way is to visualize a seesaw with two equally weighted persons on each end. If the goal is to keep the seesaw parallel to the ground, there must be minor adjustments made by each side to ensure balance is maintained. Even with both parties weighing the same, one end can rise or fall due to factors such as a party's shifting or other external factors. Emerson and Lewis (2019) explain that developing and standing in the Third Way can be uncomfortable because there is a legitimate fear that the things valued, the benefits of our preferred pole, could be lost. There is a sense that living with the downsides we might be experiencing is preferable to risk giving them up. In addition, moving into the Third Way may challenge the way we assume the world works and that can create a fear that we are losing the things that define a part of who we are. When another person or situation threatens a part of our identity, the natural reaction is to fight and resist, and we often do so by viewing those persons who hold our point of view in terms of their benefits and those who prefer the other pole in terms of their overuse.

Johnson (2014) explains that there are many reasons for people to feel attached to a particular pole. For individuals, the pole might be an expertise or where we feel comfortable and less threatened. In organizations, the reason might be that the levels of management tilt toward a particular pole as they examine how best to achieve the organization's mission. Living in the poles can also occur on a societal basis due to the adoption of ideologies or the experiences groups or individuals may have encountered. Living in a pole is a natural occurrence, and the point is that living in a pole is only a negative if it is overused and there is little consideration given to the benefits of the opposite pole. He describes those who try to move the action from overuse in one pole to the benefits offered by the other pole as crusaders and those who fear moving from their pole, even though the overuse may diminish their benefits, as tradition-bearers.

The development and use of the sensemaking tool can help persons better understand the benefits of the pole to which they attach as well as the benefits of the opposing pole. The tool is also helpful because it can provide a visual depiction of the positives and overuses of each pole. Having a concrete place to list each pole's benefits and overuses can help people diagnose the dilemma and avoid overuse of one of the poles. The tool is also important because, ideally, it is created by persons on both poles, and that can help ensure buy-in to the process of balancing the poles to achieve the greater purpose statement, the goal, developed by the participants. Emerson and Lewis (2019) argue that "in short, a good map of polarity helps people more fully see the polarity and, thereby, have it instead of it having them" (loc. 777). They also believe that taking action to create a map, even if it is not thorough, is better than trying to move ahead in managing the polarities without one. Creating the map at least generates conversation between the polarities, which can provide some relationship building and attempts to understand better.

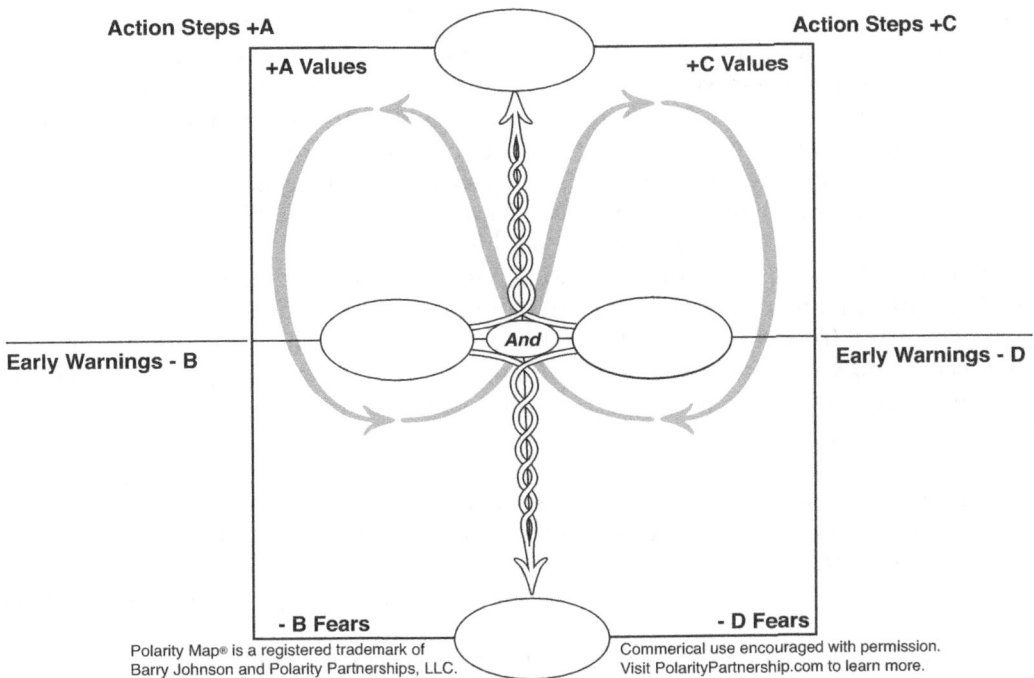

Figure 3.1 Polarity Diagram.

While polarity management is introduced here in the chapter on policing, it can be utilized throughout the criminal justice system (Figure 3.1).

The Outward Mindset

The Arbinger Institute (2016) has an approach that could be beneficial for building meaningful relationships between the police and the communities they serve. Arbinger (2016) argues that the mindset of that individual drives any behavioral changes made by an individual. Arbinger uses the term "mindset" to refer to the way "people see and regard the world – how they see others, circumstances, challenges, opportunities, and obligations" (pp. 15–16). This mindset then manifests itself in the behaviors of the individual. The premise of the argument is that any behavioral changes must begin with an examination and a change in the individual's mindset. In other words, merely implementing policies that direct behavioral changes will not ensure that the individual makes those changes or that others will receive them as sincere. Forced behavioral changes are usually not long-lasting or effective because they are dependent upon rewards and punishments for implementation. Arbinger posits that meaningful behavioral change must come from internal motivations, not external ones and that internal motivations come from the individual's mindset.

Arbinger (2016) proposes two mindsets: inward and outward. In an inward mindset, the individual concentrates on his or her own perceived needs and challenges and considers only options that would advance their own agenda. In an outward mindset, individuals consider the needs and challenges of others as well as behave in a manner that achieves the collective results to which they are committed. The two mindsets can be seen as two ends of a continuum. While few would operate only at either end of the continuum, the goal for the individual and the larger organization is to move from the inward mindset toward the outward mindset. Those individuals who move toward the outward mindset should find themselves more interested in others' needs, objectives, and challenges and less interested in their own. Arbinger argues that people with an inward mindset do things, but those with an outward mindset help others to be able to do things.

The outward mindset approach is possible only if individuals are willing to turn their mindsets toward others without expecting others to change their mindsets in return (Arbinger 2016). In interpersonal relationships, it is natural for individuals to wait until the other person changes first to make a behavioral change, so this approach is counter to conventional behavior. To help individuals change to an outward mindset, Arbinger proposes that the principle to apply is,

> as far as I am concerned, the problem is me. *I* am the place to start. Others' responses will depend mostly on what they see in *me*. The most important move is for *me* to *make the most important move.*
>
> (p. 103, italics in original)

One of the foundational principles of the outward mindset is that individuals must see others as persons, not as objects to be used to achieve their own personal needs. Seeing others as persons allows one to understand better the needs, objectives, and challenges the other person faces. Arbinger argues that concentrating strictly on the behavior of another toward us leads us to use that behavior to justify why we may feel that we are right, and the other is wrong. Being able to understand better the causes of those behaviors should lead to dialogue that addresses the concerns of the other individual. In general, individuals tend to respond to others' ways of being toward them rather than their actual behavior (Arbinger 2016). In other words, individuals in an interpersonal interaction are more likely to become offended or feel justified based on the other person's attitude or tone than the actual spoken words.

Another factor that supports the Arbinger model is the work done by Colwell and Huth (2010) in adopting the Arbinger model directly to policing. Both authors served as police officers with the Kansas City, Missouri Police Department, so their writing introduces the Arbinger model principles with application examples in policing. Colwell and Huth posit that "the profession of law enforcement requires a relentless striving for a personal anima (inner way) which sees others as people and is rooted in integrity, buttressed by courage, and expressed as unconditional respect for all" (p. 1). The concept of anima refers to the individual's inner self and not a persona or professional face. Colwell and Huth argue that building a personal anima involves building structures that are quantified by the following points:

> I am a human being, endowed with the gift of self-examination. In other words I have a conscience and am therefore responsible for my thoughts, words, and inactions.
>
> I am not a simple stimulus-response mechanism. I cannot simply blame others for my reactions and responses.

I must face the fact that I have prejudices, loyalties, desires, and fears that cloud my judgment and shroud me in self-deception. Said another way, when I am wrong, I will almost certainly deceive myself with self-justification and blame directed at other people and circumstances-I will naturally assume I am right in most wrong points.

(p. 5)

This approach clearly addresses the need for an officer to engage in self-reflection to develop a sense of courage that allows the individual to understand himself or herself more intimately and develop the courage to act in a manner not affected by popular thought.

Community policing is not a panacea. Although it has been one of the most important systematic changes in criminal justice in the last 100 years, it has also raised a series of questions about the functions of the police in modern society and the capacity of the police to accomplish those functions alone. As we see in the following chapters, the courts and corrections face the same questions about an expanded mission that seeks to produce greater public safety through increasing community well-being.

Box 3.2 Levels of Community Policing

Greene (2000) provides an important summary of the types of changes brought about by community policing, as well as the expected outcomes as a result of these changes. This discussion serves as a useful framework for understanding both the potential effort needed for the development of a community policing initiative and the potential rewards of such an initiative. The following table summarizes these levels and the expected outcomes.

Environmental Level

At the environmental level, the police form relationships and partnerships with local organizations, residents, social services, and businesses and focus on problem solving and crime reduction in an effort to reduce fear of crime and improve quality of life. The mobilization of the community to address crime-related issues is thought to increase the social bonds, communication, and trust between neighborhood members, thus improving community cohesion and increasing informal social control (formal social control being the police, and informal social control being community conflict resolution through nonpolice involvement). Also, when residents have more contact with police officers, and when police officers illustrate an investment in neighborhood quality of life, the residents feel safer and empowered (Greene 2000, pp. 321–324).

Organizational Level

At the organizational level, community policing affects how the department defines problems and solutions, and how the actual organization is structured, including the organizational attitude toward the police subculture and the selection and training of officers (for example, the hiring of more minority officers and language training for officers in minority communities). The organization must accept a new set of values for seeing the community as a partner and developing new problem-solving techniques to create a true community policing initiative. This also includes changes in internal communication practices and information sharing among officers (Greene 2000, p. 322).

Individual Level

Organizational-level changes must also make their way into the rank and file and be inculcated by each police officer if community policing is to succeed. Officers must develop new problem-solving techniques and learn to view the community as a partner in their crime-fighting activities. Also, crime prevention must become a higher priority for the officer. Job satisfaction should improve as the officer becomes more connected with the community, and the officer will have to use a greater range of interpersonal and problem-solving skills in his or her new role (Green 2000, p. 323).

Level of Intervention	Anticipated Changes	Community Policing Outcomes
Environmental	Form partnerships with local organizations and residents; increase public safety; improve social bonds	• Reduced crime and fear • Increased level of trust • More communication • Better problem solving
Organizational	Redefine department-wide problem-solving techniques; have officers adopt a new set of values, develop new internal communication practices	• Improved training • More diverse hiring practices • Improved internal communication • Improved analysis of problems • Change in information flow • New performance measures
Individual	Develop new problem-solving techniques and interpersonal skills; change view of the community role	• Increased job satisfaction • Increased performance • More attachment to community • Wider role in community

Source: Adapted from Greene (2000, p. 324).

Law enforcement has undergone critical evaluations since 2014, mostly generated by major events involving serious use-of-force issues by officers. Two major task forces were created by President Barack Obama in 2014 and President Donald Trump in 2019 to examine how policing can be improved to create better community relationships and address the issue of crime. A discussion and contrast of the two task forces can be found in Box 3.4. It remains to be seen how and if law enforcement agencies will adopt any of the recommendations, but the recommendations can potentially create substantial changes in how police services are delivered in the United States.

Box 3.3 2014 and 2018 Police Task Force Summaries

Since the shooting of Michael Brown by a law enforcement officer, there has been more focus on police behavior by government officials at all levels and community members, especially communities of color. In 2015, President Barack Obama formed the President's Task Force on Twenty-First-Century Policing to review the current policing status and create recommendations for improving policing in the United States. The Task Force was Co-Chaired by Charles Ramsey, former Chief of Police in Philadelphia, and Laurie Robinson, a Professor at George Mason University. Other task force members came from policing, education, and the nonprofit sector.

The task force provided recommendations organized around six main topic areas, or "pillars," as they were labeled. Each of the pillars also contained action items for implementing the recommendations contained in each pillar. The six pillars are:

1 Building Trust and Legitimacy
   - Importance of procedural justice in establishing legitimacy
   - Implementing a Guardian versus Warrior mindset for police officers
   - Proactively promote public trust by initiating positive non-enforcement activities to engage high-risk communities
2 Policy and Oversight
   - Policies must reflect community values
   - Clear policies on the use of force, mass demonstrations, racial profiling, and performance measures
   - Independent investigations of officer-involved shootings and use-of-force situations
   - Periodic review of policies and procedures
3 Technology and Social Media
   - Identify and assess new technology that can be incorporated into the work of law enforcement officers
4 Community Policing and Crime Reduction
   - Work with community residents to identify problems and collaborate on implementing solutions that have meaningful results
5 Training and Education
   - Attentiveness to training and education needs of law enforcement
   - Federal partnerships with training facilities
   - Mandatory C.I.T. training, training in implicit bias and cultural responsiveness, training in policing in a democratic society, training in procedural justice and effective social interaction and tactical skills
6 Officer Wellness and Safety
   - Length of work shifts
   - Expand information on officer deaths
   - Promote wellness and safety
   - Opportunities for officers to pursue educational

While all of the pillars are important, the pillar that appeared to receive the most attention is the one that addressed community policing and crime prevention.

In 2019, Attorney General William Bar convened the President's Commission on Law Enforcement and the Administration of Justice at the direction of President Donald Trump, with the commission's final report being issued in December 2020. The commission was chaired by Mr. Phi Keith, former Chief of Police for the Knoxville, Tennessee Police Department and Director of the Office of Community Oriented Policing Services. The final report listed fifteen areas where action was suggested, each containing a list of recommendations. The report did not contain action steps that could be implemented to achieve the recommendations. A significant difference between this report and the report of the 2015 commission is that this report utilized different work groups for each of the fifteen areas. A different person chaired each work area, and workgroup members were drawn from other areas of the criminal justice system. The work areas were:

1 Respect for the Rule of Law and Law Enforcement
   - Concern for the declining support for Law Enforcement
   - Concern about the under-enforcement of criminal law in specific locations and how it affects public safety and police morale
2 Victim Services
   - Better address the needs of victims of crimes, including victims of human trafficking and hate crimes, victims working with trauma, and victims who are elderly, homeless, youths, or who have limited English proficiency
3 Alleviating the Impact of Social Problems on Public Safety
   - How socio-criminal factors – mental illness, homelessness, and substance abuse – affect law enforcement
   - Focus is directed more on how the prevalence of these social problems affects law enforcement resources, capacity, and morale.
   - How other government resources can cooperatively tackle the social ills that contribute to crime
4 Juvenile Justice and Youth Crime
   - Focus on the principles of an effective, efficient, and balanced juvenile system that prevents juvenile crime and delinquency
5 Reentry Programs and Initiatives
   - Focus on how prisoner programming and post-custodial rehabilitation initiatives can reduce recidivism and improve the quality of life for criminal offenders and their families
6 Criminal Justice System Part ners
   - Focus on how the intersection of the entities can enhance the ability to prevent and control crime and serve victims
7 Business and Community Development
   - Focus on how law enforcement can collaborate with public, private, and academic institutions to reduce crime

8 Reduction of Crime
   - Focus on trends in crime, current use of targeted deterrence approaches, and new and developing technologies, along with integrating education, employment, social services, and public health services to reduce crime and the burden on law enforcement.
9 Homeland Security
   - Focus on domestic and international terrorism
10 Grant Programs
   - Focus on the Federal grant-making process and application as well as grant management systems and the use of Federal funds
11 Technology- Focus on lawful access to technology, implementing new technology, and facial recognition technology
12 Data and Reporting- Focus on eliminating duplicate Federal data collection, the requirement of states to collect standardized criminal justice data for reporting to the state and federal government, and implementation of EBP
13 Rural and Tribal Law Enforcement
   - Focus on funding needs, resources, and staffing for rural and tribal law enforcement agencies and the law enforcement needs in Alaska
14 Law Enforcement Health and Wellness
   - Focus on physical and mental wellness for law enforcement officers, as well as the creation of a law enforcement safety database that tracks law enforcement injuries and deaths and a National Law Enforcement Safety Board that investigates line-of-duty deaths
15 Law Enforcement Recruitment and Training
   - Focus on recruitment, retention, training, and use-of-force policies and training for law enforcement officers

Some topics overlapped in both reports, but the 2020 report appears to have taken a wider view of issues facing law enforcement and focused more on law enforcement and the criminal justice system than on involvement by the community in addressing crime and disorder. Both reports provided helpful observations and recommendations that could be implemented by law enforcement agencies to improve effectiveness and efficiency.

Suggested Web Sources for Readers

The Center for Problem-Oriented Policing – www.popcenter.org
The Office of Community Oriented Policing Services (C.O.P.S.) – www.cops.usdoj.gov Accessed 8/7/2024
The International Association of Chiefs of Police – www.theiacp.org
Policing.com – your headquarters for community policing – www.policing.com

References

ABC News. (2020). Cities across US announce police reform following mass protests against. *ABC News*.
Arbinger Institute. (2016). *The out-ward mindset: How to change lives and transform organizations*. Berrett-Koehler Publishers.

Braithwaite, J. (1989). *Crime, shame, and reintegration.* Cambridge University Press.

Brantingham, P.L., & Brantingham, P.J. (1990). Situational crime prevention in practice. *Canadian Journal of Criminology, 32*(1), 17–44.

Caplan, J.M., Kennedy, L.W., Barnum, J.D., & Piza, E.L. (2017). Crime in context: Utilizing risk terrain modeling and conjunctive analysis of core configurations to explore the dynamics of criminogenic behavior settings. *Journal of Contemporary Criminal Justice, 33*(2), 133–151. https://doi.org/10.1177/1043986216688814.

Carter, D.L., & Radelet, L.A. (1998). *The police and the community.* Prentice-Hall.

Clamp, K., & Patterson, C. (2017). *Restorative policing: Concepts, theories, and practice.* Routledge.

Clear, T.R., & Rose, D.R. (1999). *When neighbors go to jail: Impact on attitudes about formal and informal social control.* National Institute of Justice.

Colwell, J.L., & Huth, C. (2010). *Unleashing the power of unconditional respect: Transforming law enforcement and police training.* Routledge.

Connell, N.M., Miggans, K., & McGloin. (2008). Can a community policing initiative reduce serious crime? A local evaluation. *Police Quarterly, 11*(2), 127–150.

Cooper, C. (1999). *Mediation and arbitration by patrol police officers.* University Press of America.

Cornish, D., & Clarke, R.V. (2003). Opportunities, precipitators, and criminal decisions: A reply to Wortley's critique of situational crime prevention. *Crime Prevention Studies, 16*(2003), 41–96.

Crank, J. (2004). *Understanding police culture.* Anderson Publishing Company.

Emerson, B., & Lewis, K. (2019). *Navigating polarities: Using both/and thinking to lead transformation.* Paradoxical Press.

Gallup. (2022, July 5). Confidence in U.S. institutions down; average at new low. Retrieved 3/9/2024 from https://news.gallup.com/poll/394283/confidence-institutions-down-average-new-low.aspx

Goldstein, H. (1979). Improving policing: A problem-oriented approach. *Crime & Delinquency, 25,* 236–258. DOI: 10.1177/001112877902500207.

Goldstein, H. (1991). *Problem-oriented policing.* McGraw Hill.

Greene, J.R. (2000). Community policing in America: Changing the nature, structure, and function of the police. In J. Horney (Ed.), *Policies, processes, and decisions of the criminal justice system* (Vol. 3 of *Criminal Justice 2000*) pp. 299–370. U.S. Department of Justice.

Harpold, J.A. (1996). A community doctoring: A medical analog to community policing. In J.T. Reece & R.M. Solomon (Eds.), *Organizational issues* (pp. 319–333). U.S. Department of Justice, Federal Bureau of Investigation.

Harpold, J. (2000). *A medical model for community policing.* FBI Law Enforcement Bulletin, June.

Johnson, B. (2014). *Polarity management: Identifying and managing unsolvable problems.* HRD Press.

Karmen, A. (2001). *New York murder mystery: The true story behind the crime crash of the 1990s.* NYU Press.

Kelling, G.L., & Coles, C. (1996). *Fixing broken windows: Restoring order and reducing crime in our communities.* Free Press.

Kelling, G.L., & Moore, M. (1988). *The evolving strategy of policing.* Perspectives on Policing, No. 4. National Institute of Justice.

Lofty, M. (2002). Restorative policing. In *Dreaming of a new reality: The third international conference on conferencing, circles, and other restorative practices.* International Institute for Restorative Practices. Doi: https://iirp.edu/pdf/mn02_lofty.pdf.

Mastrofski, S.D., Worden, R.E., & Snipes, J.B. (1995). Law enforcement in a time of community policing. *Criminology, 33*(November), 539–563.

McCold, P. (2016). *White paper on restorative policing.* In P. McCold (Ed.). RJI Global Steering Committee.

McLeod, C. (2003). Toward a restorative organization: Transforming police bureaucracies. *Police Practice and Research, 4*(4), 361–377.

O'Hara, P. (2012). *Why law enforcement organizations fail: Mapping the organizational fault lines in policing*, 2nd ed. Carolina Academic Press.

Pereira, I. (2020). *Cities across US announce police reform following mass protests against brutality.* Retrieved 3/9/2024 from https://abcnews.go.com/US/cities-us-announce-police-reform-mass-protests-brutality/story?id=71130499

Pew Research Center (2022). *Trust in America: Do Americans trust the police?* Retrieved 3/9/2024 from https://www.pewresearch.org/2022/01/05/trust-in-america-do-americans-trust-the-police/.

Palmiotto, M.J., & Donahue, M.E. (1995). Evaluating community policing: Problems and prospects. *Police Studies, 18*(2), 33–53.

Police Executive Research Forum. (2013). *Compstat: Its origins, evolution, and future in law enforcement agencies*. PERF.

Ratcliffe, J. (2023). *Evidence-based policing: The basics*. Routledge.

Rohr, R. (2016). *The third way*. Center for Action and Contemplation. Retrieved 3/9/2024 from https://cac.org/daily-meditations/the-third-way-transformative-dance-2016-06-28/

Sampson, R.J., & Bartusch, D.J. (1999). *Attitudes toward crime, police, and the law: Individual and neighborhood differences*. National Institute of Justice.

Sherman, L.W., Gottfredson, D., MacKenzie, D., Eck, J., Reuter P., & Bushway, S. (1996). *Preventing crime: What works, what doesn't, what's promising: A report to the United States Congress*. National Institute of Justice.

Silverman, E. (1999). *NYPD Battles Crime: Innovative strategies in policing*. Northeastern University Press.

Skogan, W.G. (1992). *Disorder and decline: Crime and the spiral of decay in American neighborhoods*. University of California Press.

Skogan, W., & Hartnett, S. (1997). *Community policing, Chicago style*. Oxford University Press.

Sparrow, M. (2016). *Handcuffed: What holds policing back, and the keys to reform*. Brookings.

Trojanowicz, R., & Bucqueroux, B. (1990). *Community policing: A contemporary perspective*. Anderson Publishing Company.

U.S. Bureau of Justice Assistance. (1994). *Understanding community policing: A framework for action*. U.S. Department of Justice, Office of Justice Assistance.

U.S. Bureau of Justice Statistics. (2000). *Sourcebook of criminal justice statistics*, section 2: *Public attitudes toward crime and criminal Justice-Related topics*. U.S. Department of Justice.

Walker, S. (1992). *The police in America: An introduction*. McGraw Hill College Division.

Wilson, J.Q., & Kelling, G.L. (1982). Broken windows. *Atlantic Monthly, 249*(3), 29–38.

For Further Reading

Community-Oriented Policing

Greene, J. (1999). Zero tolerance: A case study of police policies and practices in New York City. *Crime and Delinquency, 45*(2), 171–187.

Kelling, G., & Bratton, W.P. (1993). *Implementing community policing: The administrative problem*. National Institute of Justice. A prescription of ways to create and sustain community-oriented policing systems and cultures.

Nicholl, C. (1999). *Community policing, Community justice, and restorative justice: Exploring the links for the delivery of a balanced approach to public safety*. U.S. Department of Justice, Office of Community Oriented Policing Services.

Pate, A.M., & Shtull, P. (1994). Community policing grows in Brooklyn: An inside view of the New York City Police Department's model precinct. *Crime and Delinquency, 40*(3), 348–410.

Radelet, L.A., & Carter, D. (1994). *The police and the community*, 5th ed. Prentice-Hall. A comprehensive review of literature on community and police interactions.

Solar, P.J. (2019). *Police-community relations: A conflict approach*, 2nd ed. West Academic Publishing.
Zhao, J., & Thurman, Q. (1997). Community policing: Where are we now? *Crime and Delinquency, 43*(3), 345–357.

Problem-Oriented Policing

Bayley, D. H. (1994). *Police for the future*. Oxford University Press. A challenging prescription of the methods and philosophy of policing in the coming decades.

Goldstein, H. (1990). *Problem-oriented policing*. Temple University Press. The classic description of problem-oriented police theory and practice.

Police Culture

Repetto, T. (1978). *The blue parade*. Free Press. Analyzes what it is like to be a police officer and the problems facing urban police reform.

Rubenstein, J. (1973). *City police*. Farrar, Straus & Giroux. The classic description of urban police culture.

Police Authority and Power

Bittner, E. (1990). *Aspects of police work*. Northeastern University Press. A summary of the literature of police behavior and the forces affecting police effectiveness.

Davis, K. C. (1969). *Discretionary justice: A preliminary inquiry*. Louisiana University Press. The classic essay on police power and police discretion.

4

The Courts and Community Justice

Of the three main divisions of the criminal justice system – police, courts, and corrections – the middle justice function, the courts, has the furthest conceptual distance to travel to become community-oriented. As we shall see, one reason for this is that the natural subject matter of the courts is the problems in criminal cases, not the problems of difficult places. Another reason is how the courts work, processing defendants through what looks like an impersonal assembly line of decisions, from charging to sentencing. And yet another has to do with the traditional values of detachment and impartiality in the courts, which tend to disconnect judges and lawyers from their clients and the communities in which they live.

Despite these impediments, the courts have been, in recent years, a setting for enthusiastic experimentation with community justice concepts and strategies. After decades in which change was very slow in the courts and traditional models of court processing remained virtually undisturbed by pervasive changes elsewhere in the system, courts have become a beacon for community justice thinking, especially concerning the handling of vexing problems that seemed intractable under the usual methods, such as drug abuse or minor crime.

In this chapter, we explore how the courts have embraced many major concepts of community justice and particular strategies of community-oriented court practices. We will see that innovation in the courts has resulted in fundamental changes in how the court system relates to citizens, including victims, offenders, and their families. As extensive as these changes have been, however, we will also see that some advocates call for even more far-reaching reform, and the courts have yet to begin to address the needs of multi-problem communities.

Criminal Cases, Communities, and Courts

The subject matter of the criminal courts is criminal cases, not communities, and this has been one of the main practical and conceptual impediments to community justice in the courts. The focus on individual cases is entirely understandable, as courts were established to deal solely with criminal cases. Each unit of the court's business, the criminal case, is defined by a complaint filed by the state against a defendant. What is at stake is the legal status of a defendant's conduct, and the efforts of the professional lawyers in the court triumvirate – prosecutor, defender, and judge – are designed to assess the legal consequences of the accused actions. These key actors in the court system perform their functions in interaction with one another with little direct activity by nonprofessionals. Courts are traditionally insulated from outside forces, and emphasis is given to creating an environment in which professionally trained lawyers can use their skills in a formal, solemn setting to create outcomes seen by the public as just.

We will discuss whether this view of the courts, as a formal, somber institution of deliberation about criminal accusations, is wholly accurate. Accurate or not, the image of an independent, detached judiciary has a hallowed place in American jurisprudence, and it has operated as a counterforce to community justice thinking. Whereas the traditional view of the courts is that they are stately and detached, community justice is seen as informal and involved. Whereas traditional court procedures are dominated by professionals, with everyday citizens silent, except when asked to testify, community justice is open to citizens' views and supplements the professional practice of the law with informal participation by people who are not lawyers.

Perhaps most important, whereas the traditional courts serve legal jurisdictions, such as states, districts, or municipalities, community justice devotes its attention to a particular location, such as a neighborhood, that is part of a legal jurisdiction. Courts give a high premium to the concept of equal justice under the law, which means that every person within that legal jurisdiction is to be treated the same way by the court workers. Community justice accepts the foundational importance of the concept of equal justice but sees within that idea a broad range of flexibility to tailor programs and legal strategies to fit the specific circumstances of communities affected by the law. Equal justice is essential, but justice that addresses the needs of people most affected by the court system is even more central to what the courts are called upon to do.

These two conceptual challenges have complicated the court system's adoption of community-oriented strategies. How can the courts shift their traditional focus on due process of law given to specific criminal cases to include a concern for the community-level impact of court case outcomes? Without violating well-established and profoundly critical constitutional rights that have evolved over two centuries of litigation, how can the courts embrace a growing concern for the quality of life in the communities the courts serve? These are difficult questions. Our review of the current efforts to bring community-oriented ideas to the courts will show that today's court innovators are successfully creating strategies that embrace the new court's concerns without violating its traditional values. There is nowhere a perfect community justice court to model all community-based court innovation, but neither is there a perfect traditional court. What court reformers have been doing involves rebuilding court processes, procedures, and jurisdictions so that community-oriented values can emerge within the broader context of individual protections. In the end, courts still apply the law from a larger political jurisdiction to individual criminal cases. Still, community-oriented courts do this in a way that considers the need for community justice in how these decisions are produced and carried out.

The Two Functions of Criminal Courts

Courts have two primary responsibilities: they adjudicate disputes and determine the sanctions that will apply in cases that have been adjudicated. In these two areas, issues arise concerning two core values underlying how the courts carry out their work: justice and rights. Justice issues are concerned with outcomes, asking the question, "What results best fit the circumstances of the case?" Rights issues are concerned with the procedures used to determine the outcomes of cases, asking a different question, "What practices should be employed (or prohibited) in developing the outcome for the case?"

Table 4.1 Balancing concerns for rights vs. justice in the court

	Adjudication	Sanctioning
Rights	Concern that the defendant receives due process under the law and that the innocent are not mistakenly found guilty	Concern that the "punishment fit the crime" and is equally applied in like cases
Justice	Concern that the guilty are not mistakenly exonerated	Concern that sanctions take differing circumstances into account and are not counter productive

Table 4.1 illustrates the different rights and justice issues related to the two functions of the courts. As we see in the following discussion, the concern for rights and the criterion of justice pose quite different challenges for community-oriented strategies of adjudication and sanctioning in the courts.

Adjudication of Complaints

The first function of the criminal courts is to adjudicate a criminal complaint. The criminal complaint is a formal document, called an indictment or an information, filed by the prosecution accusing a citizen of violating the law. This document brings the case to the attention of the court. The criminal complaint alleges certain conduct violating the law and calls upon the defendant to answer the allegations. In the courtroom, the defendant answers those charges and, if the defendant claims to be "not guilty," demands that the prosecution offer evidence in proof of the allegations.

One way of looking at the criminal complaint is that it creates a dispute between the citizen and the state. (That is why criminal cases are referred to, for example, as *State v. Jones.*) At the technical level, the dispute is about the defendant's legal status and whether the label "offender" may be applied to the defendant by virtue of conduct. Regarding practical implications, the dispute concerns whether the defendant may be sanctioned for the alleged conduct. Guilt must be proven before the person can be labeled an offender and before the imposition of punishment. The citizen's status must be shifted from "defendant" to "offender."

In adjudicating the dispute, the values of "justice" and "rights" play an influential role. Two types of unjust outcomes are possible in adjudication. One occurs when an innocent person is mistakenly found guilty, the other when the case against a person who committed the crime is not proven, and the verdict is "not guilty." Although both values of rights and justice are essential, the adjudication function seems to place a higher priority on rights, especially the defendant's rights, than on justice. The Constitution gives the defendant the right to reject taking the witness stand and prevents the state from using evidence obtained in violation of the defendant's rights. Legal traditions require that guilt be established "beyond a reasonable doubt."

The emphasis placed on rights is meant to make it difficult for the state to prove its case, and it suggests that when it comes to adjudication, not all forms of unjust outcomes are to be considered equal. This is illustrated by the commonly repeated aphorism,

"Better for a hundred guilty men to go free than for one innocent to be convicted" (Justice Learned Hand).

Community justice advocates do not view the adjudication function as a contest. Consequently, the community justice strategy tends to be less formal in its approach and tries to bring a concern for rights and a belief in outcomes that are just into a better balance. This poses one of the most difficult challenges for community justice as a strategy of the courts. America has a long-standing and immensely important tradition of individual rights as a starting point for adjudication of criminal complaints. How the courts can embrace a concern for community-oriented justice without discarding or depreciating the enormously important tradition of rights is, as we shall see, a significant challenge.

Sanctioning Wrongdoers

The courts must determine the appropriate sanction for those who are found guilty. The term *appropriate* is not easily defined in practice because a penal sanction that seems right to one person may seem too lenient or too severe to another. We all may want a court system that imposes penalties that fit the circumstances of the case, but there may be little agreement about the facts of the case that the penalty should be fitted to. Do the offender's personal characteristics matter? Which ones? Does it matter that the defendant is young, or intellectually limited, or poor, or a mother? What aspects of the crime itself are to be considered? Do we care if the offender was provoked? Does it matter if the way the crime occurred was particularly wanton?

When it comes to imposing a sanction, the concern for an outcome that is just rises in importance, and the prominence of rights is diminished. Of course, the offender's rights remain intact and may not be violated, but we recognize that the sanctioning process is mostly about selecting a penalty that fits the case. Whereas adjudication is about a process of law, sanctioning is about determining the proper legal outcome of that process.

There is disagreement among legal scholars about the outcome the sanction ought to be tailored to achieve. An eloquent case can be made that the purpose of a sanction is primarily to punish, to impose a penalty that fits the seriousness of the crime (Von Hirsch 1993). However, equally persuasive arguments exist in favor of sanctions that rehabilitate (Cullen & Gendreau 1989) and incapacitate (Zedlewski 1987). With this kind of disagreement about the basic aims of a penal sanction, it is not surprising that people frequently disagree about the best penalty to impose upon a newly convicted offender.

In selecting a penalty, the conversation turns from rights to justice: What penalty fits the circumstances of this offender and the offense? The formal process of the courts allows for various opinions to be expressed on the matter before the judge decides. The offender speaks, then the victim and the prosecutor. Sometimes, family members of the victim and the offender are also encouraged to offer an opinion, and occasionally, experts, such as psychiatrists, give testimony. Whatever penalty is eventually selected, however, must conform to the requirements of the law, and some choices are not allowed in a given penal code. Certain crimes are so severe that, at a minimum, a sentence to prison is required; other crimes are sufficiently mundane that financial or community penalties can be imposed.

In the last 40 years, many reformers have become concerned about disparities in penal sanctions (Allen 1996) and have tried to develop penal codes that resulted in more consistency in sentencing. These new sentencing approaches, whether sentencing guidelines or determinate sentencing (Tonry 1993), have been seen by some as successful and by others as a mistake. However, they have all reduced the range of penalties a judge may consider when imposing a sentence. In most jurisdictions across America, judges today have far fewer choices available when determining the sentence than a generation ago because legal reforms have restricted those choices.

Community justice challenges the sanctioning function of the courts in two ways. First, those who advocate for community-oriented penalties tend to desire a broader array of possible case outcomes than are now available to judges. They approve of creative sanctioning that builds a penalty based partly on the crime and the offender's circumstances. They also call for a sentence that considers the community's desire for a long-term investment in public safety. Community justice advocates also prioritize what is thought of as "voice": the victim, the offender, and the community should have an opportunity to explore and explain what is desired as the best outcome of the sanction once it is selected. Perhaps the most significant way community justice challenges the sanctioning function of the courts is that, under its model, sentences are not "imposed" by a judge who is remote to the circumstances of the case; instead, the penalty is determined in interaction with those who were affected by the crime, including the offender.

How Courts Work Today

We view the courts as a very formal, dignified process. Judges sit high above the courtroom, donned in severe black robes. Lawyers, dressed in professional respect, speak only when allowed. The decorum is at a premium. A type of ritual occurs, starting with the "Oyez, oyez," and is punctuated by the ringing authority of the judge's gavel. The courtroom is purposefully designed to symbolize the somber majesty of the law, standing in for the historical prerogative of the omnipotent Crown. Each detail of how the court is arranged speaks of the power and dignity of the law and the comparative insignificance of those assembled under its austerity.

Is That Really the Way the Law Operates in Practice?

The contemporary courtroom maintains elements of this stylish, symbolic instrument of power and authority. But in most cases, what happens bears only a minuscule resemblance to this picture. To understand how the criminal trial courts work today, we must begin with four concepts: caseload pressure, informality, exchange, and stages of decision-making.

Caseload pressure is a dominant force in contemporary courts because the number of criminal cases to be processed by the courts has grown over the last 30 years without a commensurate increase in judges, prosecutors, and defenders. State courts experienced a 45% increase in criminal filings between 1984 and 1997 (Ostrom & Kauder 1998). Court players have felt this growth. State prosecutors reported that the volume of their caseloads has increased because more offenders are being prosecuted (Nugent & McEwan 1988); and public defenders, who receive on average 80% of all criminal cases, have not had increases in staff commensurate with increases in caseloads (Spangenberg 2001). Specifically, this means that there is a premium on avoiding jury trials, which are five to ten times more costly in time and personnel than guilty pleas or even (in many cases) bench trials. Even though defendants have a Constitutional right to select a jury trial, the realities of case pressure mean that lawyers on all sides will try to resolve a case without resorting to an expensive and, in many cases, unnecessary jury trial.

Jury trials are not necessary in many cases because the defendant's factual guilt is often not in question. Of course, the state must be able to prove the defendant's guilt in a trial, but often, there is incontrovertible evidence of guilt, and the prospects of acquittal are less than slim. In such cases, what defendants have at stake is less the question of adjudication than the eventual sanction to be imposed. Here, *informality* is in the interests of all parties. Rather than leave the sanction up to the judge, it is often thought better for the state and the defendant to reach a general agreement about a sanction acceptable to both parties. To do this requires informal conversation and negotiation outside the inflexible confines of the courtroom.

Flexibility is reinforced by the reality of *exchange*, which means that each party has something to offer the other in negotiating a case outcome. The defender can promise not to demand an expensive jury trial and can promise the unparalleled efficiency of a guilty plea instead of a trial. The prosecutor can offer an opportunity to avoid some of the harsher penalties available under the law, either by reducing the charges or agreeing to make a recommendation to the court for a lenient sentence. By accepting this negotiated settlement, the judge can avoid tying up the courtroom with an unneeded criminal trial in which guilt is not at issue and can thereby avoid delaying getting to more pressing cases.

The *decision-making stages* in the courts facilitate this less formal processing of cases. In most courts, there is an initial hearing in which the charges are registered, and the primary evidence on behalf of those charges is listed. Often, an arraignment follows, with a more formal reading of charges and evidence, a formal plea by the defendant, and a date set for a trial. Some pretrial hearing dates deal with questions such as bail and the admissibility of evidence. All this occurs before the actual trial, and each event offers an opportunity for the parties to discuss, informally and outside the presence of the judge, a way of resolving the charges without going to trial. Each stage accelerates the pressure on the parties to work out a nonjury decision, and each stage offers a new opportunity to discuss how to make a nonjury agreement work.

The combination of caseload pressure, exchange, and a tradition of informality dominates the stages of the court process. Because there are repeated opportunities to reach an agreement, a trial is usually avoided in favor of a negotiated guilty plea. This means that most defendants eventually waive their Constitutional rights to a trial, to prove the charges "beyond a reasonable doubt," to avoid self-incrimination, and to have all the prosecution's evidence tested against rules of admissibility. The defendant trades these Constitutional rights in expectation of a penalty less onerous than the one threatened by the full force of the law.

Against this backdrop, the contemporary community justice movement in the courts must be evaluated. Critics of the community justice model argue that a defendant's rights are imperiled by the informality of decision-making in community-oriented courts, and the basic protections of the law are lost. They also say that negotiated decision-making results in compromises that detract from the symbolic importance of formal criminal law. There is also a concern that too much discretion will lead to sanctions in a community justice framework that suffers from extensive sentencing disparity.

The current system encourages these same problems because its procedures in full expression are so expensive, and those involved in the system have very good reasons for avoiding the most extreme implications of the provisions of the penal law. The question is not whether community justice has too much informality and negotiation of its practices but whether the informality and negotiation activity within community justice practices leads to case outcomes that are more acceptable to all parties.

The Victims of Crime

The last two decades have seen increasing importance placed on the victims of crime. This concern has expressed itself in two forms. First, there has been intense pressure to increase the severity of sanctions in the belief that harsher penalties show respect for the impact of crime on victims. Second, there has been pressure on the formal criminal justice system to listen more to victims regarding how cases are handled. Thus, prosecutors have opened victim-assistance offices, and penal code reforms have created a basis for victims to speak at sentencing and parole hearings and even to be informed of how charges are changed during plea negotiations.

Adding the victim's voice has changed the dynamics of criminal court case management practices. Victims are given a very limited role when they are encouraged to testify at trial and are allowed to make a sentencing recommendation. However, a more aggressive stance regarding victims lets them have a say about the case at every stage. It includes them as a voice in the charging process, the negotiations of a guilty plea, and the selection of the eventual penal sanction. Nowhere are victims as fully involved in the criminal justice process as they could be, but every criminal court hears much more from victims today than was the case 20 years ago.

Now that we have become more understanding of the needs of victims and more willing to give them a substantial voice in the criminal justice process, we have become more sophisticated in our appreciation of what victims need to begin to recover from the emotional and material costs of the crime. It is not always what we might think. Studies of victims find that they differ in their needs (Karmen 2019; Office for Victims of Crime 2000). Some want a kind of revenge, while others are more interested in restitution. Some want to meet and confront the offender; others do not. Some want to understand why the crime happened, and these victims often look for a way for the offender to be rehabilitated so that future criminality will not occur. Others care little about what is in the offender's head or heart. They want a meaningful punishment to be imposed by the court.

Almost all victims want to be able to speak on their own behalf, and giving voice to their experiences in the formal justice process is often an essential part of recovery from crime. By far, most victims, when given a choice, would prefer a sanction that leads the offender to a productive, law-abiding life, over a sanction that merely punishes. But almost all victims think that some form of punishment is called for to bring the case to closure. Contemporary critics of the way the court system handles victims point out that there is little capacity for the justice system to undertake the variety of strategies required to meet the diverse concerns of crime victims, and there is almost no provision for handling cases differently based on the desires of the victim. In the court's work, Constitutional guidelines take precedence over operational procedures.

We also know that the reality of the victim's circumstances does not always correspond to the popular image of the victim. We often think emotionally about the victim of crime, and in our image, we see an entirely innocent stranger victimized by a cavalier felon. However, most victims are not strangers to their victimizer – many are family members, and others are acquaintances. In these cases, there is often an understandable ambivalence about harsh punishment for the perpetrator of the offense. Just as important, crimes such as drug abuse or prostitution have no apparent victim. How to represent the voice of the victim in these quite common circumstances is an essential part of a broad victim's movement in criminal justice.

A growing number of federal and state prosecutors' offices now employ victim advocates who can assist the victim in understanding and navigating the criminal justice system. Victim advocates are helpful for not only the primary victims, the one against whom the offense occurred, but also secondary victims, close relatives of the primary victims. Victim advocates work closely with social workers and mental health professionals to provide support for those victims who are suffering. While emotional support for the victim is essential, victim advocates may do their best by talking with the victims about the technical aspects of the court processes. It can be very upsetting for a victim attending a preliminary hearing to discover that the judge has decided to suppress a piece of evidence without knowing what that process entails or how it will affect their case. Victim advocates can explain the actions of the judge and the prosecutors so victims will better understand the processes and arcane language being used (Karmen 2019).

In some jurisdictions, prosecutors consult with victims about prosecution issues and seek their input before filing charges. While this does not mean that the professional prosecutor is putting the decision to prosecute in the hands of the victims, it does ensure that the prosecutor will have the victim's support should his or her testimony be required. In a case involving the prosecution of a serial murderer in Jackson County, Missouri, the prosecutor called together all of the victims' families to discuss prosecution strategies. The suspect had committed 12 murders over an extended period, and, as is often the case, evidence was more substantial in some crimes than it was in others, especially since many of the victims led a high-risk lifestyle. The prosecutor wanted the families to understand why he had chosen to file charges in just a few of the cases so the families would not feel as though their loved one was less important than those victims whose cases would be filed. After the private meeting with the families, the prosecutor conducted a news conference to announce which cases would be prosecuted and why the decision had been made. Attending the news conference were the families of most of the victims, and after the news conference, they affirmed their support for the decision and the prosecutor. Prosecutorial actions such as this strengthen the trust between the community and the prosecutor by providing respect for the losses suffered by the victims' families. This was especially important in this situation since the primary victims were not wealthy or influential persons but instead victims who were often seen by society as less worthy of receiving justice.

The increasing role of the crime victim in the justice system is a critical development in the advent of community justice. Those who believe in community justice have had to invent new ways to incorporate victim sentiments and interests into the community justice ethic. From the community justice standpoint, the broader community suffers from crime, so delivering justice in the community helps deal with the problem of victims as they are community members. Moreover, sanctioning offenders affects their families and communities, and the community justice approach makes room for these issues. There is, however, a need for more – a need for community justice to embrace the specific concerns of specific victims of crime.

The Community Court

The idea of community-oriented strategies in the courts has become a new and vital force in recent years. Community courts are popular today, with many urban areas experimenting with community-based specialty courts. As we shall see, the community court concept applies to courts that serve specific neighborhoods within larger jurisdictions, and it also refers to courts that deal with a particular community of clients, such as domestic violence cases. However, the contemporary idea of community courts borrows some concepts from an era long past in the court system when municipal courts held extraordinary power over adjudication in communities isolated from other governmental sectors. The environment for community courts has significantly changed in modern times, but some of the values we expect of them have not.

A Historical Look at Community Courts

During most of U.S. history, trial courts have been community-based. Until the early twentieth century, American society was a rural society where county legal government was the dominant political force. Counties had a criminal court located in the county seat, and justice emanated from that venue. The benefit of these courts was their fit to the community. The judges who determined criminal cases lived in their communities, knew many residents, and understood the community's values. Their activity was far from impersonal and held firmly to themes of community values.

This was also the main weakness of the community-friendly rural court. People who were community outcasts or whose status was suspect may have found it hard to receive equal justice. This charge held mainly in the South, where Blacks encountered an often hostile court system run exclusively by the dominant White majority. The all-too-common lack of sympathy for poor Blacks in trouble with the law exposed the dark underbelly of community-friendly courts. You might have had difficulty getting justice if you were not seen as a legitimate part of the community.

This concern fueled a professional version of the courts, becoming the dominant idea in the latter half of the twentieth century. Several key issues were featured in this change, chief among them that the work of the courts was not community work but a professional task requiring technical skills. The law, it was felt, needed to be uniform across all places, and a community-friendly judiciary was inconsistent with the vision of an unvarying criminal law. Part of this sentiment came from an evolving commitment to equal protection under the law, which arose as part of an emerging concern for civil rights and the rights of the powerless. Another problem came from the sense that "amateur" justice was inadequate, often stemming from a faulty understanding of the law and a parochial application of its principles. In the last third of the century, there was also a new concern for equality in punishments. Punishment disparity was identified as a severe problem in criminal law, and the remedy was thought to be the reduction of sentencing discretion in favor of applying a set of sentencing standards in every location of the jurisdiction.

As in the early rural and agrarian United States, the romantic vision of a community-friendly court is forever gone, replaced by professional civil servants highly trained in the legal process. Yet the community court is still around. Most Americans may live in urban and suburban settings, where a sense of personal anonymity is a standard part of legal procedures. However, most jurisdictions in the United States remain small- and medium-sized, and many of America's courts serve populations that are not urban, disenfranchised, or poor. The state of Indiana, for example, has 92 counties, each with a county seat and a county court that handles criminal cases arising in that jurisdiction. Of those 92 courthouses, perhaps a dozen serve primarily densely urban populations.

However, the contemporary community court movement is designed for something other than the rural or suburban courthouse. How people describe the mission of the community court places its relevance directly within the troubled neighborhoods in our densely populated urban areas. The neighborhoods served are discrete locations within larger, more heterogeneous jurisdictions. The communities served within those neighborhoods are typically poor groups lacking access to legal resources. What has happened is that the logic of the bygone community court, which can tailor its efforts to meet better the needs of the community it serves, has been reformulated as an urban solution to distinctly urban problems.

Thus, we can distinguish between community-friendly courts that operate in smaller community settings and are composed of community leaders who handle cases involving people who mostly know each other and the modern community-oriented court. This latter version is not a happenstance of a community's nature. Still, it is an intentional innovation designed to help create a sense of community and improve the feel of the community it serves.

The Contemporary Community Court Movement

The breakthrough example was the Midtown Community Court in New York City. Developed in 1993, the Midtown Community Court was the brainchild of the Midtown Business Improvement District (BID) coalition of businesses, prominent residents, and social services operating in the Times Square area of New York City. The Times Square area has a concentration of entertainment-based businesses – theaters, restaurants, hotels, and recreational game centers – attracting many one-day "tourists." By the late 1980s, misbehavior by some of the more disagreeable visitors had become a serious concern: drunken and disorderly, the "tourists" would urinate in the streets and alleys, openly solicit prostitutes, get in fights with each other, and engage in other loud and rowdy activity. The increasingly undesirable nature of these visitors made living in the residential areas surrounding the businesses an ever more distressing experience.

One of the problems was that the criminal justice system was largely unresponsive to the situation. Arrests would be made, and perpetrators would spend the night in a holding cell nearby. Then, they would be released, only to return to Midtown and engage in the same disruptive behavior. The sentences imposed were typically for "time served," and referrals to treatment were never given, so the problem people and their problem behaviors remained. And in a classic broken windows pattern, their presence in the area attracted others like them.

A new strategy was invented, led by criminal justice innovator Gretchen Dykstra, the CEO of the BID. People arrested in the Times Square area would not be taken elsewhere to be processed by courts, which have no accountability to the Midtown community. Instead, they would be booked, prosecuted, and adjudicated by the local Midtown Community Court, newly established solely to serve cases from this Manhattan area. Not only would these cases be handled locally, but they would also be sanctioned locally. Sanctions would include requirements of public service – a typical offender sentenced by the court does community service cleaning the Midtown streets – but the offenders would also be placed in court-administered treatment programs. The latter, involving substance abuse treatment, job training assistance, job placement assistance, anger management treatment, and so forth, set the Midtown Community Court apart from the other courts in New York City. Whereas those courts focused on serious felonies that made citizens fearful of their streets and often did next to nothing about nuisance crimes, the Midtown Court reasoned that precisely these public order offenses led to deterioration in the Midtown area.

Residents and businesses banded together to form the Midtown Community Court, and they were wildly enthusiastic about its accomplishments. The popularity of that experimental court with its core clients – the businesses and residents of Midtown – was matched by the appreciation many of its criminal clients expressed for the services they received. Soon, the experiment was seen as such a complete success that community courts began to spring up in other urban locations. The Center for Court Innovation (CCI), which designed and ran the Midtown Community Court, began assisting other places in developing their community courts for problem locations. In 1999, the National Institute of Justice funded a series of community courts nationwide experimentally.

The Midtown Community Court has its critics, some of whom argue that locating social services within the courthouse merely strengthens judicial institutions at the expense of the community institutions the court was ostensibly created to help. This criticism is more meaningful considering the unavoidable added expense of establishing a community court. There are ancillary costs associated with decentralizing court services, such as the extra personnel costs for defense, prosecution, and corrections. Some critics have claimed that only in business-rich Midtown Manhattan can a community court garner sufficient resources to create an actual problem-solving court that disposes of local cases and can provide the care needed to address the complex problems faced by low-level offenders. Consequently, the community court model is only partially replicable. Community courts, most of which target low-level offenders, are also charged for "net-widening" activity. By bringing into the criminal justice arena a whole class of offenders who otherwise would have little if no contact with the justice system, community courts may be serving to criminalize and punish individuals who might be better served with more informal, community-based censure for their behavior.

Moreover, by displacing normal venues for informal, community-based censure, community courts debilitate the inherent social institutions that are the foundation of public safety in neighborhoods. However, even with the validity of these concerns, the community court movement has become a bellwether for reformulating courts to make them more accountable to their communities.

Box 4.1 Center for Justice Innovation

The CCI, now called the Center for Justice Innovation, was established as a public–private partnership and served as the research and development arm of the New York State Unified Court System. CCI pioneered the first community court in Midtown Manhattan in 1993 and was at the forefront of the movement to develop and promote community and problem-solving courts. Building on its success with the Midtown model, CCI tested the flexibility of its community court approach in two disparate neighborhoods: Red Hook, Brooklyn, and Harlem, New York. In each of these sites, CCI worked hand in hand with the community, listening to their concerns and incorporating their feedback. The Red Hook Community Justice Center, which housed the nation's first multijurisdictional court, also incorporated an adult job-training program and a youth court. Harlem residents were primarily concerned about the impact of youth crime on the neighborhood. Consequently, in addition to being a housing and re-entry court, the Harlem Community Justice Center created a youth court, a youth mediation program, and a juvenile treatment court. Thus, by incorporating outreach to the community during the planning process, CCI ensured that the courts were truly responsive to community public safety issues and laid the groundwork for ongoing community involvement.

The expanded Center for Justice Innovation has broadened its mission from focusing solely on courts to working in all stages of the justice system, starting from arrest and extending to reentry. The Center also examines methods of prevention and uses problem-solving to seek out and address the root causes of unacceptable behavior.

More information about the Center for Justice Innovation may be found at: www.innovatingjustice.org Accessed 8/7/2024.

Community-Oriented Court Functions

The two main functions of the courts are adjudication and sanctioning, and each has been open to an infusion of community justice concepts. We will explore how community justice principles have been incorporated into traditional court functions.

Community-Oriented Adjudication

Adjudication consists of three roles: prosecution, defense, and judiciary. Each can be adapted to a community context, though the most experience exists with community-oriented prosecution. Because the three roles are so tightly linked, it makes sense to consider how creating one as a community-based model leads to the logic of the other.

Community Prosecution. Michael Shrunk of Multnomah County (Portland), Oregon, had been elected as district attorney and served for nine years. Most people thought of him as having a "safe" seat. He enjoyed the electorate's wide respect, business leaders' confidence, and political independence. Yet he had a problem. In the highest crime area of Portland, the Lloyd District, people had little confidence in the criminal justice system, and his prosecutors often faced difficulty obtaining citizen support for investigations and prosecutions of everyday offenders from that area.

Shrunk decided to try something new. He opened a district attorney branch office in the neighborhood and assigned one of his more talented assistant district attorneys (ADAs) to that office. While most of his "downtown" ADAs were specialists in particular types of offenses – frauds, homicide, drugs – this ADA would handle all the cases emanating from that neighborhood. It was an experiment to see how this energetic ADA could change the relationship between the prosecutor's office and the residents of that area of Portland.

The innovation worked. After a few months, the ADA had gained the confidence of many of the area's residents, and new, productive relationships were formed between the citizenry and the prosecution. No longer did the residents of that area have an alienated, or even hostile, relationship to the prosecutor's work. The residents wanted legal help with their community problems, especially problems related to public safety and community quality of life, and the new community prosecutor could help them with that.

Just as interesting was the way the prosecutor's job changed when the office was moved to the problem neighborhood. In the downtown office, the emphasis was on significant cases, the kinds that make headlines and involve severe violence to victims: rape, murder, and assault. It was natural for the downtown prosecutors to focus on these cases because they seemed the most important. The public also considered these cases important, but there was an even more avid interest in criminal activity that was less likely to make headlines in the local newspaper. Citizens wanted crack houses to be closed, street drug markets to be moved off public space, open prostitution to be removed from their streets, and landlord violations to be prosecuted. They also wanted their kids who were in trouble with the law to get help by being placed in treatment programs and getting assistance with education and employment.

The community ADA learned that serious crime may be a high priority to outsiders, but the people who live in those problem places may have a different priority. Most people think that people in high-crime areas want tough prosecution of serious criminal cases. Still, this idea misses the daily indignities people in these places must confront. They want something like a legal service; they need access to the courts to press for solutions to their community-level problems. They have asked for help in problem-solving in addition to the prosecution of individual criminal cases. They want a legally relevant support system for their community priorities, and the prosecutor, as an official of the court, has a unique ability to provide that service. Because this kind of law is so different, some people have referred to it as "community safety law" (Conner & Griffin 1998).

The Portland lesson has been repeated in numerous other jurisdictions, where community prosecutors have begun to reshape the prosecution function in multiproblem neighborhoods. The problems vary from location to location because each community has a slightly different set of issues to be tackled. But the big picture is the same everywhere. Whenever a centralized prosecution service has opened specialized offices to serve a particular, troubled location, there has been an increase in citizen confidence in the prosecutor's activity, and there has been a shift in that activity to match better the needs and desires of the citizenry who live there.

However, there have been problems with community prosecution. Community-based prosecutors are open to co-optation by community groups by developing a relationship with a select number of citizens who are too close or comfortable. This co-optation jeopardizes their neutrality and inhibits their ability to see the full range of problems that must be addressed in a neighborhood. Community prosecutors must also be careful about burnout. In the face of communities' multiple and varied issues, prosecutors may try to take on too much. However, it must be recognized that community prosecution has emerged as a new way to provide prosecutorial services to address communities' needs for legal assistance with public safety problems.

Gray (2008) says that the growth of community prosecution since the 1990s has been significant and that community-based approaches to practicing law can now be found in law school curricula. Unfortunately, there has still been little empirical data collected on the effectiveness of community prosecution in preventing and reducing crime. Gray (2008) recognizes the difficulty in evaluating this method of prosecution through the examination of the prevention of crime. Still, she notes that the American Prosecutors Research Institute (APRI) and the Bureau of Justice Assistance (BJA) both have developed systems that prosecutors can use to measure the effectiveness of community prosecution techniques.

Gray explains that APRI suggests attention to establishing long-term and intermediate goals through community needs assessments. According to APRI, performance measures should include not only the traditional methods of measurement but also decreasing the fear of crime among residents, improving overall quality of life, and ensuring justice for victims of crime. APRI provides consulting and guides to assist prosecutors in implementing community prosecution methods. BJA recommends an evaluation model that divides impact measures into implementation and impact sections. The implementation section allows prosecutors to review progress in community prosecution and determine the program's maturity. After completing this needs assessment, future planning will be conducted before moving into the outcome measure phase. Evaluation in the impact section would focus on achieving the goals that were established during the planning phase and would include measuring impact in the areas of target problem, target area, role of the community, content of community prosecution strategy, and technical elements of the prosecutor's office such as office organization and workload. One concern cited by Gray (2008) is the lack of established and accepted guidelines to assist prosecutors in establishing community prosecution. She also notes that guidelines provided by APRI and BJA are beneficial and points out that there is no one right size or method for installing this type of program. Finally, Gray notes that community prosecution still allows for proper prosecutorial discretion, but with that discretion comes new issues about ethical concerns that should be addressed.

Community Defender Services. Much newer than community prosecution is the development of community defenders, also called neighborhood defender services. As a result, there are very few studies of this application of the community justice idea in the court area. The community-oriented defender (COD) network was established in 2003 by eight members. It has grown into a coalition of more than 100 public defender offices and related service providers. In 2014, the COD became part of the National Legal Aid and Defender Association.

Neighborhood defenders have several advantages over the traditional, downtown, and centralized defender services. For example, the neighborhood defender is closer to the community where the defendant lives, and it is often easier to obtain witnesses in support of the defendant at trial and to speak on behalf of the defendant at sentencing. Because many crimes occur in the same neighborhood where the defendant lives, it is also easier to gather evidence in those cases that result in a trial.

An equally important advantage of neighborhood-based defender services is that the defender gets to know the neighborhood. Relationships are established with vital private-sector interests – such as businesses and churches – and these can translate into valuable client support. Businesses can provide jobs for clients, and churches can provide other types of assistance. Familiarity with social service providers can also establish a foundation for clients to deal with the problems that led to their criminal involvement.

This point highlights one of the critical differences between neighborhood-based defender services and traditional services. In the latter, the lawyer sees the job as getting the best deal possible for the client – a finding of not guilty, if possible, and a short sentence, if necessary. However, the neighborhood defender looks at the broader interests of the defendant, helping the defendant get into drug treatment, for example, or arranging childcare and family services for the family members who are not under the scrutiny of the court. The approach of CODs has changed in recent years to become more holistic and less focused only on the court defense of the client. According to Ostrom and Bowman (2019), holistic defense practices include five holistic activities: high-quality, client-centered representation in the criminal case, meeting clients' social needs, consideration of collateral consequences, community programs, and systemic advocacy. In addition, three holistic ways of working have also been developed: defense team, enhanced information, and community connections. Ostrom and Bowman (2019) studied three sites that practiced holistic defense and found that each site functioned differently. They noted that the holistic practices at each site appeared to work to the defendant's benefit, and each site adjusted their work as they observed what worked and what did not. The major issues discovered in the study were that lack of funding prevented implementing a quality case management system for tracking defendant progress and hiring additional attorneys, social workers, and investigators to work on the teams.

Gottlieb and Arnold (2021) argue that keeping the caseloads of public defenders and public defender support staff manageable has the potential to lead to reductions in incarcerations. Their study generally found that smaller public defender caseloads were associated with more favorable case dispositions for clients and led to less incarceration. Unfortunately, the workload can still be overwhelming, and Hamer (2023) found that public defenders work three times too many cases, with some working upwards of ten cases too many. This can lead to public defenders not being able to spend the appropriate amount of time in case preparation for the clients.

As for neighborhood-based prosecutors, defenders who work at the neighborhood level find that their jobs change. They are no longer exclusively concerned with the tactics of the criminal case. Instead, they also develop an interest in the defendant's relationships with the neighborhood and look for ways to strengthen the client's integration into the neighborhood.

Community Judiciary. We have discussed the concept of community court, and the head of that court, the judge, might represent a type of community judiciary. However, there is no official role for a community judiciary beyond what we described for community courts. However, as community courts gain acceptance, there is reason to think that a community-oriented judiciary will grow.

Such a judiciary would be very different from today's centralized, disconnected judges. They would work closely with citizen groups and neighborhood interests to develop a judicial practice for neighborhood concerns. This role would constantly test their commitment to judicial impartiality. Still, it would also open the door to a deeper and more effective level of citizen participation in the work of the courts.

In effect, the judiciary can follow the orientation of the defender and prosecutor. If they have devoted themselves to a community justice model, how they develop their cases and hope to resolve disputes will be oriented toward the community. The judicial role will then be presented with case decisions and caseload priorities that reflect the orientation of the attorneys.

Community-Oriented Sanctioning

It is one thing to identify and prioritize criminal complaints with an eye to community issues; it is quite another to try to resolve them with that same vision. Community justice sanctioning offers a significant departure from the usual strategy because the sanction's aims and the stakeholders involved in the outcome differ.

Under traditional sanctioning models, the criminal sentence's aims are primarily punitive, especially for serious crimes. The sentence may include recognizing the possibility of rehabilitation if an offender must attend a treatment program or be placed under some form of community supervision with treatment conditions. But the overarching value expressed by the sentence is punitive, as its centerpiece is a loss of freedom. The secondary aims of traditional criminal sentences may be incapacitation or deterrence, depending upon the circumstances of the case. The main point is that the object of the sentence is to do something *to* the offender that will communicate blame and reprobation through an intentionally unpleasant penalty. (For a discussion of this idea, see C. S. Lewis, *The Abolition of Man*.)

In this model, the sentence is determined with little attention paid to anyone but the offender. There may be sympathy expressed to the victim and an emotional appeal to community values, but the sentence is about the offender's conduct and the requirements of the law. The crime is seen as a trespass against the state's laws, and the resolution of the crime is for the state to reassert its authority by imposing a penalty for the trespass.

Community justice changes the aims of the sentence. Punishment of the wrongdoer is not eliminated as a goal. Still, it takes a second priority to the community's needs for an outcome that restores some losses from the crime. Instead of viewing the crime as a legal dispute between the accused and the state, a criminal act is seen as an unfair loss (or harm) imposed by one citizen upon another. The problem to be solved is to overcome the unfairness by restoring the loss and repairing the harm. In most crimes, there are multiple victims – a citizen, the community, relatives of the offender, and the victim – and restoring all their losses is a priority. In this way, the stakeholders in a criminal event are not just the state and the accused but everyone affected by the crime.

Thomson (2009) argues that much of the courtroom workgroup's use of the penalty-oriented model is due to mundane decisions where the group exercises comfortable and familiar actions. He boldly suggests that a large amount of sentencing is guesswork because of the lack of information considered by the court in pronouncing sentences, and that, together with considerations of liberty and equality, should lead us to err on the side of avoiding incarceration whenever possible. Thomson (2009) cites the growing body of research over the past 30 years that indicates public opinion supports moderation in criminal sentencing. He believes that a model of progressive justice that emphasizes moderation in punishment pursued in conjunction with a restorative justice perspective would provide community well-being sentencing with a solid grounding in traditional jurisprudence. The goal for Thomson (2009) would be to lower the number of offenders sentenced to incarceration and allow community input into the proper sentencing that would strengthen the community and rehabilitate the offender.

The Role of Victims. In this philosophy of sanctioning, the role of the victim is radically changed. Traditional justice models tend to see the victim as aligned with the punitive agenda of the state. They stand mostly at the sidelines of the criminal case, offering testimony to support the conviction and being allowed to argue for the most punitive sanction available to the court. The extent of harm or loss due to the crime tends to be expressed as anger at the offender and a call for a more punitive penalty.

Studies of victims find that many have a much more complex view of how they would like the sanctioning process to proceed and what they expect from the penalty (Office for Victims of Crime, 2000). Most want the offender to be punished for the crime, but they also want to be able to tell their story so the offender can see how the criminal act was harmful. They want to understand why the offender committed the crime and to see a sanction imposed that makes it less likely that the offender will repeat the crime. If some rehabilitation program is in order, the victim usually supports its inclusion in the sanction, and victims want some support that will help to repair the harm they have encountered because of the crime.

> **Box 4.2 Parallel Justice**
>
> The movement toward incorporating victims' voices in the justice process is best represented by Susan Herman, the former executive director of the National Center for Victims of Crime, who called for a system of parallel justice for victims. She argues that most victims don't get a chance to participate in the justice process because their offenders were never arrested or prosecuted, and even those that do participate are likely to be disappointed because the justice system is focused primarily on instituting appropriate treatment of offenders. Rather than tie the dispensation of victims' services to the court process and offender restitution, local government authorities should provide all victims with resources ranging from counseling to new door locks to victims' compensation. Herman sees the creation of this parallel system for victims taking place on the local level. Local leaders would be "challenged to assess the needs of victims in their community, establish a process for meeting those needs, and combine federal and local resources to make parallel justice a reality" (Herman 2000).

These views are like those of citizens at large (Gorczyk & Perry 1997). Most people want a penalty that "makes sense," which will help restore the victim. They also want the offender to recognize the harmfulness of the act and regret it. This desire translates into an "instrumental penance," where the offender is so sorry for the act that he or she takes strong steps to deal with the problems that led to the act so it will not be repeated. In this sense, the community expects an offender to repent, make restitution to the victim and the community, and become a better citizen. The desire is for a three-way restoration – of the victim, the community, and the offender.

To achieve this three-way restoration, community justice must place the victim and the community at the center of the sanctioning process, not at the sideline. Instead of a process that emphasizes the voice of the prosecution and the protests of the offender, community justice seeks a process that gives voice to victims, offenders, and communities and moves the role of the judge and prosecutor to the sideline. This approach is known as "restorative justice."

Restorative Justice. Restorative justice is a newer version of an ancient idea: the outcome of a transgression against the community ought to be some process that restores the community from the effects of that transgression and thereby allows the transgressor to be restored. There are four main versions of restorative justice (Bazemore & Umbreit 2001).

Victim-offender mediation is an approach to sanctioning that enables the victim to confront the offender with the harm that has been done and then invokes a process whereby the victim and offender come to an agreement about the appropriate sanction to be imposed due to the wrongful conduct.

Community reparative boards are citizen tribunals that receive criminally convicted referrals from the court, for which they determine the appropriate sanctions through a process of conversation with the offender and others affected by the crime.

Family group conferencing is derived from ancient practices of the Maori people of New Zealand, in which the family of the offender, the victim, and the community come together with a trained facilitator to develop an appropriate sanction for the offender's misconduct.

Circle sentencing is based upon traditional practices of aboriginal peoples of North America, in which community leaders, the offender, and the victim come together in a circle to seek sanctions that will lead to healing from the crime on everyone's part.

There is a growing body of research on restorative justice approaches. These studies find that most restorative justice processes are limited to nonviolent, less serious crimes, although there are a handful of projects that apply these principles to interpersonal violent crime. Almost all studies report a significant improvement in the satisfaction of both victims and offenders with the process and the sanction it produced. Several studies show that offenders who go through restorative sanctions have lower failure rates than those who go through the traditional process, though other studies find no difference. Interestingly, there is some evidence emerging that the most successful restorative justice projects are those that allow cases involving serious interpersonal violence and that are not restricted to property crime (Coates & Umbreit 1999). A more in-depth discussion of restorative justice principles and theory can be found in Chapter 5.

Methods of alternative dispute resolution (ADR) have assisted in the growth of reconciliation programs. Three elements of ADR are conciliation, mediation, and arbitration. Conciliation involves using a contact person to facilitate information flow from one disputant to another. Mediation, also discussed in Chapter 2, requires negotiation between disputants with an independent third party, helping the parties arrive at a mutually acceptable compromise. The process involves discussion, sharing viewpoints, and discovering areas of common interest. Arbitration involves using a neutral individual who hears both sides of the dispute and then imposes a decision based on the information gathered during the investigation.

Karmen (2019) argues that several beliefs further the growing interest in informal justice. First is the belief that centralized government coercion has yet to bring about social change. Secondly, there is the belief that nonstranger conflicts should be settled in arenas outside of the formal court system. The final assumption is that the traditional punishment and rehabilitation efforts behind bars have failed to "cure" offenders. According to Karmen (2019), with courts and prisons facing capacity constraints, informal alternatives to dispute resolution are appealing.

Karmen also recognizes that there could be problems with the increased use of restorative justice techniques. If caseloads grow too large, there could be a temptation to adopt procedures that hurry cases through the process, causing less than thorough treatment of the disputes brought for resolution. Another concern is that restorative justice programs remain victim-centered, with an emphasis on offender responsibility for the offense committed. Finally, restorative justice cannot be sold as a cure-all that will apply to all criminal matters. Restorative justice has been successful in many juvenile cases and property-oriented crimes. Increased use of the techniques in interpersonal crime should, and are, being explored, but it must be recognized that not all interpersonal crime is amenable to this resolution technique. Restorative justice appears to be a viable tool for a justice system that prides itself on the proper administration of justice while allowing sentencing that strengthens the fabric of the community.

Courts for Specialized Communities

As new adjudication practices emerged and sanctioning schemes broadened, more attention was paid to how the courts were structured to accommodate these processes. When increasing specialization of treatment and intervention protocols that address the needs and circumstances of specific populations, such as substance abusers or juvenile delinquents, were added to the mix, courts began to tailor their work to these particular communities of offenders.

Drug Courts

Drug courts emerged in response to the crack epidemic of the late 1980s, which flooded court dockets with drug offenders. The initial drug-court models were established to overcome the backlog of cases through expedited case processing. These courts, however, did not address the "revolving door" phenomenon of the many addicted offenders who inevitably became recidivists upon release. As commonly implemented today, drug courts coordinate legal case processing with various treatment modalities. These courts build on the experience of pioneers such as Treatment Alternatives to Street Crime (TASC), which brought a treatment link into the courtroom but took this treatment intervention one step further through a codified model of "therapeutic jurisprudence." According to the Office of Justice Programs, as of May 2023, there are now more than 4,000 drug courts in operation across the country, a number that includes juvenile treatment courts and family treatment courts, as well as drug courts (see U.S. Department of Justice, Office of Justice Programs, Drug Courts, Special Feature at http://ojp.gov).

In a drug court, the judge plays an active role in helping defendants conquer their addiction by teaching consequential thinking through a series of graduated sanctions and rewards. Defendants must appear in front of the judge at frequent and regular intervals, at which point they recount how they are progressing with their treatment and other life goals. Compliance with the court requirements is celebrated by rewards, such as having to appear in court less frequently, and noncompliance is marked by sanctions that vary in severity depending on the gravity of the violation. A low-level offense might trigger a temporary remand to jail, while a urine test positive for drugs will bring a day spent in court watching the proceedings. These graduated sanctions incorporate an understanding that relapse is an almost unavoidable component of the recovery process, and rather than terminate someone from treatment for relapse, the court incorporates an appropriate therapeutic response. Defendants who complete the drug court often receive a reduced sentence, a lowered or dismissed charge, or some combination.

As in most community justice models, the roles of justice players are redefined. To operate a drug court effectively, the traditionally adversarial roles of the prosecutor, defense, and judge are shifted so that the three represent a coordinated team. This team then acts both to safeguard public safety and to treat defendants for their addiction problems. Drug courts also serve as community justice models, not because they are located within a geographic community and therefore concern themselves with the issues of that community, but because their approach to justice problems incorporates a context much larger than the case at hand. Drug courts work to solve the problem of drug-addicted offenders who cycle in and out of the justice system. The court must form strong links to community-based treatment programs by bringing them into the courtroom and the justice process. Additionally, drug courts often develop connections to other community-based support services such as job training and education. In the ideal drug-court model, community volunteers would be brought into the court to provide continual support for defendants in court and upon their return to the community. According to the Nelson A. Rockefeller Center for

Public Policy and the Social Sciences at Dartmouth University, drug courts show a 69% success rate versus a 25% success rate through traditional incarceration (www.rockefeller.dartmouth.edu).

Domestic-Violence Courts

Domestic violence continues to be one of the most intractable public safety issues with which communities and the justice system grapple daily. The National Crime Victimization Survey revealed that in 1998, an estimated 1 million violent crimes were committed against intimate partners (Rennison & Welchans 2000). The justice system has responded to this crisis by developing specialized court processes to handle domestic violence cases. These courts, which are still in their infancy, vary widely in their structure and goals (Keilitz 2000). One court that has received national attention was implemented in 1996 in Brooklyn, New York, by the New York State Unified Court System in partnership with the CCI.

The Brooklyn Domestic Violence Court was designed to promote swift and certain responses to domestic violence offenders while also ensuring the victim's safety. Defendants must appear regularly in the court, where they are subject to ongoing monitoring of court-ordered programs, such as batterers' intervention programs and compliance with orders of protection. Defendants remain accountable to and continue to appear in front of the same judge, even after case disposition and during the term of probation. A resource coordinator helps the judge monitor compliance by obtaining information from the district attorney, the Department of Probation, and the batterer's programs. A victim advocate, who works in partnership with the prosecutor, ensures that victims have a safety and housing plan and are linked to counseling and other social services.

Another successful domestic violence court can be found in Lexington County, South Carolina. Gover et al. (2007) found that the court's success appeared to result from emphasizing procedural justice principles. Victims and defendants were provided opportunities to participate in the judicial process, and they reported high satisfaction with the court's operation and the sentences pronounced. Procedural justice examines the processes and not just the outcomes of a case. The idea of procedural justice is based on the concept that processes strongly affect how people obey the law. Paternoster et al. (1997) suggested that the subsequent behavior of the offender was affected more strongly by how the sanctions were imposed than by the sanctions themselves. It has also been recognized that punishment can create unintended results if it is inappropriately administered. Resentment and anger could occur if the person punished is demeaned, embarrassed, or diminished.

In the Lexington County court, the judge and prosecutor communicated regularly, and the judge more often accepted sentencing recommendations made by the prosecutor due to the collaboration. Observations and surveys conducted by Gover et al. (2007) revealed that 90% of the victims and 68% of the defendants felt that the court gave adequate time to explain their side of the story, 77% of victims and 68% of defendants believed the outcome of their case was fair and just, and 67% of victims and 58% of defendants thought at the Lexington County domestic violence court's response to domestic violence cases was just right. It appears that the use of ADRs and the emphasis on rehabilitation and treatment positively affected both victims and defendants. According to the researchers, the focus on collaboration between the judge, prosecutor, victim advocate, mental health counselor, sheriff's investigators, victim, and defendant led to a significant reduction in rearrests for domestic violence offenses. The court also established an active approach to addressing domestic violence that emphasized victim safety, offender accountability, and batterer treatment.

Domestic violence courts provide a critical step in a continuum of response that begins with local police intervention and continues through ongoing community correction monitoring of the offender and community-based services for victims. As can be seen, when courts become more collaborative with professionals outside of the courtroom workgroup, the results become more beneficial for the victim, the offender, and the community.

Mental Health Courts

The creation of mental health courts is a recent action that creates collaboration between the criminal justice system and mental health professionals to address the needs of mentally ill persons who have been charged with nonviolent crimes. Because of decreased funding for mental health, persons who have mental illness and commit nonviolent crimes are placed in the criminal justice system instead of treatment facilities or programs. The criminal justice system is not equipped to handle mentally ill patients. So, they do not receive the proper care and are eventually returned to the community, where they often offend again. This begins a revolving door cycle that does not benefit the criminal justice system or mentally ill persons.

According to the BJA, mental health courts are still few, only about 450 in 2020, according to the American Psychiatric Association. They are usually structured similarly to drug courts, where professionals outside the courtroom work group collaborate with the workgroup to establish individualized plans to address the defendant's needs. Often, mentally ill persons who are arrested suffer from homelessness, lack of family support, substance abuse, and lack of finances to seek appropriate treatment or medication. The work teams establish treatment plans and provide monitoring and often financial assistance to assist the individual in staying on the plan and avoiding being arrested again.

The following case study chronicles the establishment of a mental health court in a poor, rural area of southwest Georgia. Because most high-impact areas are in economically depressed communities, the success of this court is encouraging for those officials who work to implement community justice principles in deprived areas. Although the court was launched in an impoverished area with few resources, creating such a court could be accomplished in any jurisdiction, regardless of financial status, if collaboration between the courts and mental health professionals is established.

There are arguments, pros and cons, for using mental health courts. The American Psychiatric Association (2020) argues there is evidence that mental health courts improve recidivism by providing and engaging individuals with treatment services. They also argue that the mental courts should be administered in a manner that values the offender's well-being and honors the concept of therapeutic jurisprudence. This argument holds that even if mental illness is not the underlying variable in the case, people with mental disorders should be routed to treatment and provided psychosocial support to help them avoid future encounters with the criminal justice system. Those who oppose mental health courts argue that mental disorders do not necessarily cause crime and that people with mental illness have the same risk factors and reasons for offending as the general population. They believe that the goal should be to reduce recidivism in individuals with mental disorders by using the same approaches that have been effective in other offender populations. Another argument against the use of mental health courts is that their very existence perpetuates a stigma by implying a link between mental disorders and criminal offending. Overall, they do recommend continuing the development of mental health courts with the use of evidence-based approaches to any applicable treatment interventions to promote mental health. They also cite the need for ongoing research since the current data does not clearly indicate how effective the courts have been. Dean (2017) conducted a systematic review of mental health courts and found that the courts effectively reduce recidivism for participants, but there did not seem to be an indication of how or why this is the case. An additional concern cited by Dean was that in her study and numerous previous studies, it has been shown that mental health courts vary widely in their policies and procedures, making comparisons between courts challenging.

Box 4.3 Albany, Georgia Mental Health Court Case Study

Because those with mental health issues often end up in the criminal justice system, Stephen Goss, a trial judge in rural southwest Georgia, started a felony mental health court. Judge Goss served in an area where poverty is rampant and resources in the mental health field have been drastically decreased. The goal of the court is to help the appropriate agencies coordinate their efforts in addressing mental illness so that arrests and mental health facility stays are decreased and the overall health of the patient is improved.

Albany, Georgia, is a rural community located in southwestern Georgia. The population of the city is approximately 77,000 persons composed of approximately 68% African-American, 29% white, 2% Hispanic, and less than 1% Native American, Asian, Pacific Islander, and other races. The yearly median income is $29,000 for households and $33,000 for families, but the median income per capita is only $16,000. About 22% of families and 27% of the population were below the poverty line. Owner-occupied housing is one indicator of how healthy a community is, and Albany has 43% owner-occupied housing, with 57% of the housing being renter-occupied. The national average is 67% owner-occupied and 33% renter-occupied, so it appears that Albany is not particularly healthy in this area (U.S. Census Bureau, 2008). Overall, it can be seen that while the city has strengths, it also has a weakness in the economic conditions of the city and surrounding counties. The region is one of the poorest congressional districts in the country and has been designated as a federal health care professional shortage area (Goss, 2008).

Judge Goss recognized that the criminal justice system had become the de facto mental health treatment center for many of the offenders arrested. Those with mental health problems who were arrested were not usually under the care of a health professional and did not have prescriptions to address their afflictions. These factors led to a revolving door process where the arrested persons were treated at the jails or admitted to mental health facilities where treatment costs were high. After the treatment, the persons were usually given credit for time served and then released from custody. Because they had no support system at home, they would often relapse and be rearrested for violating the law.

A meeting including members from the local judiciary, law enforcement, jail staff, mental health professionals, and disability advocates was organized by Judge Goss. After that meeting and further discussion lasting several months, two needs were identified. The first was the need for better training for first responders, such as police officers and paramedics, and the second was to develop a systematic approach to court cases involving those with mental illness issues. The group recognized that the symptoms were being treated by the criminal justice system when the real need was to develop actions to address the underlying mental health and substance abuse problems of the offenders.

Judge Goss and the task force realized that a major factor in their problem was that the United States has moved from institutional based treatment to more community-based treatment. While this move appears to be more humanitarian, there are some negatives associated with such a move. In many cases, those who are placed in community-based treatment do not have stable living arrangements or family support, and they often have financial issues that affect their ability to seek medical treatment and purchase needed prescriptions. Because of these unstable living conditions, many individuals begin to self-medicate with street drugs or just cease looking for treatment options.

The group identified two general case scenarios that are usually experienced. The first is that the mentally ill person is in the community with outpatient counseling and treatment. In this scenario, a stressor event occurs that overloads the ability of the person to cope with the stressor. The person may begin to act out, quit taking prescribed medication, increase alcohol consumption, and cease seeking professional treatment. Often, the behavior of the individual becomes problematic enough that the police are called. When they arrive the individual may feel threatened and become combative, leading to an arrest and entrance into the criminal justice system. In the second scenario, the mentally ill person is homeless. Here, the mentally ill person lives on the street and often sleeps in doorways or other warm areas of buildings. When proprietors arrive the next morning, they discover the individual and call the police. Officers who respond to the call usually realize the person has nowhere to go and often an arrest is made for loitering, entering the person into the criminal justice system. Many times, those individuals arrested are gainfully employed, but their incarceration prohibits them from going to work. If those individuals are receiving governmental disability payments, the benefits are suspended because the individual is not working. It can be seen how this cycle can create financial hardship not only for the individual but for the family as well.

Judge Goss also realized that many of the professions that are involved in this process are not accustomed to communicating with each other. He found that much of the problem stemmed from medical and legal professionals being trained on confidentiality issues. He also discovered that very often the problem involved the lack of sharing information, causing these professionals to be unaware of existing programs that could address the problem.

The program developed in Albany contains a court coordinator and two case managers on staff at the community mental health organization. Those staff members coordinate with jail nurses and help determine the appropriate actions that should be taken to address those mentally ill persons already in custody. The results have been a reduction in the jail population and medication costs for the county, along with respect shown to the mentally ill individuals.

In the postadjudication process, entrance into the court program is a voluntary process since being mentally ill is not illegal. If the person opts to participate in the program, the treatment professionals make a recommendation to the judge and a case plan is tailored to the individual's needs. The probationer has an assigned state probation officer and a treatment case manager, ensuring proper support mechanisms are in place. Borrowing from the drug court model, periodic judicial reviews are held to keep the judge informed on the progress of the individual and the need for any modifications to the treatment plan. Such hearings also allow the judge to praise an individual for making progress and emphasize the need to follow the program to those who do not appear to be engaged in the process. It is also recognized that those with mental illness often do not have stable living arrangements because during their care they move from family member to family member. The program helps to stabilize these family settings so that the individual does not miss medication times or treatment appointments.

The program includes mandated participation in group or 12-step programs in cases where alcohol or substance abuse is a problem. There is also outreach to the community, which generates support and material goods for those in the program. Local churches have provided clothing items for homeless participants, and housing options have been developed through personal care homes operated by community organizations.

To assess the effectiveness of the program, administrators vertically studied the results of persons in the postadjudication felony probation program. The important issue examined is the number of times the participant has returned to jail or has to be admitted to an expensive in-patient stay at the mental health hospital. Administrators also look at a comparison of a participant's jail stays before coming into the program compared to after coming into the program. In a review conducted after the first 30 months of operation, it was found that 41% of the program participants were not rearrested after coming into the program. Participants in the program are felons, and one of the positive steps has been probationers suffering from a mental health disorder only without a co-occurring substance abuse problem. It was also discovered that the probationers do well if their living arrangements can be stabilized, allowing them to have consistency in medication regimens.

Teen Courts

Teen courts turn peer pressure on its head, using young people to censure teens who have broken the law. With the earliest documented teen court established in Grand Prairie, Texas, in 1976 (Godwin 1996), teen courts have blossomed across the United States, with approximately 1,400 courts nationwide (Mary Baldwin University 2023). These courts, by providing an alternative to more formal case processing for young offenders, serve to craft a more meaningful response to low-level teen offending and positively involve young people in the justice process. Teen courts fit into the rubric of community justice by creating a "community of teens" that works to promote and enforce appropriate standards of behavior for young people in their neighborhood.

Although there are many types of teen courts, in the basic model, young offenders who have already admitted their guilt to low-level offenses such as vandalism, truancy, shoplifting, and trespassing participate voluntarily in a process in which their case will be heard by a judge and jury of their peers, who determine the appropriate sanction. Schools, probation departments, police, nonprofit agencies, and courts all may operate a teen court. Some teen courts use adult judges with youth juries and/or youth "attorneys," while young people fully staff other courts. Typical sanctions might include community service hours, essay writing, a letter of apology, service on the teen court jury, and/or restitution. Teen courts may also work to incorporate family participation, with parents being required to take the stand or with mandated parental attendance at the hearing. Teen courts frequently draw on the principles of restorative justice by incorporating a social service assessment of the young person before or after the hearing and subsequent linking to social services. One of the primary philosophical underpinnings for using teen courts is that youth continually cite peers as having the most influence on them as they are growing up. With this in mind, designers of teen courts argue that sentences pronounced by peers will have more of an effect on the future behavior of a defendant than a sentence pronounced by an adult who is seemingly unconnected with the trials and tribulations of being a teenager.

Most youth courts rarely accept offenders with a previous arrest record. Still, it is known that repeat offenders tend to band together with other offenders to commit 50% of the juvenile crime (Forgays & DeMilio 2005). Forgays and DeMilio (2005) studied the Whatcom County Teen Court Program in Bellingham, Washington, which did take repeat offenders into their program, and found that through a cohort comparison, recidivism was not a problem. The researchers attribute much of the program's success to the restorative justice principles on which it was founded. The critical fact to be gleaned from the study is that inclusion of multiple offenders into a teen court program can yield success.

The most common evaluations of teen courts focus on the recidivism of the young offender, which disregards the multiple functions teen courts fulfill. These recidivism analyses fail to indicate a clear connection between lowered recidivism and teen court participation. A summary (Butts & Buck 2000) of studies of youth courts found inconsistent results from recidivism analyses: some supported the idea that teen courts are more successful than regular juvenile courts, and others found no differences between the two in overall outcome. A study by Gase et al. (2016) also found inconclusive evidence that teen courts have a measurable effect on recidivism. However, teen courts also serve to make justice processing more accessible to communities, to provide a community-based forum for the handling of youth crime, to increase public awareness of the legal system, to teach young people about the justice system, and to help young people feel responsible for their neighborhoods. The realization of these last goals will serve the most valuable community justice function by planting positive seeds in the community that will grow into increased community engagement in overall public safety. As with many other specialized courts, researchers recommend more robust research be conducted to determine the effectiveness of these courts.

> **Box 4.4 Red Hook Youth Court**
>
> Dave sits facing a jury of ten at-risk neighborhood youth all wearing Red Hook Youth Court T-shirts in the basement of a local church. The community advocate has already made an opening statement about the harm done to the community by Dave's recent truancy, mentioning that Dave not only is jeopardizing his own future but has also set a bad example for other young people in the neighborhood. The youth advocate has also made an opening statement, stressing that Dave is generally well-behaved and promises not to do it again. The judge just opened the questions to the jury. In a free-style manner, the jurors start asking about Dave's life – what he does instead of going to school, what he likes and doesn't like about school, and how his relationships are with his family. During the course of their wide-ranging questions, they discover that Dave is frequently truant, that he smokes pot at home when he's not at school, and that he really likes art but doesn't like his teachers. Upon finishing their questions, the jury exits to deliberate and returns with a sanction that incorporates a letter of apology to Dave's mother, a drug assessment, and a goal-setting workshop. Several weeks later, some of the jurors talk about seeing Dave in the neighborhood and asking how he is doing, and one juror said that he took Dave to his after-school art class. After completing their six months of service, many of the jurors mention that they feel more responsible for their neighborhood and will stop other kids when they see them writing graffiti or doing other vandalism.

Re-entry Courts

Re-entry courts take the drug-court model of intensive court monitoring, therapeutic jurisprudence, graduated sanctions and rewards, and the combination of services with justice case processing. They then apply it to offenders returning to the community from extended stays in jail or prison. Their goal is to stabilize parolees and probationers in the community when they first exit prison or jail to prevent future recidivism. Spearheaded by an Office of Justice Programs initiative, re-entry courts were established. As of 2020, 64 adult and two juvenile re-entry courts were in operation in the United States. Although evaluation results are still sparse, re-entry courts hold the promise of alleviating the pressures of one of the fastest-growing prison populations across the United States: technical parole violators. Carey et al. (2017) studied eight reentry court sites and found mixed results across them. They noted that in the sites where the program showed good effectiveness, there were high levels of consistency and intensity of substance abuse treatment. They believe sites with less positive results were possibly because they needed to have the appropriate level and type of services that were consistently available to best serve the varying risk levels of their participants. Lawson et al. (2021) conducted a cohort study for a sample of 340 participants who exited a reentry court. The study's objective was to determine if their reentry court completion status affected their likelihood of recidivating three years after exiting the program. The results indicated that successful program completion did continue to shape recidivism outcomes up to three years after their reentry court exit.

Even though re-entry court models differ, they combine similar elements. Offenders are assessed before release, and a re-entry plan is developed. Once released, the offender appears in a "court" established in partnership with parole or probation, often headed by a magistrate or administrative law judge rather than a sitting judge because the offender's case has already been adjudicated. The offender must attend appropriate social and drug-treatment services established by the court, be law-abiding, and engage in education or employment training. The offender will return frequently to court for parole and judicial monitoring and will be subject to a graduated system of sanctions and rewards in response to compliance with the court's mandates.

Re-entry courts may be in a downtown courthouse, but they necessarily concern themselves with the successful reintegration of offenders into their home communities. To achieve this, the courts must draw on neighborhood-based community supports, including community-based social service agencies, family networks, or faith-based institutions. Ideally, by drawing on these informal community institutions, re-entry courts will also strengthen them, improving prospects for overall public safety in the neighborhood.

Veterans Courts

Another specialized court that has been established is the Veterans Court. The purpose of this court is to assist retired military members who may be at risk for arrest and entry into the criminal justice system. In many cases, an arrest and conviction in the criminal justice system can put many veterans' benefits in jeopardy and exacerbate an already serious situation.

According to the American Addiction Centers (2023), as of 2023, there are 461 Veteran treatment courts in the United States. The treatment courts have proven to be effective, with participants being more likely to have improved outcomes in mental health, social functioning, housing, and employment. Data shows that only about 20% of veterans who participated received sanctions involving jail time during the duration of the program, and 14% had new incarcerations compared to 23%–46% of defendants in traditional court. Nearly 90% of veterans with co-occurring post-traumatic stress disorder (PTSD) did not have any arrests while involved in treatment court. This is significant because often, issues involving veterans with PTSD can become violent or physical.

Veterans Courts are operated similarly to drug courts, with opportunities for participants to attend individualized treatment programs that address substance abuse disorders (SUDs) and mental health issues rather than going to jail. Another important piece is that participants see the same judge at every scheduled court session, creating familiarity between the judge and the participants. Participants have support sources such as the Veterans Administration (VA), volunteer mentors who are also veterans, and organizations that offer resources designed to assist veterans.

The courts can intake participants involved in public intoxication, DUI (driving under the influence), domestic disputes, delinquency or failure to pay child support, drug possession, vandalism, theft, robbery, manslaughter, and sexual assault issues. Many of these offenses are serious, and admission to the courts is on a case-by-case basis. Overall, the most common offenses reported by participants are DUI, public intoxication, disorderly conduct, and drug possession.

DUI Courts

Another court established based on the drug court treatment model is the DUI court. The objective of this court is to identify first- or second-time offenders who may be deterred from recidivism if offered treatment and intensive supervision. Harron and Kavanaugh(2015) state that DUI courts reduce recidivism and general recidivism by approximately 12% better than other sentencing potions. They add that the best DUI courts are as much as 60% better and argue that these courts do not cost more to administer than traditional probation because they can shorten the time period required to supervise offenders and reduce the overreliance on incarceration, which has a poor record of treating substance abuse.

DUI courts, also called DWI courts in some states, combine alcohol and drug treatment with increased court supervision. Plumb (personal communication, July 5, 2024) shares that in some states, drug courts hear both drug and DUI cases, while in other states, the two courts are separated. He notes that therapists tend to prefer separation of the courts because one substance, alcohol, is legal while drugs tend to be illegal. Because accessing alcohol is much easier than accessing illicit drugs, treatment challenges may be different.

Plumb explains that DUI courts address the underlying substance abuse of participants by holding them accountable for their actions. The ultimate goal of the DUI Court is to reduce recidivism and make it less likely that participants will commit crimes like DUI in the future. Plumb says that a team, including a judge, prosecutor, defense attorney, probation officer, law enforcement representative, and program coordinator, monitors the participant's progress in addressing the substance abuse problem. Substance abuse treatment providers are in regular contact with the team members, and the participants must come to court frequently for progress reports.

Plumb believes peer support can be a factor in helping clients complete the program, and most DUI courts include opportunities for program participants to meet with each other and share challenges. An issue that participants frequently face is that DUI arrests often result in driver's license suspensions, which can affect their ability to attend treatment and court sessions. Plumb says that one of the benefits of establishing a separate DUI court is that the judge can grant limited driving privileges, which can mitigate some of the transportation issues encountered by participants. He did agree that another possible drawback is the program's community supervision aspect, which means that supervision personnel could visit them at home or their place of employment.

Again, as is the case in other treatment-based courts, there needs to be more evidence that can accurately assess the effectiveness of DUI courts. Miller et al. (2015) found that some evidence supports the effectiveness of programs that utilize intensive supervision and education. They argue that a more rigorous research design should be established to determine the program's effect.

The community court movement is at the center of tension that surrounds the idea of community justice. Do concerns about rights or concerns about justice take priority when they are in conflict? In practice, community courts are splitting the difference. The concern for rights during the adjudication process still predominates in the courtroom, while a concern for justice is gaining preeminence during the sanctioning process. One important reason for the increasing concern for justice during the sanctioning process is that the argument for rights has steadily weakened as the cumulative effects of individual sanctioning decisions have become more apparent. In communities where people suffer poverty, substandard education and health services, and few economic opportunities, the same sanctions given to offenders add up to a more disproportionate impact on the community and the individual than they do in communities characterized by more resources and healthier community well-being. Despite continuing and prospective conflicts, community courts show that a fair balance can be struck between individual rights and community justice. As the discussion

> **Box 4.5: Multicultural Community Justice**
>
> One of the promises of community justice is its ability to be responsive to cultural and racial differences among community residents. For community police, it might mean looking at a group of people hanging out in front of a building, not as potential drug dealers but as community members seeking companionship and cooler air outside cramped apartments. For community defenders, it might mean treating a client as a member of an elaborate family network who will not make decisions about the case without considering the needs of this network. Community mediators must regularly grapple with racial and cultural differences as they facilitate the direct communication of parties in conflict. Mediators must be adept at helping parties understand each other through a fog of disparate communication styles. They must also be sensitive to the role that racism can play in initiating and escalating conflicts and then in inhibiting the fair and reasonable resolution of conflict (Umbreit & Coates, 2000).

about specialized courts revealed, it will be necessary for the specialized courts to develop some standardized practices and focus on rigorous evaluation of the programs to determine effectiveness and if there is a need for modifying operations.

Thielo et al. (2019) noted that no national-level study has been conducted that assesses the degree to which the American public supports problem-solving courts. Their study, which involved data from a survey conducted by YouGov America, Inc. in 2017, examined public support for five problem-solving courts: drug, mental health, veterans, homeless, and domestic violence. Although problem-solving courts tend not to have directive or unifying theories that guide their operations, the study discovered that the problem-solving courts examined did tend to share a set of common principles that included the principle of diversion from imprisonment, the principle of problem-solving, the principle of individualized treatment, the principle of accountability, and the principle of effectiveness. The results of their data analysis revealed that the respondents believed that correctional sanctions should accomplish multiple goals with priority placed on rehabilitation and protecting society. Approximately 88% of the respondents agreed that treating offenders supervised by the court and living in the community was a good thing. Key findings from the study revealed that respondents supported problem-solving courts across all five special offender populations. There was also strong support for offenders with military service, and support was most pronounced for domestic violence offenders. The results indicated that support for treating offenders remains strong, even though punitive sentiments still exist. Americans want the correctional system to punish and protect but also to try to save offenders from a life of crime. The good news is that the public is supportive of the use of problem-solving courts, which is positive news for developing and using these types of courts.

Suggested Web Sources for Readers

Center for Justice Innovation – innovatingjustice.org
National Association of Drug Court Professionals – www.nadcp.org
National Association of Youth Courts – www.youthcourt.net
National Council of Juvenile and Family Court Judges – www.ncjfcj.org

References

Allen, F. (1996). *The habits of legality: Criminal justice and the rule of law*. Oxford University Press.

American Addiction Centers. (2023). Veterans treatment courts: Treatment and alternatives to prison. Retrieved 3/9/2024 from https://americanaddictioncenters.org/veterans/veteran-treatment-court.

American Psychiatric Association (2020). Resource document on mental health courts. October 2020. Accessed from www.psychiatry.org on February 15, 2024.

Bazemore, G., & Umbreit, M. (2001). *A comparison of four restorative conferencing models*. Juvenile Justice Bulletin (February). U.S. Department of Justice, Office of Justice Programs, Office of Juvenile Justice and Delinquency Prevention.

Butts, J.A., & Buck, J. (2000). *Teen courts: A focus on research*. Juvenile Justice Bulletin (October). OJJDP.

Carey, S.M., Rempel, M., Lindquist, C., Cissner, A., Hassoun Ayoub, L., Kralstein, D., & Malsch, A. (2017). Reentry Court Research: An Overview of Findings from the National Institute of Justice's Evaluation of Second Chance Act Adult Reentry Courts. Retrieved on April 20, 2024 from https://innovatingjustice.org/sites/default/files/media/documents/2018-02/reentry_courts_findings_overview_nij.pdf

Coates, R.B., & Umbreit, M.S. (1999). *Research & resources review: Victim offender mediation empirical studies*. Center for Restorative Justice & Peacemaking, University of Minnesota.

Conner, R., & Griffin, P. (1998). *Community safety law: An emerging legal specialty*. National Institute of Justice.

Cullen, F., & Gendreau, P. (1989). *The effectiveness of correctional rehabilitation: Reconsidering the 'Nothing Works' debate*. In L. Goodstein & D. MacKenzie (Eds.), *American prisons: Issues in research and policy* (pp. 23–44). Plenum Press. https://doi.org/10.1007/978-1-4684-5652-3_3

Dean, R. (2017). *What is the impact of mental health courts? A systematic literature review*. Unpublished MSW Clinical Research Paper, St. Catherine University and the University of St. Thomas.

Forgays, D.K. & DeMilio, L. (2005). Is teen court effective for 1st time offenders? *International Journal of Offender Therapy and Comparative Criminology*, 49, 107–118.

Gase, L.N., Schooley, T., DeFosset, A., Stoll, M.A., & Tony, K. (2016). The impact of teen courts on youth outcomes: A systematic review. *Adolescent Research Review*, 1, 51–67. https://doi.org/10.1007/s40894-015-0012-x

Godwin, T. (1996). *Peer justice and youth empowerment: An implementation guide for teen court programs*. National Highway Traffic Safety Administration and the American Probation and Parole Association.

Gorczyk, J.F., & Perry, J.G. (1997). What the public wants from corrections. *Corrections Today* (September).

Goss, S.S. (2008). Mental health courts in rural and nonaffluent jurisdictions. *Criminal Justice Review*, 33(3), 405–413.

Gottlieb, A., & Arnold, K. (2021). The effect of public defender and support staff caseloads on incarceration outcomes for felony defendants. *Journal of the Society for Social Work and Research*, 12(3), 569–589. https://doi.org/10.1086/712924

Gover, A., Brank, E., & MacDonald, J. (2007). A specialized domestic violence court in South Carolina: An example of procedural justice for victims and defendants. *Violence Against Women*, 13(6), 603–626.

Gray, K.B. (2008). Community prosecution: After two decades, still new frontiers. *The Journal of the Legal Profession*, 32, 199–214.

Hamer, E. (2023, September 12). As milestone studies and new data show, public defenders work 3 times too many cases. *St. Louis Post Dispatch*. Retrieved 3/9/2024 from https://www.stltoday.com/news/nation-world/crime-courts/public-defenders-attorneys-dangerously-overworked/article_5a63628b-63d0-56dc-bc91-ce908820ac75.html

Harron, A. & Kavanaugh, J.M. (2015). Research updates on DUI courts. NCDC: The Bottom Line, National Institute of Corrections, Accessed January 20, 2024 from https://nicic.gov/resources/nic-library/all-library-items/research-update-dwi-courts.

Herman, S. (2000). *Seeking parallel justice: A new agenda for the victims movement*, speech given at the National Press Club luncheon, December 15, Washington, DC.

Karmen, A. (2019). *Crime victims: An introduction to victimology*, 3rd ed. Wadsworth Cengage.

Keilitz, S. (2000). *Specialization of domestic violence case management in the courts: A national survey*. National Center for State Courts.

Lawson, S.G., Grommon, E., & Ray, B. (2021). Does reentry court completion affect recidivism three years out? Results from a retrospective cohort study. *Corrections: Policy, Practice, and Research*, 6(4), 288–304. Doi: 10.1080/23774657.2019.1663562.

Mary Baldwin University (2023). Retrieved 5/2/2024 from https://marybaldwin.edu/news/2023/04/20/senior-pitches-regional-teen-court-program/

Miller, P.G., Curtis, A., Anders, S., Day, A., & Droste, N. (2015). Effectiveness of interventions for convicted DUI offenders in reducing recidivism: A systematic review of the peer-reviewed scientific literature. *The American Journal on Drug and Alcohol Abuse*, 41(1), 16–29. Doi: 10.3109/00952990.2014.966199.

Nugent, H., & McEwan, J.T. (1988). *Prosecutors' national assessment of needs*. National Institute of Justice, U.S. Department of Justice.

Office for Victims of Crime. (2000). *New directions from the field: Victims' rights and services for the 21st century, strategies for implementation*. Tools for Action Guide Series: Training Manual. U.S. Department of Justice.

Ostrom, B.J., & Bowman, J. (2019). Examining the effects of indigent defense team services: A multisite evaluation of holistic defense in practice. *Justice Systems Journal*, 41(2), 139–184. https://doi.org/10.1080/0098261X.2020.1723842

Ostrom, B.J., & Kauder, B. (1998). *Examining the work of state courts, 1997: A national perspective from the court statistics project*. National Center for State Courts.

Paternoster, R., Bachman, B.R., & Sherman, L.W. (1997). Do fair procedures matter? The effect of procedural justice on spouse assault. *Law and Society Review*, 31, 163–204.

Rennison, C., & Welchans, S. (2000). *Bureau of justice statistics special report: Intimate partner violence*. U.S. Department of Justice, Office of Justice Programs, Bureau of Justice Statistics.

Spangenberg Group. (2001). *Keeping defender workloads manageable*. U.S. Department of Justice, Office of Justice Programs, Bureau of Justice Assistance.

The Nelson A. Rockefeller Center for Public Policy and Social Sciences. (2021). Drug court: Where justice meets treatment. Retrieved 2/21/2024 from rockefeller.artmouth.edu.

Thielo, A.J., Cullen, F.T., Burton, A.L., Moon, M.M., & Burton, V.L. (2019). Prisons or problem-solving: Does the public support specialty courts? *Victims and Offenders*, 14(3), 267–282. https://doi.org/10.1080/15564886.2019.1595243.

Thomson, D. (2009, September 25). *Infiltrating the criminal justice mystique: Citizen engagement with local criminal courts to end mass incarceration*. [Conference session]. Annual Meeting, Midwest Criminal Justice Association, Chicago, IL.

Tonry, M. (1993). *Sentencing commissions and their guidelines. Crime and Justice*, 17, 137–195.

Umbreit, M., & Coates, R. (2000). *Multicultural implications of restorative justice: Potential pitfalls and dangers*. U.S. Department of Justice, Department of Victims of Crime.

United States Census Bureau, 2006–2008 American Community Survey. Retrieved 3/9/2024 from http://www.census.gov/acs/www/

Von Hirsch, A. (1993). *Censure and sanctions*. Clarendon Press.

Zedlewski, E.M. (1987). *Making confinement decisions*. U.S. Department of Justice.

For Further Reading

Courts Culture and Caseload

Eisenstein, J., & Jacob, H. (1977). *Felony justice: An organizational analysis of the courts*. Little, Brown. Still the best description of the social organization of the courts and how it affects court processes.

Harlow, C. (2000). *Defense counsel in criminal cases*. Bureau of Justice Statistics.

Lewis, C.S. (2001). *The abolition of man*. Harper.

McCoy, C. (1993). *Politics and plea bargaining: Victim's rights in California*. University of Pennsylvania Press. An analysis of the ways court culture affected the implementation of victims' rights in California.

Rosset, A., & Cressey, D.R. (1976). *Justice by consent*. Lippincott. Classic study of the way the courts' caseload affects court processing.

Sentencing Reform

Byrne, J. M., Lurigio, A.J., & Petersilia, J. (1992). *Smart sentencing: The emergence of intermediate sanctions*. Sage. A description and evaluation of various alternatives to incarceration.

Griset, P. (1991). *Determinate sentencing: The promise and reality of retributive justice*. SUNY Press. A critical assessment of the determinate sentencing movement.

Tonry, M. (1996). *Sentencing matters*. Oxford University Press. An explanation and analysis of contemporary issues in sentencing in the United States.

Innovation in the Courts

Feeley, M. (1983). *Court reform on trial: Why simple solutions fail*. Basic Books. A special report on the reasons why court reform in the United States has not succeeded in improving court performance.

Shapiro, M. (1986). *Courts: A comparative and political analysis*. University of Chicago Press. A classic description of various court systems and the social and political issues they raise.

Stone, C. (1996). Community defense and the challenge of community justice. In *Communities: Mobilizing against crime, making partnerships work*. August, National Institute of Justice Journal. 41–45.

5
Corrections and Community Justice

The system of criminal justice is at its core a human services occupation. It is a "people business," and those who work in the field are considered public servants. Police officers, judicial officials, and corrections officers all engage with individuals experiencing some of the most difficult moments in their lives. With perhaps the exception of career criminals who comprise only 2% of criminal offenders (United States Sentencing Commission 2022), most people involved in the criminal justice system did not foresee or plan for such involvement. While no aspect of the criminal justice system is pleasant for offenders, it is important to recognize that convicted offenders generally spend more time under correctional authority fulfilling their sentence than they do in the custody of law enforcement or in navigating the court proceedings. This places correctional workers in a critically important position where they often have a significant amount of time to work with those under their supervision.

The field of corrections has traditionally been seen as the punitive arm of the criminal justice system, yet it is important to acknowledge its wider potential. Corrections is ideally positioned to aid offenders in transitioning from merely law-abiding citizens to individuals who can lead healthy and fulfilling lives within the community. The relational approach, which is at the heart of community justice, is instrumental in transforming corrections from a solely punitive entity into a catalyst for positive change, community health, and well-being. Community justice is not about "softening" corrections; it is about recognizing, as Holsinger (2023) states, "that there is benefit in viewing correctional supervision and rehabilitative efforts as real 'human services' that hold tremendous potential for affecting the lives of justice-involved people and others to whom they are connected" (p. 21).

In the context of correctional operations, we distinguish between two types: institutional corrections, which include jails, state prisons, and federal penitentiaries, and field-service corrections, which mainly involve probation and parole. Probation is a court-ordered period of correctional supervision in the community. Probation may take the form of either a suspended imposition of sentence or the suspension of an incarcerative sentence, which can later be imposed if the offender fails to successfully complete the probation term. Parole, or post-release supervision, is a form of community supervision meant to monitor the reintegration of offenders into their home communities as they return from prison. While institutional corrections and field-service corrections may appear to have competing priorities, they are, in fact, interconnected pieces of a larger system that aims to uphold justice and maintain societal order.

Institutional corrections, despite their obvious retributive goals, also play a key role in beginning the process of rehabilitation for incarcerated individuals. The most prevalent forms of corrections – probation and parole – are inherently community-based. They are not just about monitoring and supervision but also about fostering relationships, promoting positive change, and facilitating reintegration. This is where the goals and principles of community justice come into play.

Community justice, with its emphasis on strengthening community cohesion, nurturing relationships, and creating partnerships, aligns with the overarching goal of corrections, which is, according to the State of Missouri Department of Corrections (DOC), *Improving lives for safer communities.* Community justice underscores the importance of collaboration between justice-involved citizens and various community stakeholders, including correctional officers, probation and parole officers, community reentry organizations, and the broader community. When these relationships are built on trust and mutual respect, they play an integral role in giving justice-involved citizens the tools and confidence they need to reestablish ties with their families and the community.

Therefore, it is important to view corrections and community justice as two sides of the same coin with the same objectives – successful rehabilitation and reentry of justice-involved individuals and the safer communities that come as a result.

Community justice within correctional settings is fundamentally centered on the fostering of relationships and partnerships. Whether it is the interaction between a probation and parole officer and their client, a correctional officer and an incarcerated person, or the collaborative efforts between corrections agencies, community reentry organizations, and the returning citizens they serve, such relationships are crucial. These relationships and partnerships serve as the cornerstone for fostering trust, promoting rehabilitation, and facilitating the successful reintegration of offenders into society.

In this chapter, we begin with a brief overview of the pillars of traditional correctional service. We then explore the pillars of community justice in correctional settings and the ways in which traditional correctional thought is being integrated into the community justice framework. We then introduce the value and transformative power of relationship building in community and institutional correctional settings. We conclude with a consideration of the challenges faced by formally incarcerated women.

Pillars of Traditional Correctional Services

Before we can determine the steps, we should work toward and implement in terms of correctional effectiveness, it is important to first understand the present state of corrections. Therefore, to set the stage for discussing the relational aspect of community justice and its relevance to correctional services, we will briefly consider the five primary pillars of traditional correctional practices: offender management, risk assessment, treatment, surveillance, and punishment. Each of these pillars are a fundamental aspect that underpins and supports the system of corrections.

Offender Management

In traditional corrections, the technical core focuses on managing offender behavior through the application of criminal sanctions. Correctional workers are held accountable for the way they deal with individual offenders. Computerized information systems track offenders from the point they are sentenced by the judge to the point they are terminated from correctional programs, whether through successful completion or revocation. Indeed, every aspect of correctional activity is designed for how it assists correctional workers in managing the offenders assigned to their care.

The offender-management pillar dictates that correctional focus be primarily on the individual offender, not the community, the victim, or the system. This offender-orientated approach permeates correctional action: institutional officers are assigned to oversee cell ranges or housing units, where they are held accountable for the well-being and behavior of individual offenders. Likewise, community supervision is organized into caseloads which consist of groups of offenders, generally grouped according to the way a classification system suggests they be handled. Under correctional authority, offenders are processed through stages of correctional work – pretrial, postconviction, and community re-entry. The essence of correctional management is operationalized through interactions between correctional staff and each client.

Risk

The central concern correctional officials emphasize in managing offenders is their risk. High-risk offenders are treated one way – managed with care and with an emphasis on control; and low-risk offenders are dealt with in another way – given less restrictions and controls. Average-risk cases fall in the middle. Most correctional programs allow for dynamic risk assessment, where an offender's level of risk can evolve throughout the penal process. Initially, a strategy emphasizing tight controls may be implemented, but as the offender exhibits improved behavior, a less restrictive approach may be adopted to reflect the reduced level of risk. Risk permeates correctional thinking. When a case fails, especially when a new crime is committed by a person under correctional authority, questions usually follow about why the risk was not anticipated. This means that it is unwise to underestimate risk, and correctional officials are encouraged to treat any risk indicator as important. At the same time, however, there are far too many cases under correctional control for all of them to be handled as high risk. Correctional leaders are therefore caught in a bind – they must find a substantial body of low-risk cases that justify diverting their attention to the more problematic cases. But whenever there is a problem with any of these cases, correctional officials are made to answer for not anticipating the risk.

Treatment

The idea of rehabilitation, particularly in the context of corrections, has waxed and waned over the past number of decades. Rehabilitating offenders was a primary goal of corrections until the early 1970s due, in part, to rising crime rates and the prevailing notion that rehabilitative efforts were ineffective (Martinson 1974). Nonetheless, the importance of correctional programming remains significant. Most offenders have significant personal problems that, left unchanged, undermine their ability to reintegrate into community life after correctional authority ends such as drug abuse, mental health issues, absence of family support, poor impulse control, lack of job skills, educational deficits, and so on. All correctional settings are required to assess offender needs for treatment and provide basic programs that meet those needs. Unfortunately, the success of correctional treatment programming is notoriously poor. It is not so much that "treatment doesn't work," as Martinson (1974) alleged, but rather that even the best treatment programs work for only some of the clients, and all treatment programs have some failure. There is no "silver bullet" in correctional rehabilitation. Treatments are at their most successful when they address the needs of high-risk (rather than low-risk) clients, so we can see that treatment programming poses an inherent dilemma for corrections: the treatments are all going to have failures, and if they are applied correctly (to high-risk cases) to start with, they will have a larger number of failures overall.

Surveillance and Control

Traditional correctional programs have a basic concern for the safety of the community. This implies the need for a minimum level of surveillance and control and suggests that as program failures mount and as risk levels of clients get higher, the need for surveillance and control also increases. For correctional administrators, there are no excuses for losing control of cases. A basic requirement is to know where a client is supposed to be and to know if the client is actually there. Institutional correctional officials conduct counts several times a day to maintain surveillance and control, while community corrections workers (CW) utilize home visits, employment checks, and drug testing to attain comparable oversight. With the advent of new technologies, the emphasis on surveillance and control has grown in recent years. From electronic monitors that identify a person's whereabouts to drug screens and lie detector tests, correctional officials have at their disposal an ever-increasing array of methods to assert control and aid surveillance. Whenever there is a problem in a particular offender's case, the question always seems to be, "Why wasn't this person's behavior under closer scrutiny?" It isn't possible to watch every offender all the time, but it is possible to give greater emphasis to watching particular offenders more closely, especially those of high risk or those who have complicated or significant treatment needs – in the former case, to make sure that the rules are being followed, and in the latter, to make sure the treatment program is working.

Punishment

Corrections is often viewed as the punitive branch of the criminal justice system. While the police identify and apprehend suspected wrongdoers and the courts adjudicate cases and affix sentences upon conviction, it is the responsibility of the corrections system to administer punishment. If there is one thing that citizens expect from corrections, it is that offenders will be sanctioned for their misconduct. This has two levels of meaning for correctional officials. Firstly, correctional officials are responsible for ensuring that court-ordered punishments are carried out according to the judge's directives. Secondly, when offenders fail to adhere to the rules of correctional programming, the consequences must be sufficiently painful that the offender will be persuaded to rethink their errant ways. The metric of punishment has changed in recent years. Sentences are longer, correctional program conditions are more stringent, and expectations for compliance are higher than they used to be only a scant generation ago. This has caused some observers to consider punishment as the most important function of corrections. It is certainly true that the public's expectations of effective punitive approaches have been accepted by correctional authorities as a strong mandate in the correctional agenda. The five foundational pillars of traditional corrections – offender management, risk, treatment, surveillance and control, and punishment – constitute something of a modern language in the field. Any useful description of current correctional policy must inevitably consider and grapple with these issues. However, it is important to note that these pillars do not hold the same level of prominence in the context of community justice as they do in the traditional correctional framework.

Pillars of Correctional Community Justice

The pillars of community justice consist of a set of guiding principles and perspectives, all aimed at addressing crime and criminal behavior within the context of the community. While community justice has significant differences from the traditional approach, it is not in opposition to it. The most significant difference is that unlike the traditional criminal justice system, which often operates independently, community justice actively seeks alignment and builds capacity with informal social controls at the community level. Formal social controls – police, courts, and correctional enforcement – are seen as of secondary importance in building a safer society than informal social controls – such as families, personal associations, social organizations, and the private sector. The heart of community justice lies in recognizing the importance of and building upon the strength of these informal networks. Through such collaborations, community justice aims to create a stronger community capacity for public safety. Below, we examine five fundamental pillars of community justice within the framework of corrections.

Neighborhoods and Communities

In a community justice model, corrections maintain a focus on neighborhoods and local communities. This focus stems from the recognition that neighborhoods are a central aspect of contemporary life, and ensuring public safety requires treating neighborhoods as stakeholders. Under the community justice model, the scope extends beyond the offenders under correctional supervision and control; it also encompasses the places where these individuals live and work and the people with whom they interact. The importance of neighborhood and community is particularly evident in correctional functions that operate while offenders reside in the community, such as probation and parole. The actions of these individuals have significant implications for community life, especially in relation to their struggle to remain crime-free. In addition, the presence of offenders in the community affects the lives of many other residents, as offenders also have roles as family members, employees, neighbors, parents, peers, and friends to those around them.

The concentration of offenders in certain locations is great enough that, as a result, correctional authorities may have a substantial impact on the lives of many residents. However, the neighborhood connection also extends to institutional correctional function. Communities consist of interconnected social networks that form the basis for collective community activities – it is through the social networks that groups form, resources are shared, and supports are provided. Criminologists agree that informal social controls form the basis for public safety in community life; the capacity of a community to achieve a degree of public safety through collective activity is referred to as collective efficacy (Sampson et al. 1997). Without strong, broad networks, there is little collective efficacy. Every time an offender is removed from the community for incarceration, those networks are affected. While incarceration may eliminate behaviors that damage the capacity of the network to support its members, it also removes contributions by the offender that may have assisted the networks such as familial support, participation in the local labor force, informal caretaking roles, and community involvement. Likewise, when an offender re-enters the community from prison or jail, those networks are called upon to reintegrate the individual as a resident. Thus, high rates of incarceration can significantly affect the capacity of social networks in these communities to perform their public safety functions (Sampson et al. 1997). For example, when large numbers of men are locked up from a particular area, their children may lack male supervision, and their parental partners are forced to take on additional responsibilities as financial and personal supports. Similarly, communities with a high concentration of residents fresh from prison or jail must develop their informal capacities to address the challenges of reentry and workforce integration for these returning citizens. For these reasons, correctional functions under a community justice approach are concerned with particular neighborhoods and the people who live there. The focus extends beyond offender behavior to encompass the broader impact of an offender's situation, whether incarcerated or reintegrating into the community, on those not under correctional authority.

Partnerships

Community justice organizations, including correctional agencies, do not work in isolation. Those organizations, each with specific objectives such as rehabilitation and public safety, partner with other organizations to achieve their goals. The rationale for these partnerships is clear: the issues faced in communities are complex and interconnected, and addressing them in isolation is unlikely to bring about significant change. When organizations begin to work together, greater change can occur.

One of the most common correctional partnerships is with other criminal justice organizations, particularly the police. Within the framework of community justice, police become natural partners to probation and parole officers, and public defenders can work alongside correctional authorities to pursue the interests of the client, especially regarding treatment, employment, and family relationships. However, when it comes to forming partnerships in community justice, institutional corrections face the greatest challenge, but the idea that careful transition planning can improve re-entry success automatically suggests a role for community partners, even with institutional correctional functions. Box 5.1 is an illustration of a successful partnership between the Massachusetts DOC and the Massachusetts Parole Preparation Partnership (MPPP), demonstrating how institutional corrections can collaborate with community organizations to assist inmates in preparing for reentry into society.

Non-criminal justice agencies also make valuable partners. For example, treatment providers become natural partners for the jail, as offenders prepare for release and seek to maintain continuity in treatment programming. Social services, such as welfare, child-protective services, and employment-related services, may also work closely with correctional activity under community justice approaches. Juvenile correctional workers align themselves closely with the schools. Overall, partnerships with non-justice agencies are designed to encourage "seamless" service systems in which comprehensive strategies are concentrated in communities whose residents suffer from significant deficits. Finally, community justice strategies seek private-sector partners. Among the most important partners are for-profit businesses that operate (or might operate) in the neighborhoods targeted by community justice initiatives. In making community quality of life a priority, community justice seeks to help transform troubled communities into places where businesses can succeed because this helps create employment opportunities (for offenders and nonoffenders alike) and bolsters a solid economic foundation for residents. In addition, community justice organizations build partnerships with private nonprofit organizations, such as foundations, to carry out community development initiatives that build a firmer foundation for public safety.

> **Box 5.1 Public–Private Partnership Delivers Support to Incarcerated Individuals Navigating the Parole Process and Returning to the Community**
>
> In July 2023, the Executive Office of Public Safety and Security (EOPSS) unveiled a groundbreaking collaboration between the Massachusetts DOC and the MPPP, a local nonprofit dedicated to aiding parole petitioners in their hearing preparations. This new partnership signifies a concerted effort to support individuals seeking parole by providing them with comprehensive transition plans, thereby demonstrating their commitment to successful reintegration into society.
>
> Through this initiative, MPPP, with the backing of the DOC, closely collaborates with a select group of petitioners to craft detailed transition plans. These plans are intended to be presented to the Massachusetts Parole Board during hearings, showcasing the individuals' dedication to sustainable reentry and contributing to enhanced public safety, decreased recidivism rates, and positive community re-engagement. The pilot project will specifically cater to parole petitioners at MCI-Norfolk serving life sentences with the possibility of parole. MPPP will pair eligible applicants with two partner paralegals who will aid in various aspects of hearing preparation, including
>
> - Organizing petitioner information for submission to the Parole Board
> - Identifying potential family and community support systems for post-release integration
> - Facilitating connections with potential supporters
> - Crafting robust reentry plans
>
> "This collaborative initiative strives to effectively prepare incarcerated individuals for the transition into communities to reduce crime, victimization, and recidivism while promoting successful reentry," said Public Safety and Security Secretary Terrence Reidy. "EOPSS is proud to introduce this unique collaboration to help participants with community reintegration." According to Undersecretary for Criminal Justice Andrew Peck, "The partnership between DOC and MPPP will help break through barriers that can impede successful reentry and impact a returning individual's ability to lead a healthy and productive life."
>
> "This partnership with MPPP is an important step toward fostering positive transitions for incarcerated individuals seeking a second chance," said DOC Commissioner Carol Mici.
>
> "Parole systems should be designed to facilitate and support individual success. That starts with ensuring that people are prepared for their parole hearings and the start of their parole sentence," noted Kendra Bradner, Director, Probation and Parole Project at the Columbia University Justice Lab.

> "Most people serving a life sentence with parole eligibility go to their hearings without representation. They are not prepared to present their best case for parole", said Kim Jones, MPPP's Director.
>
> This program will help parole petitioners not only prepare for their hearings, but it will also provide support to them upon release from prison. Petitioners who receive assistance with parole hearing preparation are more likely to be granted parole than those without assistance, and parolees who have formed solid connections with community members have much lower recidivism rates than those who do not.
>
> [https://www.mass.gov/news/new-public-private-partnership-delivers-support-to-incarcerated-individuals-navigating-the-parole-process-and-returning-to-the-community]
> Accessed 3/2/2024

Victims and Communities

Unlike traditional justice services, community justice initiatives focus on clients beyond the offender directly under correctional supervision. The community justice agenda extends its responsibilities beyond mere offender management. Community justice strategies recognize that crime and its consequences profoundly impact both victims and communities. For these clients, crime represents a significant challenge that needs to be overcome. In contrast, traditional correctional practices indirectly address victims and communities – by prioritizing public safety interests. While traditional corrections benefit victims and their communities indirectly, community justice takes a more direct approach. It actively embraces the interests of victims and communities. The problems victims encounter as a result of the crime and the difficulties encountered by communities resulting from the removal and return of resident offenders are made a part of the community justice agenda. The approach to these issues taken by community justice is one of problem solving.

Problem Solving

Community justice is a problem-solving philosophy. The orientation contrasts with traditional criminal justice, which is adversarial. Under community justice, preference is given to amelioration of problems and long-range solutions to entrenched difficulties rather than the mere adjudication of legal disputes. This concern for identifying problems and finding solutions enables community justice strategies to embrace a concern for victims and communities. The problem-solving orientation of community justice means that an unusual set of questions may be addressed by community justice through its partnerships. The community justice orientation allows correctional agencies to consider diverse questions: In what ways can community justice partnerships address the issue of food insecurity among justice-involved individuals and their families? What tailored solutions can be developed to address the specific mental health needs of incarcerated veterans? How can communities, families, and corrections officials work together to help convicted sex offenders reintegrate into society safely while making sure our community stays secure? In what ways can prisons help inmates stay connected with their families? What approaches can we use to encourage offender accountability, repair the harm caused by the crime, and strengthen relationships between offenders, victims, and the community? One of the reasons partnerships are so important to community justice is that problem solving is so important. Rarely are important problems simple. The important problems faced by communities and their residents are sufficiently complex that no single organization can resolve them in isolation. Therefore, the community justice orientation requires correctional agencies to reach out to other groups – police, social services, and the private sector – to fashion solutions to complicated problems.

Restoration

Every solution to crime involves some level of restoration because crime is destructive to society. It is destructive in tangible ways, as victims lose property and suffer personal injury. It is destructive in meaningful but less tangible ways, as citizens lose faith in societal institutions and residents isolate themselves from one another in order to remain safe (Zehr 1989). This dual level of loss – tangible and social – suggests that restoration has two aims. One aim is to repair the losses suffered by victims of crime. This is accomplished by restitution, usually from the offender but often from the community as well. But the social damage of crime can be addressed only through social reparation. This involves offenders "giving back" to society by recognizing that the crime they committed was a wrong done, not just to the victim, but to everybody. As an objective of community justice action, restoration replaces punishment at the top of the priority list. Community justice correctional action will include punishment, because community justice advocates recognize that one of the ways reparation is achieved is through legal sanction. But in selecting sanctions, there is often significant latitude, and, all else being equal, community justice strategies give highest preference to sanctions that restore the victim and repair the frayed social fabric that results from crime.

Box 5.2 Platte CARES (Community Alternative with Restorative and Educational Services)

In 2021, Platte County, Missouri Prosecuting Attorney Eric Zahnd, introduced a pioneering program called Platte CARES that offers a second chance to first-time, non-violent misdemeanor or felony offenders. Platte CARES is a prosecutor-led diversion program that stands for Platte Community Alternative with Restorative and Educational Services.

"The goals of Platte CARES are to reduce court caseloads, decrease incarceration, and lower recidivism by intervening with lower-risk offenders, hopefully diverting most participants from future involvement with the criminal justice system for the rest of their lives," said Zahnd. "And because a misdemeanor or felony record can have adverse consequences for a lifetime, Platte CARES is designed to achieve these goals while participants avoid their first misdemeanor or felony criminal conviction." To participate in the program, the offender must acknowledge their mistakes and take responsibility for their actions. Over six to 12 months, offenders perform community service as part of their commitment to restitution. They must remain crime- and

> drug-free and either continue their education or secure employment. Participants must also complete educational assignments tailored to their specific crimes and, in some cases, participate in restorative justice (RJ) processes. Those who fail to complete their assignments will be expelled from the program, and the prosecutor's office will file the criminal charges originally submitted. Since the program's inception, 510 individuals have been considered for admittance, 285 have been accepted, 73 were accepted but declined, failed to respond, withdrew, or were removed, 141 were rejected, and 11 are pending.
>
> The Platte County Prosecuting Attorney's Office is no stranger to diversion programs, as they are the only jurisdiction in the Kansas City, Missouri metro to have implemented four of the most-recognized treatment courts: drug, DWI, mental health, and veterans' courts. "I've always believed dangerous people deserve long prison sentences to preserve public safety and protect law-abiding citizens," Zahnd said,
>
>> But every prosecutor's office deals with far more people who have made mistakes that can be corrected without serving time. I now think there is a category of people we may not even have to charge in order to achieve justice ... Platte CARES is for good people who have made mistakes.
>
> As of March 2024, 165 participants have graduated from Platte CARES, reflecting a graduation rate of 87%. The 100th graduate reflected on how Platte CARES impacted their life. "Platte CARES transformed my life," they said.
>
>> I was on the wrong path, and the program pushed me to consider it from a different perspective. I'm very relieved the Platte CARES team believed my mistake didn't define who I am. I've discovered from Platte CARES that good people do make mistakes, but they learn and grow from them.
>
> https://plattecountylandmark.com/2021/06/03/program-helps-low-risk-offenders-avoid-charges/
>> https://www.co.platte.mo.us/plattecaresdiversionprogramcelebrates100thgraduate
>> Accessed 3/2/24

Integrating Traditional Correctional Thought into the Community Justice Framework

While the traditional pillars of corrections (i.e. offender management, risk, treatment, surveillance and control, and punishment) remain relevant under community justice, they are incorporated into the community justice priorities. The most important of these priorities is the neighborhood and community focus of community justice, as most of the traditional correctional agenda is shaped by this orientation.

For example, offender management adopts a community-focused approach. Rather than focusing solely on whether offenders are obeying the conditions of their criminal sanction, the focus becomes how can they be assisted in their reintegration into the community. For this reason, community corrections apply most powerfully to the traditional activity of probation and parole, with more complex implications for institutional corrections. Because offenders live with their families and in relationships with their neighbors and others who share their context, their integration into community life becomes a central focus of community justice offender-management strategies. Correctional workers become involved with key members of the offender's interpersonal network, and they also work to establish and strengthen new network ties – associates, organizations, and family members are important sources of support for reintegration. In working with those in the offender's social network, community justice workers must bear in mind the *risk* the offender represents to people in that network and to others in the community. Building strong community ties cannot ignore the fact that offenders have shown, through their past behavior, a willingness to damage those ties through criminal behavior. Part of what makes working with offenders under supervision so complex and challenging is the need to balance a realistic concern for risk with the direct need to establish supportive relationships and interdependencies that are vulnerable to that risk. Community justice workers thus give a significant importance to the need to monitor the progress of those relationships, both to make sure that they are remaining supportive of continuing progress toward full reintegration and to pick up signals of potential problems that may put those networks at risk. Offenders can hardly be expected to achieve the aims of repairing broken relationships and restoring the costs of their past crime unless criminal behavior has stopped. And neighborhoods and communities have a legitimate expectation that offenders have desisted criminal behavior.

The three most significant ways that community justice workers ensure progress toward reintegration are through the combined strategies of treatment programs, problem-solving efforts, and fostering a collaborative bond between themselves and the client. Treatment programs control and reduce risk. Problem-solving strategies identify ways that risk may be overcome through new offender and community approaches. Collaborative relationships between CW and clients, among other things, help to foster trust and facilitate the achievement of behavioral change goals. For example, an offender who has difficulty finding and keeping a good job can benefit from job-training programs, but these can be carried out in such a way that the offender earns some wages during on-the-job training in work that also benefits the wider community. Some of those wages can go to restitution, while some of the work can translate into community improvements, such as trash removal or housing renovation. Thus, community justice workers may wish to connect with community partners who offer on-the-job training programs that provide a beginning level of wages and include some degree of community service.

Both punishment and surveillance and control play roles within the framework of community justice. However, they serve as a means to an end – the reintegration of offenders – rather than as ends in and of themselves. When the offender is placed under correctional authority, punishment has *already occurred*. This includes any loss of liberty (such as jail time or a prison sentence) and restrictions on freedom (imposed through conditions of supervision). These aspects constitute the punishment, and no further sanctions need to be imposed. Similarly, surveillance or control are used to facilitate reintegration. Surveillance and control are not seen as having value except that they are helpful in guiding the offender toward a fully reintegrated status. The decision to apply specific kinds of surveillance or control is influenced by risk assessments, which takes into account the unique circumstances of the client and the community and are therefore not a general part of the overall correctional program for every offender under community justice supervision. Finally, the collaborative relationship between CW and individuals under their supervision is important to the success of reintegration strategies. Building a collaborative relationship involves developing "buy in" from the client. It is about empowering them so that they are involved in the decision-making process regarding their supervision. Even when specific conditions of supervision are mandated, it is important for clients to feel empowered to contribute their ideas on how to meet these requirements.

In the context of community justice, traditional correctional pillars persist but undergo a transformation, becoming secondary to the central principles of community justice. When observing a community justice system in action, one may still detect remnants of traditional correctional thinking. What is different is the larger and broader sense of client – including victims and the community – and the central concern for reintegration as the offender-management aim. Moreover, the question posed to assess the value of particular actions (Will this strategy help the offender adjust to the community more successfully?) is not directed mainly at the offender but is instead focused on the question of community quality of life (Will this strategy help strengthen this community and the offender's circumstances within it?).

How Community Justice Changes the Traditional Correctional Functions

The pillars of community justice can reshape traditional correctional practices, fundamentally altering their nature. Correctional functions traditionally operate within two main settings: the community and institutions. In each of these settings, there are distinct functions: regarding the community, there are probation and parole (re-entry); regarding institutions, there are jails and prisons. Though this classification is somewhat simplified, it provides a useful framework for understanding how the pillars of community justice can enhance and transform correctional tasks.

Community Justice and Probation and Parole

Probation, alongside parole, involves community supervision, indicating that its operations occur within a community setting where its clients reside. Indeed, the term "community-based corrections," encompassing probation and parole activities, as well as residential community facilities, underscores the natural connection of these functions to the community. Probation and parole share several commonalities in their community management. For example, in many states and jurisdictions, both are overseen by the same office and handled by the same correctional officer, known as a probation and parole officer. Their conditions of supervision may align (e.g. obey all laws, maintain residency, and report as directed), and establishing connections with community partners is crucial for both probationers and parolees. As a result, the principles of community justice applied in probation essentially parallel those applied in reentry.

Despite probation and paroles' apparent connection to the community, traditional community supervision has not fully embraced a community justice orientation. Indeed, the predominant approach to probation has been described as "Fortress Probation" (Schaefer et al. 2022). This term, while primarily referencing probation, applies equally to both probation and parole supervision. Fortress Probation is characterized by the placement of probation offices adjacent to the courthouse, downtown, far away from the communities where clients live. Officers seldom conduct visits to clients' homes or workplaces, except as mandated by agency policies regarding contact protocols. Instead, clients are required to come to the office for scheduled appointments. During these visits, they report on their activities since the previous office visit and provide urine samples for alcohol and drug testing to determine compliance with the conditions of their supervision. Unfortunately, this arrangement hinders officers from gaining insight into the many and varied opportunities clients face to engage in criminal activity. Moreover, "fortress supervision limits the influence that officers can have on their clients" (Schaefer et al. 2022, p. 3).

In Fortress Supervision, the caseloads are organized to make the reporting process easier. Typically, caseloads either contain a balanced number of high-, moderate-, and low-supervision cases to manage the workload effectively, or they consist of "specialized" clients representing particular problems or supervision issues, such as intensive supervision. This organization aims to make the management of these cases more manageable.

The Fortress Probation approach to supervision is certainly not without its critics. They point out that studies of probation effectiveness continually show the futility of the traditional caseload system of supervision (Manhattan Institute 1999), and they complain that the reactive style of Fortress Probation means that problems are not prevented but simply managed. One of the most significant criticisms of this traditional approach is that office-bound officers cannot engage in the kinds of community services that are needed to support their clients' adjustment to the community, and they fail to get to know anything meaningful about their family, work circumstances, or living situation (Schaefer et al. 2022). Yet, these are the factors that will have more effect on the offender's eventual adjustment than almost any others.

Under a community justice model, probation and parole move out of the office and into satellite offices opened in the neighborhoods where most clients live, and officers operate from them. Sometimes they work in the office, but more often they are in the community, working not just with offenders, but also with others who live and work in that neighborhood. Operating "in the field" makes it much easier for community justice probation and parole to broaden its scope beyond mere surveillance and control of court-sentenced offenders and returning citizens – individuals released from prison. It enables officers to engage more effectively with clients and to cultivate the kind of positive prosocial relationships conducive to the betterment of the client and the community in which they live.

In 2022, approximately 448,432 prisoners were released from state or federal prisons in the United States (Korhonen 2024), and their collective impact on the communities they reenter is significant. Studies show that successful reintegration is not just a concern for the returning citizens (released inmates); it is also a matter of public safety and economic necessity. Schanzenbach et al. (2016) argue that "a criminal justice system that emphasizes incarceration but does not support the journey home does a disservice to the formerly incarcerated as well as to the public" (p. i).

Relationship Building in Probation and Parole

In many ways, probation and parole are the correctional functions ideally suited to incorporate the values of community justice. With over 4 million US citizens on probation and parole at any given time (Still et al. 2016), community corrections is singularly poised to play a significant role in preparing individuals under supervision to not simply complete the terms of their supervision but to help prepare them to live meaningful lives full of hope, fulfilling work, and healthy relationships. However, if we are to be successful in our endeavors, we need to conduct business differently, and building strong relationships is crucial. Alameda County, California Chief Probation Officer Still holds,

> We know that our officers can help promote positive change in our clients' lives. But a prerequisite for that change is a relationship built on trust. It's a cultural shift, to have faith in people's ability to change, to treat people with dignity and respect, to recognize that our clients are members of our communities—and we know that cultural shift is foundational to our officers' wellness, to the success of individuals on our caseloads, and to healing for survivors of crime.
>
> (Gavel 2016. p. 1)

To establish trust and legitimacy within community corrections, Still et al. (2016) outline six core principles:

- Treat each individual on community corrections with dignity and respect. Recognize our common human capacity both to make mistakes and to make a change for the better.
- Realign incentives in the criminal justice system. Cost considerations at the local level should not systematically favor incarceration over alternative sanctions.
- Impose the least restrictive sanctions necessary and minimize the collateral consequences associated with criminal processing and conviction.
- Restore communities and facilitate their health and safety in a holistic way. This community perspective requires us to view public safety differently. The authors state, "Community corrections should serve as ambassadors to the business community to help them view justice-involved individuals differently" (p. 18).
- Reduce institutional bias and work to ensure that all individuals receive fair, equal access to the justice system – including opportunities for diversion and alternatives to incarceration.
- Evaluate what we do, invest more in practices that work, and abandon practices that do not. We should rely on data-driven decision-making and evidence-based practices to provide the most effective and efficient resources to people on our caseloads, victims, and communities.

Of course, adopting new principles of community supervision may necessitate agencies reconsidering their mission, reorganizing supervision practices, and redefining the role of supervision officers. In many agencies, there has been a historical focus on a surveillance and control approach, which aligns with the traditional correctional pillar. However, transitioning toward a mission-centered approach, which prioritizes relationship-building and the success of clients over solely punishing their failures, represents a significant and challenging shift in the traditional functions of probation and parole. This will entail a commitment by correctional agencies to train and prepare officers to build collaborative relationships with clients and their families.

The community justice probation and parole officer understand the significant impact of relationships or informal social controls on their client's success or failure. These informal social controls encompass the positive relationships that reinforce an offender's ties to conventional living, such as family members, employers, associates, and community organizations. Extensive research is clear on the pivotal role of informal social control in shaping both criminal and law-abiding behavior. Despite the probation and parole officer's greater *legal* authority, community-supervised offenders may be more inclined to heed the counsel and guidance of their loved ones. Studies indicate that informal sanctions, such as disappointing your boyfriend or inconveniencing your mother, can be more influential in controlling offenders' behaviors than formal sanctions (Mullins & Toner 2008; Williams & Hawkins 1986; Zimring & Hawkins 1973). Consequently, to effectively steer offenders toward desired behaviors, probation and parole authorities must leverage the support of the offender's loved ones to help communicate the rules and consequences of breaking them (Still et al. 2016).

While community justice probation and parole aim to establish various support networks within the community to assist their clients, a primary emphasis is often placed on family relationships. As mentioned, when the offender's primary relationships are supportive of the offender's overall adjustment, the chances of success improve. Nevertheless, it is important to recognize that family members do not automatically know how to provide the best support. Hence, it is important for community justice officers to talk with family members to help them understand how they can contribute to their loved one's success. Community justice probation and parole play a crucial role in strengthening and amplifying these social controls by emphasizing their importance, fostering the offender's connection to them, and providing guidance on how they can contribute to the offender's rehabilitation.

Community justice supervision is also concerned about victims of crime, as they are also residents of the community. In many cases, probationers are required to provide restitution to their victims, and community justice officers recognize that ensuring restitution can go a long way to increasing the community willingness to participate in this form of community supervision. From this perspective, the community is also a victim of crime, and offenders can be expected to make some form of restitution to the community, not just to the specific victim. Restitution to the community is usually some type of community service, such as repairing property, cleaning parks, or restoring damages in the neighborhood infrastructure.

In essence, community justice, probation, and parole aim to positively impact the lives of more than the clients under their supervision. It extends its concern to encompass the broader neighborhood and those individuals who may influence the offender's reintegration. Community justice corrections seeks to build ties to various community organizations, such as neighborhood councils, social clubs, and churches, and it relies upon those various organizations to develop a better relevance to residents who are under criminal justice authority. Each of these targets can be a part of a probationer's or returning citizens "making it": business managers can become employers, churches can become support groups, and community organizations can become advocates for community services and even host them.

The Transformative Power of Relationships in Probation and Parole

Correctional workers possess oftentimes untapped potential for facilitating successful offender reintegration. While training in risk assessment, safety protocols, and agency policies remains vital, a similar emphasis should be placed on fostering collaborative relationships with correctional clients. Such relationships have the power to serve as models of prosocial behavior, provide emotional support and encouragement, facilitate trust and mutual respect, and improve compliance. Drawing from personal experience as a former probation and parole officer, I've witnessed firsthand the transformative power of relationship-building in correctional settings.

From the first time, I met with new clients, I let them know that I was not out to "get them" and that I genuinely cared and was invested in their success on supervision. To emphasize their agency in the supervision process, I would share the analogy of "The Supervision Journey," which went along the lines of:

> "I am going to start out by putting you in the driver's seat of your own supervision. I am your "wing man" sitting in the passenger's seat. Our road map on this journey is the conditions of your supervision. I am here to guide and assist you, but this is *your* supervision. I am not going to do the driving unless or until such time that your 'driving' is putting us in danger. If your choices or actions threaten to drive this supervision off a cliff, I will take hold of the wheel through the use of sanctions." I meant every word of it and clients knew it. It was often the case that by the time I finished my "story" the client was in tears. The comment I most frequently heard was "I think this time, I might make it (i.e., successfully complete supervision). In the past, my other POs did all the driving."

Relationship building has transformative power. I have seen past clients, in violation status in their new jurisdiction, come to the office of their old, trusted PO to turn themselves in. I have observed clients threatening to abscond who would return when the officer said, "if you value the relationship we have built, you will come and talk to me." I know many clients who valued the relationship with their PO to such a degree that even when better housing opportunities arose, they refused to move outside their officer's jurisdiction. These kinds of experiences do not just happen; they are the product of the time and effort an officer puts in to building positive relationships grounded in mutual respect. I watched officers conduct visits in homeless encampments with clients who could not meet them at the office as a way to help their clients stay out of violation status. Many officers had open-door policies or stayed late to meet with clients after they got off work. I saw "Zoom" computer visits conducted so the officer could virtually meet and get to know their client's family and officers who (in pairs or more) met with clients at a local park while the clients' children played nearby. In my district, many a warm day found officers and clients outside sitting in lawn chairs while they completed lengthy risk assessments. An atmosphere, one could argue, that was more conducive to having the kind of difficult conversations that arise during an assessment than an impersonal conference room. These are all efforts to meet the clients where they are, to learn more about them – beyond the case file with its criminal history – (not that this information is not important, but it does not provide the whole story), and to build the kind of relationships that can be drawn on when the journey gets tough.

Research suggests that strong, positive working relationships that are based on mutual respect, openness, honesty, and warmth, among other qualities, can increase compliance and engagement with supervision and decrease recidivism (Center on Sentencing and Corrections 2013). Community justice in corrections is, after all, "a human service." The dynamics within the officer–client relationship have been linked to likelihood of supervision failure, the effectiveness of rehabilitation efforts, and the satisfaction levels of probationers (DeLude et al. 2012; Kennealy et al. 2012). Holsinger suggests, "When community supervision officers and treatment personnel have the capacity for empathy toward the justice-involved people they are working with, the ability to motivate behavioral change increases" (2023, p. 21). In light of such findings, it may be time to consider a shift from what has been called the traditional "referee" model of supervision to a more supportive "coaching" approach.

First introduced by Lovins et al. in 2018, the Coaching Model for Change (CMC) suggests that correctional officers should view their role more from the perspective of a coach rather than a referee. They argue that traditional CW are trained to act as referees, much like the referee in a game. The client's conditions of supervision are the rule book, and the referee/officer is taught to watch for rule violations and to issue a penalty when one is observed. Conversely, a coach is a person who is "assessing for talent and potential, teaching skills, practicing repeatedly until the players understand how to use the rules in the game, focusing on development, being invested in the player, and even holding the player accountable" (Lovins et al. 2023, p. 12). The authors contend that by employing the traditional referee-type model in community supervision, we may get compliance – what some may call a "win," but we do not see genuine behavioral change. In the coaching model, a "win" involves behavioral change and improved conduct. Correctional officers employing a coaching approach address rule infractions by fostering accountability and providing educational interventions aimed at facilitating clients' learning from their mistakes. The coach/officer knows their clients' deficits (criminogenic needs) that need to be improved and the strengths they have that can be built upon. They have a supportive and trustworthy relationship with their client and are seen as someone who is "warm but restrictive." Coach/officers interact with their clients through training and encouragement as they help them to develop skills to perform more successfully. The coach/officer follows core correctional practices (CCP) for more on CCP, see Dowden and Andrews (2004) and is part of a correctional culture that views their work as a human service with the goals of fostering positive behavioral change and a good life for their clients. Lovins et al. (2023) propose,

> If we can change the context in which our interventions are delivered, hire and train coaches to help people change, and give them skills found to be effective in changing cognitions and behavior, we believe we can increase the success of the criminal justice system. This will result in stronger communities, safer neighborhoods, supportive families, and ultimately, fewer victims.
>
> (2023, pp. 29–30)

Box 5.3 Neighborhood Opportunity Network (NeON) Initiative (New York City, USA)

The National Institute of Corrections lists "engagement with the community" as one of seven essential ingredients for successful reentry initiatives. The New York City Department of Probation (DOP) took this mandate to heart when it developed a community-based program, called the Neighborhood Opportunity Network, or NeON. NeON aims to improve outcomes for individuals on probation by shifting supervision to local neighborhoods, fostering community engagement, and connecting clients with essential services.

As with the New York City Model of Probation overall, the process of creating the NeON has been an agency- and community-wide effort. Informed by an emerging body of theory and research about what works, the aim was to establish a community-oriented practice rooted in strength- and desistance-based theories of change (Maruna, 2001) and principles of justice and equality that would yield successful results for probation clients and their communities.

Under the NYC Model, the primary objective is to enhance access to essential opportunities such as education, employment, and civic engagement for probation clients. By prioritizing these resources, the aim is to support individuals in achieving their personal and professional aspirations, ultimately bolstering public safety. Rather than focusing solely on "fixing" individuals, the approach seeks to overhaul DOP operations. This entails implementing policies and practices that incentivize staff to facilitate client success, promote community safety, and minimize instances leading to revocation and incarceration.

In sharp contrast to the "get tough on crime" mantra prevalent in the United States criminal justice system as a whole, New York City DOP Commissioner Schiraldi states, "Do no harm. Do more good. Do it in the community." One way DOP does "it in the community" is through decentralization of probation services. This has involved relocating key personnel from downtown court buildings to local NeON offices situated within or near the neighborhoods where clients reside. This strategic shift ensures that Branch Chiefs, Supervising POs, and other staff members are embedded within the community they serve. These NeON offices are often co-located with or adjacent to nonprofit organizations to enhance accessibility for clients.

When determining the locations of NeONs and NeON Satellite offices, multiple factors are taken into account. These include the density of residents serving probation terms, the presence of community assets such as robust service provider networks and institutions, the level of community and political support or opposition to the NeON initiative, existing deficits in healthcare, education, and other services, elevated rates of unemployment and homelessness, as well as considerations related to real estate costs.

To achieve this vision, the NYC Model sets out five goals, each with several related strategies:

GOAL 1: SAFER COMMUNITIES Strategy 1 – Target Resources to People on Probation at High-Risk of Reoffending Strategy 2 – Create and Rapidly Administer a Continuum of Graduated Responses

GOAL 2: OPPORTUNITIES, RESOURCES AND SERVICES Strategy 3 – Establish the Neighborhood Opportunity Network Strategy 4 – Prioritize Education, Work and Strength Based Development Strategy 5 – Realign Juvenile Justice Services Strategy 6 – Broker Opportunities and Eliminate Barriers to Success

GOAL 3: ORGANIZATIONAL EXCELLENCE Strategy 7 – Strengthen Professional Development Strategy 8 – Adopt Best Practices Strategy 9 – Embrace Organizational Culture of Client Success

GOAL 4: STRONG PARTNERSHIPS AND COMMUNITY ENGAGEMENT Strategy 10 – Establish Partnerships with Communities Strategy 11 – Collaborate with City, State and National Partners Strategy 12 – Build Broad Support for DOP Priorities

GOAL 5: MEASURING SUCCESS Strategy 13 – Streamline Data Collection and Improve Analysis Capacity Strategy 14 – Promote Accountability

In a recent comparison study (Center for Court Innovation, 2020), NeON clients reported having fewer challenges related to probation reporting, receiving more services, and being referred to more neighborhood-based services and diverse treatment options when compared with a matched sample of clients reporting to central probation offices. NeON clients also had more positive perceptions of procedural justice – fairness regarding their criminal justice experiences overall. This suggests that the NeON initiative has a positive impact in terms of increased access to local services, reduced barriers to reporting, and increased sense of fairness. More may still need to be done in terms of relationship-building. While clients in both groups reported positive relationships with their POs, those reporting to centralized probation offices generally reported better overall relationships, potentially reflecting less stability in PO assignments in NeON sites during early implementation of the initiative.

10-neighborhood-opportunity-network.pdf (ojp.gov)
https://www.nyc.gov/site/neon/programs/programs.page
NeON Works (nyc.gov)
Accessed 3/4/2024

Community Justice and the Jail

Jails are very important to the community. Over 3,000 jail facilities are operational across the United States. Before the COVID-19 pandemic, these jails processed about 10 million bookings annually. The overall number of incarcerated individuals has seen a substantial increase over the last four decades, escalating from around 220,000 in 1983 to over 750,000 in 2019 (Washington II 2021). While jails experienced a 24% reduction in population during the first half of 2020, by June 2020, national jail populations had begun to rise once more. By the end of 2020, the population had surged by over 50,000 individuals (Washington II 2021). Most jails are community based in that they operate within the confines of a particular community, but turning a jail into a community justice correctional operation is not a simple matter.

Jails handle offenders that are confined for various reasons: some are in lockup for only a night or two, until they make bail; others stay incarcerated until they are sentenced, then go to probation or prison to complete their sentences; still others receive jail terms as sentences and switch from being detained to doing time for a few months before they are released. If the processes of removal and return are important to community life, then jails are a major part of those processes.

Most often, the typical jail inmate stays inside for only a few days or weeks and then returns to the community. What can be done about those cases from the perspective of community justice? Three principles would seem to be important in the application of community justice to the jail: informal social controls, transition planning, and restoration/restitution.

The jail stay, no matter how short, always represents a disruption in the offender's life, and the disruption can imperil the ties to informal social controls (family and others) that will prove so important after the offender leaves jail. If the person serves a reasonable period in jail – several weeks or a few months – there will often be profound consequences regarding informal social controls and community supports: loss of a job, break in relationships, eviction from housing, conflict with intimates, and so forth. These can be quite problematic for later adjustment, even if they are very recent changes. A community justice orientation to a jail will try to minimize these losses. It will work to keep employment prospects strong, reach out to family members so they may retain contact with the person in confinement, assist community groups in reaching out to the jailed offender, and so forth. The broad aim of targeting these informal social controls is to try to create a situation in which the inmate, upon release, will be surrounded by supports that will tend to reinforce a positive adjustment. Perhaps most important, the jail staff can help set up treatment programs for drug and alcohol abuse or anger management that will continue to be a part of the offender's life after release.

Transition planning, therefore, is very important. In the typical case, a jailed inmate is released with no support or assistance. In New York City, for example, inmates are released in the wee hours of the morning and put on a bus to the center area of the borough where they live. They dismount the bus into an awaiting gathering of drug dealers and prostitutes. Under community justice, the plan for return to the community – especially its impact on family, neighbors, and potential employers – is carefully factored into the way the release is conducted, and the idea is to use release as the first positive step in the overall adjustment to the community.

Jails can also play an important role in restoration and restitution. One of the ironies of incarceration is that locked-up offenders cannot make restitution to their victims. But a community justice jail finds ways to make restitution possible: inmates are allowed to work for income that partly goes to a victim's fund, trustee programs are created that allow the offender to perform restorative services in the community, and inmate programs that benefit the community are encouraged.

The jail can also be decentralized to local levels, and facilities like halfway houses can be part of the offender's initial stay in the community. These facilities enable offenders to work during the day, sustain their family contacts, and provide income to the family and restitution to the victim, all while becoming gradually more involved in the neighborhood and its system of informal social controls. Jails are not community-based correctional facilities, but they can be reconfigured to have a community justice relevance.

Box 5.4 Community-Based Alternatives to Jails

Around 70% of individuals detained in US jails are facing charges related to drug, property, or public order violations; less than one-third are charged with violent offenses. Unlike prisons, where inmates have been convicted, approximately two-thirds of those held in local jails are awaiting trial. A number remain incarcerated pretrial as they are unable to afford bail. In addition, many incarcerated individuals are homeless or suffer from behavioral health issues. Approximately 44% of jail inmates report having at least one mental health condition. Individuals in jails also experience homelessness at rates ranging from 7.5 to 11.3 times higher than the broader population (Washington II, 2021). Nationally, there has been a call to create a network of services to help people manage conflict, address health issues, and promote socioeconomic stability and public safety without relying on the criminal legal system. The key to success lies in establishing partnerships with nonprofit organizations and advocacy groups. A number of communities have found innovative ways to address these issues without involving the criminal justice system.

Non-Jail Crisis Response

Eugene, Oregon, has long been at the forefront of addressing behavioral health issues by adopting methods that minimize the reliance on law enforcement intervention, unless expressly sought. In 1989, they implemented a mobile crisis response program called Crisis Assistance Helping Out On The Streets or CAHOOTS. The program is integrated into, and funded by, the Eugene Oregon Police Department and uses two-person teams pairing a medic and a behavioral health crisis worker. CAHOOTS units are equipped to deliver "crisis intervention, counseling, mediation, information and referral, transportation to social services, first aid, and basic-level emergency medical care."

The demand for CAHOOTS services has increased significantly over the years. In 2014, CAHOOTS was dispatched and arrived at 9,646 calls for service, while in 2021, CAHOOTS was dispatched and arrived at 16,479 calls for service. It is important to note that if the situation involves a crime in progress, violence, or life-threatening emergencies, police will be dispatched to arrive as primary or co-responders.

However, of the estimated 24,000 calls CAHOOTS responded to in 2019, only 311 required police backup.

When a call arrives at Eugene's communications center, through either 911 or the community's non-emergency line, call-takers listen for details that might identify whether CAHOOTS would be the appropriate response. As Eugene communications supervisor Marie Longworth put it, sending CAHOOTS rather than police is often regarded as "better customer service" for community members requesting assistance for themselves or others.

https://www.vera.org/behavioral-health-crisis-alternatives/cahoots
https://www.vera.org/beyond-jails-community-based-strategies-for-public-safety
https://www.eugene-or.gov/4508/CAHOOTS
Accessed 3/5/24

Tackling Homelessness

The Supportive Housing Social Impact Bond Initiative (SIB) was implemented in Denver in 2016 to provide targeted interventions to individuals heavily reliant on emergency services. SIB uses funds from private and philanthropic lenders to provide housing and supportive case management services to a minimum of 250 homeless individuals who frequently use the city's emergency services, such as emergency shelters, jails and prisons, detox centers, and hospital emergency rooms.

The Urban Institute, with partners from The Evaluation Center at the University of Colorado Denver, tracked implementation of the Denver SIB and evaluated its effects through a randomized controlled trial between 2016 and 2020. The study found

- Participants in the Denver SIB supportive housing program received 560 more days of housing assistance over three years compared to the control group
- 86% of participants remained stably housed one year later, with retention rates of 81% at two years and 77% at three years (excluding those who passed away during the observation period)Shelter stays for program participants decreased by 40%, with 127 fewer shelter visits over three years
- Police interactions decreased, with participants experiencing 34% fewer police contacts and a 40% reduction in arrests
- Participants referred for supportive housing had almost two fewer jail stays and spent 38 fewer days in jail over three years, marking a 30% reduction in unique jail stays and a 27% reduction in total jail days
- Program participants used short-term or city-funded detoxification services less frequently compared to the control group

The study suggests that by offering housing and the right supports, this type of preventive investment can help people find stability while reducing the public costs of the homelessness-jail cycle.

https://www.coloradocoalition.org/SIB
https://www.vera.org/beyond-jails-community-based-strategies-for-public-safety
Accessed 3/5/24

Addressing Cycles of Violence

According to Williamson II (2021), "Incarceration often worsens the root causes of interpersonal violence, fails to promote accountability once violence has occurred, and doesn't allow communities to lead their own peaceful conflict resolution" (p. 9). Various stakeholders have considered approaches to prevent, defuse, and address interpersonal violence by focusing on root causes and prioritizing the individuals affected. Such approaches include community mediation services and public health–based violence intervention programs. While leaders of these initiatives may coordinate with criminal justice agencies referring individuals to services or engaging with communities, their primary support comes from alternate channels.

Community Mediation Centers

Community mediation is a method for resolving disputes among individuals, groups, and organizations. It provides an opportunity for participants to address their concerns and needs while fostering stronger relationships and connections within the community. Mediators facilitate challenging conversations, allowing participants to retain decision-making authority. One example of a community mediation center is the Ku'ikahi Mediation Center, located in Hilo on Hawaii's Big Island.

Since 1983, Ku'ikahi Mediation Center has sought to bring peaceful resolutions to community conflicts – first as a program of the YMCA of Hawaii Island and since 2006 as an independent nonprofit organization. Ku'ikahi Mediation Center provides mediation services for individuals, families, businesses, and organizations to resolve disputes and conflicts peacefully. In Hawaiian, the word Ku'ikahi means a treaty, covenant, agreement, feeling of unity, peace, or reconciliation (Puki and Elbert, 1986). Ku'ikahi offers both mediation and facilitation services. Mediation programs include family, landlord–tenant, workplace, and community mediations.

Facilitation involves collaboratively guiding small or large group discussions to help participants identify and solve problems, make decisions, and accomplish tasks. By fostering a cooperative atmosphere, facilitation facilitates the group in fulfilling its objectives. Facilitation also cultivates an environment conducive to creative thinking, shields individuals from criticism, and stimulates idea generation to aid the group in achieving its goals.

In 2020, Ku'ikahi mediated and facilitated a combined total of 447 cases, conducting 220 sessions and serving 761 clients. Forty-eight percent of these clients had household incomes under $20,000. Additionally, 95% expressed satisfaction with the mediation process, while 97% would recommend it to others. As noted by one participant,

> When faced with any situation that becomes a legal issue, anxiety and stress erupt. Small things become big things and communication between parties becomes strained. Lawyers and courtrooms are intimidating and expensive. Ku'ikahi Mediation Center was a welcome alternative. The mediator assigned to my case truly understood my angst and made sure I was comfortable and understood the decisions being made in mediation.

In terms of educational initiatives, Ku'ikahi organized eight public and six private trainings and workshops, engaging 314 participants, of whom 98% reported learning something new and useful. Furthermore, nine brown bag talks on topics such as "Understanding and empathizing with differing conflict style" attracted 223 participants, with 87% reporting similar gains. Additionally, 24 in-house continuing education programs were conducted for volunteer mediators.

https://hawaiimediation.org/
https://archive.org/details/hawaiiandictiona0000mary
Accessed 3/6/2024

Public Health-Based Violence Prevention

The Aim4Peace (A4P) Violence Prevention Program, adapted from the evidence-based Cure Violence program, uses a public health approach to prevent and reduce killings. The main components of the A4P program are to detect, interrupt, and mobilize the community to prevent and reduce violence. Identifying and mediating conflicts between community members and groups is a core component of the A4P approach. Personal altercations were the primary reason for conflict in 66% of the 446 mediations supported by A4P from 2018 to 2020. One A4P member shared,

> About an hour after a homicide, we went to speak with the victim's family. Several male family members were out when we approached the block. I knew most of them from staying in this neighborhood for years. We sensed the tension in the air and noticed that just about all of them had handguns and rifles. As I approached the men and expressed neighborhood affection, I also expressed my condolence for the family. I spoke with the leader and asked to have his men stand down and show support to the victim's mother, spouse, and child. He and all the other men agreed. We will follow up by stopping by the family's house, deploying the street team to the neighborhood, calling and regularly visiting family members.

Aim4Peace also supports a hospital-violence intervention program in partnership with University Health and Research Medical Center. The program offers supports to survivors of violence-related intentional injury, their families, and friends while at the hospital and post-discharge, including to deescalate conflicts and prevent further involvement in violence. Commonly, A4P responders receive a phone call from the hospital chaplain when a shooting or blunt force trauma injury occurs. Hospital responders conduct initial and follow-up visits to help the patient navigate the hospital system and to offer case management supports, including safety planning, identifying short- and long-term goals, and providing referrals to reduce their risk for retaliation, reinjury, and hospital readmission. The goal is to continue to offer supports to the patient and family post-discharge for at least 6 months. From 2018 to 2020, partner hospitals made 908 intentional injury patient referrals to Aim4Peace, of which approximately 75% were related to a gunshot wound. A4P facilitated 1,544 case supports, including referrals, to patients and their loved ones. Aim4Peace continued providing services to 155 patients post-discharge who became participants of the program.

Aim4Peace provides a continued presence in the neighborhood, including after the occurrence of violent incidents, to build rapport with residents in the neighborhoods through outreach activities. During the report period, Aim4Peace provided supports to 146 participants enrolled in the program through 10,127 contacts which were primarily in-person (55%). Although in-person contacts substantially decreased after the onset of COVID. Nearly 36% of the 121 participants for whom changes in risk levels were examined showed a decrease in risk.

In 2023, the U.S. Department of Justice awarded Aim 4 Peace $2 million to continue its fight against the root causes of violence in the community. A significant portion of the grant – $600,000 – will fund a contract with the Mattie Rhodes Center to assemble a Hispanic and Latino response team, which will meet with survivors of violent crime and reach out to Hispanic neighborhoods. Kansas City Missouri Mayor Quinton Lucas said.

> This is the most important thing we can do. Making sure that children in (KCPS Superintendent) Dr. (Jennifer) Collier's school have resources, know about conflict resolution opportunities, have mentorship opportunities like those from Mattie Rhodes. That is why we're here today, and that's why we're trying to do the work.

https://www.kcmo.gov/home/showpubvlisheddocument/1183/636956956461630000
https://fox4kc.com/news/kansas-city-program-receives-2m-grant-to-fight-against-violence/
https://communityhealth.ku.edu/sites/communityhealth/files/documents/Aim4Peace%20Evaluation%20Report%202018-2020.pdf
Accessed 3/6/24

Community Justice and the Prison

Of all the correctional functions, the prison is the most removed from a community justice orientation. Yet prisons are an important part of community justice, even though they seem to be remote from community life. One reason is that each prisoner comes from a community, and concentrations of inmate populations often come from certain communities. At yearend 2022, an estimated 32% of sentenced state and federal prisoners were black; imprisonment rates for white were 188 per 100,000, while black US residents were imprisoned at a rate of 911 per 100,000 (Carson 2023). While Colorado, Michigan, and Iowa have lower incarceration rates than many states, counties containing their major cities – Denver, Detroit, and Des Moines, respectively – have some of the highest incarceration rates in the US. These counties send disproportionately high numbers of people to prison (Widra 2019). These kinds of concentrations of removal and return pose important issues for the communities in which the effects are most concentrated.

Incarceration sets in motion numerous adverse physical, psychological, and economic consequences for individuals who undergo imprisonment, their families, and the broader community. Being imprisoned results in diminished employment prospects and leads to lower long-term earnings (Apel & Sweeten 2010). Additionally, prior incarceration is associated with food insecurity, housing instability (Abosy et al. 2022), and reliance on public assistance (Halushka 2020). Children with incarcerated parents endure significant academic and health setbacks (Miller & Barnes 2015; Poehlmann & Turney 2021). Furthermore, high rates of incarceration destabilize entire communities, causing the breakdown of informal networks that typically deter neighborhood crime (Nellis 2024).

The typical state-convicted prisoner is away from the community between one and three years (Kaeble 2021), while the average convicted federal offender is gone for approximately 12 years (United States Sentencing Commission 2023). This is certainly long enough to suffer severe disruptions in ties to informal social controls back in the community, and long enough to allow significant changes in the circumstances of those left behind. Children grow, spouses form new relationships, families move, loved ones die, jobs dry up, and society slowly changes in the technologies and everyday practices the released offender will encounter. For many prisoners, the seriously disrupted social ties are a major obstacle to overcome in their eventual adjustment back to the community. Prisons can help make that process of adjustment easier. An emphasis can be placed on facilitating the maintenance of family ties through visitation programs and access to long-distance telephone services. (Currently, operator-assisted collect calls from prisons to home are among the most expensive calls in the industry.) Prisoners can receive the kinds of wages that enable them to contribute some money back to the family and to pay a portion of the necessary restitution as well. Inmates can also be allowed to interact with community groups and communicate with outsiders who might play a role in social supports upon release. As the offender nears release, a process of planning for transition can occur. This process can help create linkages to the community by involving family members, employers, and residents' groups (such as churches) in the preparation for the transition. Prison time can shift to the community, as offenders move from the secure confinement of a remote facility to semi-secure halfway-house facilities in transition neighborhoods. Treatment programs can be in the community, and other supportive resources can serve halfway-house inmates and community members equally. The point of any community justice initiative in prison is to reduce the isolation of prisons from community life. Prisoners are being incarcerated because of their crimes, but with only minor exceptions, they will eventually return to the community. It is common sense to organize the incarceration term in a way that makes return to the community more likely to be successful.

> **Box 5.5 Houses of Healing Program in California State Penitentiaries**
>
> The importance of preparing offenders to return to the community cannot be overstated. Many rehabilitation programs, including Therapeutic Communities (TCs), use group processes as a cornerstone of their curriculum. However, there is a distinct population of inmates, such as those in Solitary Confinement and on Death Row, who are segregated from the general population or who will not be returning to the community at all. For these individuals, traditional rehabilitation approaches may not fully address their unique circumstances and needs. The Houses of Healing Program (HOH) is a comprehensive curriculum focused on social-emotional learning (SEL) specifically tailored for prisoner rehabilitation. At its core lies the book "Houses of Healing: A Prisoner's Guide to Inner Power and Freedom." As a trauma-informed, mindfulness-based, and cognitive behavioral curriculum, HOH aims to enhance

incarcerated individuals' self-awareness while bolstering their ability to manage challenging emotions.

In 2015, The Lionheart Foundation created The Houses of Healing One-on-One Correspondence Course for Prisoners in Solitary Confinement. The goal of this *revised version* of the HOH was to offer people in solitary confinement a tool that would help minimize the harmful effects of solitary confinement while teaching skills and perspectives to empower them to take greater charge of their lives, participate in their own emotional well-being and healing, and move forward in a more positive way. Program volunteers are matched with participants who offer encouragement and feedback on the participants "self-work" assignments.

In 2016, Lionheart was awarded an "Innovative Grant" from the California Department of Corrections and Rehabilitation (CDCR) to bring the Houses of Healing Self-Study Course to incarcerated individuals in the CA Special Housing Units (SHUs) in Pelican Bay, CA State Prison – Corcoran, and the CA Correctional Institution (CCI) – all prisons with large isolation units. During the grant period (1/2016–6/2017), 464 participants voluntarily registered and participated in The Houses of Healing Self-Study Course for Incarcerated Individuals in the SHU. Course evaluations from 160 participants showed significant positive change and progress including

- 93% of respondents reported being able to remain in control of their behavior when upset since taking the course, compared to 18% before the course.
- 91% of respondents reported using healthy ways to make themselves feel better when upset, compared to 13% before the course.
- 95% of respondents reported feeling hopeful about life since taking the course, compared to 29% before the course.
- 95% of respondents reported the ability to take responsibility for their actions since taking the course, compared to 30% before the course.
- 100% of respondents stated that they would recommend the Houses of Healing Self-study Program to others.

Participants in the program reflected on their transformation, expressing insights and gratitude for the impact of the Houses of Healing Self-Study Program. One participant shared,

> It's given me understanding which has allowed me to be more accepting, to relax. Accepting myself has let me accept the hurt I've caused. I'm now making some amends. I might not be able to change the beginning, but I can change the ending.

Another participant found solace and hope within the program, remarking, "HOH self-study program could give someone a light of hope in Ad seg as it did to me. 2 months ago a man down the tier committed suicide. Maybe HOH course have given him some hope to live."

Reflecting on the program's impact, one participant emphasized its potential for broader positive change, stating, "I have recommended the H.O.H. self-study course to other prisoners for the good of the world."

> Participants' testimonies highlight the effect of the HOH in fostering self-awareness, healing, and hope within correctional facilities.
> https://lionheart.org/lionheart-programs/houses-of-healing
> https://sanquentinnews.com/houses-healing-self-study-program-death-row-shu
> Accessed 3/6/24

Relationship Building in Prison

It is undeniable that correctional work is challenging. Corrections officers are working with a population basically held against their will and who are potentially violent. Correctional officers shoulder numerous, what can appear to be, competing responsibilities as they are tasked with safeguarding the public from convicted individuals while also being expected to help inmates change their lives for the better. Such concerns as well as organizational issues like recruitment, retention, and high staff turnover can further burden correctional officers, leading to burnout.

Despite the many challenges they face, there is evidence to suggest that corrections officers play a crucial role in the correctional system, not only in helping to ensure the safety and security of the institution but also in serving as role models capable of guiding and supporting inmates as they prepare to return to the community. Studies indicate that prosocial relationships between CW and inmates not only positively impact offenders but can also bring a renewed sense of purpose and meaning for correctional officers in their jobs.

In recent research by Abdel-Salam et al. (2023), the dynamic between correctional officers (COs) and incarcerated persons was explored in the context of a prison-facilitated Therapeutic Community (TC). TCs focus on issues related to substance use and other conditions that lead to criminal behavior. The environment is one that fosters rapport and relationship building between participants and treatment staff. It is believed that prison programs that foster collaborative processes and social acceptance among participants may increase perceptions of "justice, fairness, and quality of life among incarcerated persons, thereby providing resilience and desistance from reoffending" (Abdel-Salam et al. 2023, p. 44).

Interviews were conducted with 26 current and former TC participants; subjects were asked to describe the quality of interactions and relationships they had with correctional officers (COs) and their perceptions of and attitudes toward the treatment staff. In particular, the focus was on the "positive social elements" (p. 44) between prison staff and inmates. It was found that overall, participants took a neutral or negative view of COs. Common themes centered on the minimal involvement that COs played in the lives of the inmates, as they mostly focused on their custodial duties. TC participants expressed disappointment when corrections officers did not appear to take an interest in how they were doing in the program.

Even with such unfavorable views, participants still believed that COs could be trained to be more understanding and sympathetic to the needs of those who are incarcerated. As one participant commented,

> Let them understand what we are doing. Yeah, we're inmates, but let them know we are in a treatment program. Not be as harsh. They come off other blocks, with regular people (general population), and come over here with an attitude. They don't care as much as they should.
>
> (p. 56)

The authors hold that when COs realize that inmates hope to be treated with understanding and compassion, they can better engage in the treatment process and serve as a motivating force in the lives of TC participants.

The desire that inmates expressed for corrections officers to exhibit respect, compassion, and interest in their efforts toward change is illustrative of the importance of creating collaborative relationships between correctional workers and inmates. A robust working alliance in corrections can not only promote improved communication but also encourage inmate participation in programs, creating a safer, more rehabilitative institutional environment.

Core Correctional Practices (CCP) are, according to Dowden and Andrews (2004), designed to "increase the therapeutic potential of rehabilitation programs for offenders" (p. 204). One such principle holds that offenders are more likely to engage in treatment, and treatment is more likely to be effective when a good therapeutic alliance has been created. The importance of the therapist–client relationship has been extensively reviewed in psychological literature, where it has been found to play a key role in therapy and the process of facilitating change (Horvath & Luborsky 1993; Yalom 1980). A therapeutic alliance refers to the collaborative bond between a therapist and their client that helps facilitate positive change in the client that exists independent of the treatment they received. Bordin (1979) extended the application of the therapeutic alliance when he formulated a trans-theoretical framework of the therapeutic alliance, what he coined as the "working alliance." The working alliance assessed the relational advantages present in various forms of "helping relationships."

Bordin (1979) identifies three key ingredients for the working alliance: (1) agreement on the goals; (2) consensus on the tasks to achieve the goals; and (3) an overall bond between client and helper that helps to facilitate collaboration. In the context of correctional work, an agreement on goals would focus on the mutual understanding between the correctional worker and the client in terms of the rehabilitative goals for the client. This ensures that each party is on the same page regarding the desired outcomes. There then needs to be a consensus between both parties as to how the goals will be achieved. For example, if maintaining sobriety is one of the goals, a decision must be agreed upon as to the specific substance use treatment, how often the client will attend, and how accountability and successful completion of the program will look. The relational bond between the corrections worker and the client is a critical component of the working alliance. This bond will be exhibited through the building of trust, respect, and rapport – clear communication and efforts made to understand each other's perspectives.

Of course, not all agree that a therapeutic alliance can be forged in a mandated environment, such as a correctional setting, as opposed to a voluntary therapeutic environment (Skeem et al. 2007). Obstacles exist, including the challenge of building trust when officers must report rule violations by offenders. Issues of power and authority inherent in the role of the officer further create a "lopsided" dynamic that can impede relationship building. Finally, the "convict code" is a force to be reckoned with in terms of forging a working alliance with inmates. The convict code refers to a set of informal rules, norms, and values that govern behavior among those who are incarcerated, including no snitching, do your own time, do not get too friendly with the "police" (corrections officers), and mind your own business. These may be useful strategies for managing one's stay in prison, but less so for building prosocial relationships. While these are all concerns to keep in mind, they are not in and of themselves reasons to refrain from building working alliances between corrections officers and individuals who are incarcerated. As Haas and Smith (2019) point out, correctional workers such as corrections officers, probation and parole officers, counselors, and case managers are expected to develop a "working alliance" with clients.

A strong working alliance between CW and those under their supervision is crucial. According to Dowden and Andrews (2004), CCP are essential, as offenders learn "prosocial and anticriminal altitudinal, cognitive, and behavioral patterns from their regular interactions with front-line staff" (p. 205). As illustrated in the following study, strong working alliances also contribute to the overall well-being and job satisfaction of CW.

Ricciardelli et al. (2023) recently explored, from the perspective of CW, what forms of positivity emerge from their work. Interviews were conducted with CW in Canada, including corrections officers, probation and parole officers, nurses, rehabilitative staff, other health care staff, administrative staff, managers, teachers, and other employees within the correctional community. Participants answered the following open-ended question obtained from data gathered from the CW Mental Health and Well-being Study, *Please tell us how you think your job contributes to your overall well-being and outlook on life.*

The results indicate that while correctional workers experience many challenges including psychological impacts due to occupational stress, there were many positive aspects to correctional work. Some shared how their work afforded them a sense of self-awareness and empathy for others, as they saw themselves as making a positive impact in the lives of those with whom they worked. Many diligently worked to create positive change and found meaning and happiness in the successful integration of persons who are incarcerated (PWAI). For some their positive perspective extended to those under their supervision. One worker commented, "I really do love my job and my clients."

Of course, not all CW took such positive views of their occupation. There were those for whom the financial remuneration was the only good aspect of the job. As one mentioned,

> There is nothing positive about this job but the paycheck and the time off. I am a changed individual and rarely find pleasure in life anymore. This place sucks the soul out of you for a half-baked pension at the end.
>
> (p. 390)

While it is widely acknowledged that corrections work can take an emotional toll, most participants expressed a deep-seated commitment to the compassionate aspects of their work.

Some described their role as a "service," "vocation," and even a "ministry." One participant further stated,

> It helps me to love people who are hard to love and gives me more compassion and understanding to human suffering. Which I would not trade for anything. I would not change the fact that I went into justice, even though it has changed parts of my personality that I liked about myself.
>
> (p. 292)

The understanding that correctional workers can make a significant and positive difference in the lives of incarcerated persons was not lost on most of the participants.

In sum, most participants shared a desire to instigate genuine change and contribute positively to the lives of PWAI such that they found fulfillment upon seeing the success of offenders in prison and in their reintegration into the community. Ricciardelli et al. (2023) noted,

> CW's internal commitment to care and care work in the context of their occupational responsibilities—a commitment tied to a positive sense of self and awareness—is

a necessary step toward creating healthier living and working conditions in correctional spaces.

(p. 300)

This is a terrific reminder of the connection between compassion and personal well-being. When we extend kindness, we not only help the recipient of our kindness, but we also nourish ourselves. Zoroaster could have been talking about CW when he stated, "Doing good to others is not a duty, it is a joy, for it increases our own health and happiness."

Box 5.6 Center for Conflict Resolution (CCR) and Transition Center of Kansas City (TCKC)

The CCR is a nonprofit, 501(c)3 organization that provides mediation services, facilitation, and training to individuals and organizations. By using RJ processes and providing safe, structured, and positive environments, CCR empowers people to solve conflict in their lives, giving them the tools they need to find peaceful solutions and choose understanding over escalating conflict.

CCR is currently engaged in an innovative collaboration with the Missouri DOC known as the Restorative Reentry Community (RRC) at the TCKC. The RRC, spearheaded by CCR, operates as a community-focused transition management model grounded in RJ principles in a college campus atmosphere. Seeing the dignity of each human being is at the core of this collaboration, breaking down the "us versus them" mentality found in correctional institutions to foster successful transformations founded in trust, compassion, empathy, and healing.

Within TCKC, the RRC endeavors to cultivate an environment free from the negative influences typical of prison settings. It promotes cooperation and collaboration among residents, staff, and administration, fostering successful transformations rooted in trust, compassion, empathy, and healing.

The RJ approach at TCKC focuses on principles such as repairing harm, restoring relationships, conflict resolution without violence, and circle processes. These principles are integrated into the reentry preparedness process to instill accountability, personal development, civic and social engagement, and a commitment to a crime-free life in each resident.

Over 50 community partners play an important role in providing residents with diverse opportunities for growth and transformation. They offer programs, classes, employment, and learning opportunities both inside and outside the facility. The program is structured into four phases:

- Orientation: Acquaintance with the program and resources at TCKC
- Discovery: Discovering passions and purposes
- Journey: Learning unique skills and building a future
- Transition: Successfully transitioning into the community

During the Discovery, Journey, and Transition phases, community partners assist residents in completing core classes, choosing individual tracks (education, employment, or self-improvement), and developing personal transition plans. They also help coordinate services to facilitate a seamless reentry process.

Following their time at TCKC, program graduates receive continued support from case managers, parole officers, and community partners. Additionally, TCKC organizes Citizen Circles, where community members provide additional support and resources to returning citizens. Graduates are encouraged to return to TCKC to mentor current residents based on their personal experiences.

https://www.ccrkc.org/tckc
https://doc.mo.gov/divisions/probation-parole/transition-center-kansas-city
Accessed 3/6/24

Community Corrections and Restoration

One of the values that sets community justice apart from traditional criminal justice is a concern for restoration. A consequence of crime is damaged relationships; therefore, true justice would involve "the restoration to wholeness of those whose lives and relationships have been broken or deeply strained by criminal offense" (Dickey 1998, p. 107). Crime damages the fabric of mutual trust that is necessary to the very idea of community, and it generates fear of association that makes community harder to achieve. Doing something to prevent crime is a part of building community, but doing something about the damage that results from crime is an essential part of community justice. Community justice approaches restorative justice (RJ) as problem solving.

The RJ paradigm holds:

- Crime is a violation of people and interpersonal relationships.
- Violations create obligations.
- The central obligation is to put right the wrongs.
- Dialogue and negotiation are normative.
- Justice is defined as right relationship outcomes.
- Victim and offender are engaged in the process; victims needs are recognized; offender accountability.
- There is a possibility for repentance and forgiveness (Zehr 1995).

RJ is significantly different from the "contest" version of traditional criminal law, which is illustrated by the very name given to its cases: for example, State v. Wilson. By contrast, community justice conceptualizes a criminal case not as a contest between two disputants, but as a problem between three parties: the offender, the victim, and the community. What is needed is a way to design case outcomes that best meet the legitimate interest of each party to the problem at hand.

In community justice, the offender has a legitimate interest in being allowed to find a way to re-establish ties to the community; the victim has an interest in having the losses suffered at the hands of the offender restored; and the community has an interest in developing some confidence that the offender will refrain from this kind of conduct in the future.

Each interest connotes an obligation as well. The offender is obliged to repair the damage and to provide some tangible assurance that criminality will not recur. The victim has an obligation to identify the losses that need to be restored and to entertain the possibility of a reconstituting community with the offender (note that this is not an obligation to rebuild community with the offender, just to entertain the possibility of this rebuilding under the "right" circumstances, regarding which the victim has a voice). The community has an obligation to identify the circumstances under which both the victim and the offender can be restored to the community.

A key advantage of a community-based restorative program lies in its emphasis on facilitating direct communication with the parties involved. The focus on dialogue is critical, as instances of crime "ruptures right relationships and creates harmful ones" (Van Ness et al. 2022, p. 7). Crime tears apart what is referred to as *shalom*. The word *shalom* in the Judeo-Christian tradition, signifies an optimal state in which the community should function. Van Ness et al. (2022) hold that shalom "is much more than the absence of conflict, it signifies completeness, fulfillment, and wholeness – the existence of right relationships among individuals, the community, creation, and God" (p. 6).

Restorative community justice is an important, different way to conceive of justice. It gives both the community and the victim an active role in determining the appropriate sanction in a case, and it gives the offender a voice in that same process. By opening the process to those who are most affected by its outcome, the restorative model seeks to develop solutions both to the problems that result from crime and to the impediments to community that accompany the existence of crime.

Women: Transitioning Between Incarceration and Reentry

Much has been written about the effect of imprisonment on the fabric of the community. The continual movement of people into and out of the community creates instability within families and the community at large. Often overlooked in that discussion is the effect of the imprisonment of women on families and the community. Because males are seen as income earners, their absence can be quantified more easily than women. Kajstura and Sawyer (2024) state, "Like so many other aspects of life in America, the unique experiences of women in the criminal justice system are obscured by those of men, treated as an afterthought" (np).

Women find themselves being incarcerated for a variety of reasons, but in many cases, the arrests come because of a boyfriend or significant other who uses the women and her residence as a base for illegal activity. The relationship is often characterized by emotional abuse and the insistence of the male that if it was not for him, the women would not be able to find companionship. Often, the male provides just enough financial support for the women and the children to allow her to stay at home and watch the "business" while he goes out to conduct illegal activity. In low-income areas, the place of residence is often public-subsidized housing or rental property, and when the illegal activity is discovered, the women and her children are evicted. Once the eviction is completed, the male usually disappears, leaving the woman to care for the children with no stable place to live. If the evidence indicates that the woman was aware of or participated materially in the criminal activity, they too are arrested.

Recent statistics indicate that the number of incarcerated women increased by more than 525% from 1980 through 2021, with women of color being disproportionately incarcerated at 1.3 (for Hispanic women) to 1.6 (for Black women) times the rate of white women (Monazzam & Budd 2023). While there are more men in prison than women, the rate of growth for female imprisonment, since 1980, has been twice as high as that of men. The increase in females being placed under state or federal jurisdiction clearly presents many problems for the stability of communities since over half (58%) of imprisoned women have a child under the age of 18 (Maruschak et al. 2021), and of those, most are single mothers who were living with their children prior to their incarceration. For many women, incarceration leads to a permanent breakup of the family as children are shuffled off to live with this family member or that friend. Many children are placed in foster care or, should parental rights be terminated, they are considered for adoption.

For both females and males released from prison, family relationships are critical to providing the necessary support for the prisoner to continue employment, refrain from using illegal substances, and reoffending. Research has shown that males are able to reestablish family ties with immediate relatives and significant others in their lives. Women, on the other hand, appear to have more difficulty in reestablishing relationships with immediate family, and the researchers theorize that this tenuousness in the relationships may center on the minor children that have been cared for by the family during the prisoner's incarceration.

For women fortunate enough to have family or friends taking care of their children, this does not automatically mean that they will be able to maintain a relationship with them while incarcerated. The location of prisons poses a big challenge for families when it comes to visiting their loved ones. Since most prisons are located in rural areas of the state, over 63% of prisoners are incarcerated approximately 100 miles from their homes and families (Lockwood & Lewis 2019). Relatives of individuals who are incarcerated revealed that many lacked sufficient time, financial resources, childcare arrangements, or access to transportation to visit the prison as frequently as they would have liked. Some said they simply could not afford to go at all (Lockwood & Lewis 2019).

Gordon (2018) explored the challenges facing two women (Lia and Rebecca) during their post-incarceration life in St. Louis, Missouri. Lia, a mother of five children, was fortunate in that her children were living with her husband during the time she was in prison. Yet, she still found it difficult to keep in contact with her family, as her husband and children could not make the two-hour drive to prison to visit her. Despite the desire to be a mother to her children upon release, she worried as to how this would work out as she had missed a significant portion of their growing up years. Lia expressed,

> If a woman has children and is trying to step back and regain that relationship, sometimes it is not there for them. I didn't know if my [relationships] were going to be like that, but I was sure hoping and praying that it was because I wanted to step back into that role.
>
> (np)

Rebecca considered the importance of relationships and connection in terms of being successful in addiction recovery. She stated,

> I am glad that I have a wonderful, wonderful sponsor. That loves me. That I can call her anytime of the day ... that is one thing you have to do ... You have to get connected because this does not work alone ... you have to get connected in order to grow in this process.
>
> (np)

Rebecca further cherishes the bond she has created with women in *Let's Start* – a program providing addiction and reentry support for formally incarcerated women. She comments,

> *Let's Start* is like a family to me. I belong to *Let's Start*. As long as I keep going, hopefully I can help someone else out. That's my intention. I want to save the world! I want to save all the females that have ever been affected with drug, addition, abuse, rape or anything. I want to let them know that there is some hope.
>
> (np)

The strong connections made by Rebecca have motivated her to help support and empower other women facing similar challenges.

Theorist and author Jean Baker Miller asserts that women inherently seek meaningful connections, stating, "Women stay with, build on, and develop in a context of connections with others." According to Miller's Relational-Cultural Model RCM) (1976), our interactions and connections with others significantly influence our self-perception, resilience, and overall mental well-being. She affirmed, "all of living and all of development takes place only within relationships" (1986 [1976] p. xxi). Jean defines growth-fostering relationships as characterized by at least "five good things" (1986, p. 3):

- Each person feels a greater sense of "zest" (vitality, energy).
- Each person feels more able to act and does act.
- Each person has a more accurate picture of herself/himself and the other person(s).
- Each person feels a greater sense of worth.
- Each person feels more connected to the other person(s) and feels a greater motivation for connections with other people beyond those in the specific relationship.

Lia and Rebeccas' stories illustrate how women reentering the community post-incarceration have a keen yearning for family reunification and growth-fostering connection; they thrive on relationships that promote growth and empowerment. These connections provide women with vital support, encouragement, and opportunities for self-discovery and create a desire to help and build connections with other women in similar circumstances.

Moving Forward

The field of corrections, like each component of the criminal justice system, is fundamentally a "human service" vocation with its focus on helping those under correctional supervision. Because of this, it is well aligned with the idea of building relationships, which is central to community justice. Those who are so fortunate as to work in corrections should never feel like they are simply a small cog in a very large wheel. CW, both in the community and in institutions, hold a privileged position to help unlock their client's potential for positive change.

To cultivate positive prosocial relationships with those under correctional supervision, facilitating their successful reintegration into the community such that they can take care of their families, maintain employment, and live law-abiding, productive lives, does not mean that we have to abandon the fundamental tenets of traditional corrections – namely, offender management, risk assessment, treatment, surveillance and control, and punishment. Rather, it entails establishing strong and collaborative relationships with our clients such that the principles of community justice – engagement with neighborhoods and communities, restoration, problem-solving, acknowledgment of victims and communities, and forging partnerships – are purposefully incorporated into our operational strategies. Community justice in corrections requires relationship building to be foundational to our mission. This means we must be intentional in our efforts to connect with clients. This intentionality first starts when we can view them through the lens of fellow neighbors and community members because that is who they are and will become upon their release.

References

Abdel-Salam, S., Antonio, M.E., Bratina, M.P., & Kilmer, A. (2023). Rapport and relationship building in a therapeutic community: Examining the dynamic between correctional officers and incarcerated persons. *Criminal Justice Policy Review, 34*(1), 43–64.

Al Abosy, J., Grossman, A., & Dong, K.R. (2022). Determinants and consequences of food and nutrition insecurity in justice-impacted populations. *Current Nutrition Reports, 11*(3), 407–415.

Apel, R., & Sweeten, G. (2010). The impact of incarceration on employment during the transition to adulthood. *Social Problems, 57*(3), 448–479.

Bordin, E.S. (1979). The generalizability of the psychoanalytic concept of the working alliance. *Psychotherapy: Theory, Research and Practice, 16*(3), 252–260.

Carson, E.A. (2023). *Prisoners in 2022—Statistical tables*. Retrieved 3/6/24 from U.S Department of Justice Office of Justice Programs Bureau of Justice Statistics website https://bjs.ojp.gov/document/p22st.pdf

Center on Sentencing and Corrections, Vera Institute of Justice Source: Federal Sentencing Reporter. (December 2013). *New momentum for federal sentencing reform, 26*(2), 128–144. Published by: University of California Press on behalf of the Vera Institute of Justice Stable URL. Reviewed 03-04-2024 from https://www.jstor.org/stable/10.1525/fsr.2013.26.2.128

DeLude, B., Mitchell, D., & Barber, C. (2012). The probationer's perspective on the probation officer-probationer relationship and satisfaction with probation. *Federal Probation, 76*, 35.

Dickey, W.J. (1998). Forgiveness and crime: The possibilities of restorative justice. In R.D. Enright & J. North (Eds.), *Exploring forgiveness* (pp. 106–120). The University of Wisconsin Press.

Dowden, C., & Andrews, D.A. (2004). The importance of staff practice in delivering effective correctional treatment: A meta-analytic review of core correctional practice. *International Journal of Offender Therapy and Comparative Criminology, 48*(2), 203–214.

Gavel, D. (2016). Community corrections can improve public safety, reduce costs, and promote justice, according to report. Retrieved. 2/26/24 from https://phys.org/news/2016-12-safety-justice.html

Gordon, A. (2018). Getting out: Women in transition. Retrieved 3/9/2024 from *Washington University in St. Louis* website https://amcs.wustl.edu/news/getting-out-women-transition

Haas, S.M., & Smith, J. (2019). Core correctional practice: The role of the working alliance in offender rehabilitation. In P. Ugwudike, H. Graham, F. McNeill, P. Raynor, F. S. Taxman, & C. Trotter (Eds.), *The Routledge companion to rehabilitative work in criminal justice* (pp. 339–351). Routledge.

Halushka, J.M. (2020). The runaround: Punishment, welfare, and poverty survival after prison. *Social Problems, 67*(2), 233–250.

Holsinger, A.M. (2023). Evidence-based correctional practice: What works, and what should be next? *Journal of Community Justice, Summer 2023*(6), 7–24.

Horvath, A.O., & Luborsky, L. (1993). The role of the therapeutic alliance in psychotherapy. *Journal of Consulting and Clinical Psychology, 61*, 561–573.

Kaeble, D. (2021). *Time served in state prison, 2018*. Retrieved 3/6/24 from *Bureau of Justice Statistics* website https://bjs.ojp.gov/library/publications/time-served-state-prison-2018

Kajstura, A., & Sawyer, W. (2024). Women's mass incarceration: The whole pie 2024. Retrieved 3/9/2024 from *Prison Policy Initiative* website https://www.prisonpolicy.org/reports/pie2024women.html

Kennealy, P.J., Skeem, J.L., Manchak, S.M., & Eno Louden, J. (2012). Firm, fair, and caring officer-offender relationships protect against supervision failure. *Law and Human Behavior*, 36(6), 496.

Korhonen, V. (2024). Number of sentenced prisoners released from jurisdiction U.S. 2000–2022. Retrieved from *Statista* website 3/18/24 https://www.statista.com/statistics/252905/number-of-sentenced-prisoners-released-from-jurisdiction-in-the-us/#:~:text=In%202022%2C%20about%20448%2C432%20prisoners%20were%20released%20from,prisoners%20were%20released%20since%202000%2C%20at%20443%2C740%20prisoners

Lockwood, B., & Lewis, N. (2019. The long journey to visit a family member in prison: Remote prison towns and strict visitation policies make it hard to stay in touch. Retrieved 3/9/24 from *The Marshall Project* website https://www.themarshallproject.org/2019/12/18/the-long-journey-to-visit-a-family-member-in-prison

Lovins, B.K., Brusman-Lovins, L., & Williams, T. (2023). The integration of a coaching framework into the risk, need, and responsivity model for corrections. *Journal of Community Justice, Summer 2023*, 11–31.

Lovins, B.K., Cullen, F.T., Latessa, E.J., & Jonson, C.L. (2018). Probation officer as a coach: Building a new professional identity. *Federal Probation*, 82(1), 13–19.

Manhattan Institute. (1999). 'Broken Windows' probation: The next step in Crime Fighting. *Civic Report*, 7(August).

Maruschak, L.M., Bronson, J., & Alper, M. (2021). Parents in prison and their minor children: Survey of prison inmates, 2016. *Bureau of Justice Statistics*. Retrieved 3/9/2024 from https://bjs.ojp.gov/library/publications/parents-prison-and-their-minor-children-survey-prison-inmates-2016

Martinson, R. (Spring 1974). *What works?—Questions and answers about prison reform*. Retrieved 3/9/2024 from https://en.wikipedia.org/wiki/Robert_Martinson

Miller, J.B. (1986[1976]). *Toward a new psychology of women*. Beacon Press.

Miller, J.B. (1986). *What do we mean by relationships?* Work in Progress, No. 22, Stone Center Working Paper Series, Stone Center, Wellesley, MA.

Miller, H.V., & Barnes, J.C. (2015). The association between parental incarceration and health, education, and economic outcomes in young adulthood. *American Journal of Criminal Justice*, 40, 765–784. https://doi.org/10.1007/s12103-015-9288-4

Monazzam, N., & Budd, K.M. (2023). Incarcerated women and girls. Retrieved 3/8/2024 from *The Sentencing Project* website https://www.sentencingproject.org/fact-sheet/incarcerated-women-and-girls/

Mullins, T.G., & Toner, C. (2008). *Implementing the family support approach for community supervision*. American Probation and Parole Association.

Nellis, A. (2024). Mass incarnation trends. Retrieved 3/6/24 from *The Sentencing Project* website https://www.sentencingproject.org/reports/mass-incarceration-trends/

Poehlmann-Tynan, J., & Turney, K. (2021). A developmental perspective on children with incarcerated parents. *Child Development Perspectives*, 15(1), 3–11.

Ricciardelli, R., Johnston, M.S., & Maier, K. (2023). Making a difference: Unpacking the positives in correctional work and prison life from the perspective of correctional workers. *The Prison Journal*, 103(3), 283–306.

Sampson, R.J., Raudenbush, S.W., & Earls, F. (1997). Neighborhoods and violent crime: A multilevel study of collective efficacy. *Science*, 277(August), 918–924.

Schaefer, L., Townsley, M., & Hutchins, B. (2022). Can family and friends improve probation and parole outcomes? A quantitative evaluation of triple-S-social supports in supervision. *Trends and Issues in Crime and Criminal Justice*, 654, 1–21.

Schanzenbach, D.W., Nunn, R., Bauer, L., Breitwieser, A., Mumford, M., & Nantz, G. (2016). Twelve facts about incarceration and prison reentry. *Hamilton Project*. Retrieved 3/18/24 from *Brookings* website http_20161020_twelve_facts_incarceration_prisoner_reentry.pdf

Skeem, J.L., Louden, J.E., Polaschek, D., & Camp, J. (2007). Assessing relationship quality in mandated community treatment: Blending care with control. *Psychological assessment, 19*(4), 397.

Still, W., Broderick, B., & Raphael, S. (2016). Building trust and legitimacy within community corrections. US Department of Justice, Office of Justice Programs, National Institute of Justice. Retrieved 3/26/24 from *Harvard Kennedy School* website https://www.hks.harvard.edu/centers/wiener/programs/criminaljustice/research-publications/executive-sessions/executive-session-on-community-corrections/publications/building-trust-and-legitimacy

United States Sentencing Commission. (2022). Quick facts: Career offenders. Retrieved on 3/4/24 from the *United States Sentencing Commission* website https://www.ussc.gov/sites/default/files/pdf/research-and-publications/quick-facts/Career_Offenders_FY22.pdf

United States Sentencing Commission. (2023). Federal offenders in prison. Retrieved on 3/6/24 from the *United States Sentencing Commission* website https://www.ussc.gov/research/quick-facts/federal-offenders-prison

Van Ness, D.W., Strong, K.H., Derby, J., & Parker, L.L. (2022). *Restoring justice: An introduction to restorative justice.* Routledge.

Washington II, M. (2021). Beyond jails. Retrieved 3/20/24 from *Vera* website https://www.vera.org/downloads/pdfdownloads/beyond-jails-full-report.pdf" beyond-jails-full-report.pdf (vera.org)

Widra, E. (2019). How America's major urban centers compare on incarceration rates. Retrieved 3/6/24 from *Prison Policy Initiative* website https://www.prisonpolicy.org/blog/2019/03/28/urban-incarceration/

Williams, K.R., & Hawkins, R. (1986). Perceptual research on general deterrence: A critical review. *Law & Society Review, 20*(4), 545–572. https://doi.org/10.2307/3053466

Yalom, I.D. (1980). *Existential psychotherapy.* Basic Books.

Zehr, H. (1989). VORP dangers. *Accord: A Mennonite Central Committee Canada Publication for Victim Offender Ministries, 8*(3), 13.

Zehr, H. (1995). *Changing lenses: A new focus for crime and justice.* Herald Press.

Zimring, F.E., & Hawkins, G.J. (1973). *Deterrence.* University of Chicago Press.

Suggested Web Sources for Readers

Center for Justice Innovation: Community Justice Today: Values, Guiding Principles, and Models | Center for Justice Innovation (https://www.innovatingjustice.org/publications/community-justice-today)

Community Justice Scotland: Community Justice Scotland: Community Justice Scotland

Institute for Community Solutions: Community Solutions to Justice Report – Institute for Community Solutions

National Center on Restorative Justice: Home – National Center on Restorative Justice (ncorj.org)

Prison Policy Initiative: Prison Policy Initiative

Restorative Justice Council: Restorative Justice Council | Promoting quality restorative practice for everyone

Sentencing Project: We change the way Americans think about crime and punishment (sentencingproject.org)

6
The Future of Community Justice

Community justice is still a relatively new idea. Although many elements of community justice have a rich heritage in social thought – reparation, community, pragmatic problem solving – the idea of community justice as an expression of criminal justice is about 20 years old. We are in a time of rapid changes in criminal justice, but nobody can know with certainty where any changes will lead. What role, if any, will the community play in developing criminal justice in the coming years?

To answer this question, we must shift our level of analysis from the specific to the general. The preceding chapters investigated specific applications of community justice to the three main functions of the criminal justice system: apprehension of offenders, adjudication of charges, and imposition of sanctions – police, courts, and corrections. This analysis showed that community justice concepts have been widely applied in each traditional criminal justice function. Throughout the apparatus of criminal justice, community justice ideas are increasingly common and important as foundations for new projects and innovative practices. Understanding the significance of community justice as an idea, however, requires that we reach beyond these new projects to consider the core of the idea of community justice and how it transforms the current system. In this chapter, we first consider the core ideas that compose the community justice model. We then address a series of questions about community justice as a new way of doing justice. We conclude with a comment on the future of community justice and share additional tools that may be helpful for communities adopting community justice as a practice.

The Essentials of Community Justice

Community justice is a familiar idea. Police have always walked beats, courts have tried to impose sanctions that restore the victim for years, and corrections have worked with offenders in the community since its earliest existence. Therefore, what makes community justice so new?

A great variety of activities are offered under the community justice label: from community policing to drug courts, from neighborhood probation to zero tolerance. Does it all count as community justice? What must it offer as a new way of doing business for a new idea to qualify as a community justice initiative?

Community justice has three essential components: place, adding value, and public safety. Throughout this book, we have described and analyzed many additional ideas important to specific community justice applications: partnerships, problem-solving, reinvestment, and citizen involvement. These are all critical ideas in community justice thinking, but there are good examples of community justice initiatives in which one or more need to be included. It is possible (though not necessarily advisable), for instance, to build a community justice court without community involvement; one could build a community-oriented policing approach without partnerships, and so forth. However, community justice can only occur with place, adding value, and public safety. The actuality of place makes the approach one of "community." The commitment to adding value enables the community approach to do justice. Finally, the ultimate aim of all community justice is a better public safety experience.

Place

Community is often used as an abstraction: the fellow feeling among people who share a personal characteristic, such as ethnicity; the sense of belongingness that comes from close associations and shared experiences; the mutuality of interests that binds people together in a shared destiny. These abstractions are important, for they help us understand the intuitive appeal of the term *community*. However, while it calls to mind these abstract notions, the term community justice also has a concrete meaning. Community justice refers to actions in a designated location, a neighborhood, or a section where people live and see themselves as sharing life. Community justice takes place in a specific place.

Adding Value

Most of criminal justice is about a kind of "subtraction." The police investigate crimes to find perpetrators so they may be removed from the streets; the courts determine who should be removed and for how long; corrections confine those who have been removed and oversee others at risk of removal. Communities may benefit when problematic members are removed – a kind of "adding by subtracting." However, community justice stands for two additional points. First, almost all of those removed eventually return, so the question of what to do about the people who live in the community, some of whom are ex-offenders, cannot be avoided by policies that only try to remove offenders. Second, and more importantly, dealing with offenders is not enough. Justice requires consideration of the community's broader and deeper quality of life. From this perspective, public safety is not just a matter of strategic subtraction but requires attention to improving what is left intact. Community justice attempts to overcome the problems that produce crime, reduce the impediments to a good quality of life that communities face, and improve the capacity of communities to become safer, better places to live and do business.

Public Safety

It is possible to add value to places without doing community justice. What sets the community justice ideal apart from other philosophies of community life is that community justice is involved squarely with questions of public order and public safety. However, community justice does not embrace a narrow conception of public safety, as might be suggested by simple crime rates. Community justice is interested in public safety as a broad idea: people feel free to walk the streets without fear of harassment by anyone, criminals, or agents of the state. Parents have confidence that there are good options for their children's daily activities, and young people feel they have good choices of safe and satisfying ways to pass the time. There is vibrant social (and economic) commerce, and people can pursue their dreams and aspirations. From the standpoint of community justice, public safety is not represented by an electric fence, a metal detector, or a barred window; public safety exists where there is open and accessible social commerce without personal fear. Essential to the idea of community justice is the belief that achieving such a version of public safety is a prominent public aim.

Varieties of Community Justice

These three essential elements of community justice leave plenty of room for many ways of doing the work. We can visualize many varied strategies that seek to promote public safety by adding value to places. To help illustrate this, we can further investigate the core elements described above. Place is the *setting* for community justice, and this can be any neighborhood or community small enough to have an identity distinct from other locations (especially within the same larger town or city). Public safety refers to the *goal* of community justice; adding value refers to the *means* of community justice. This enables us to investigate differences in means (adding value) for specific community justice locations and goals (public safety). Figure 6.1 depicts a conceptual model of community justice approaches based on goals and means.

Goals Continuum

The goals continuum provides two extreme values. On the one hand, there is an emphasis on the goal of crime prevention; on the other, there is community capacity. Community justice initiatives that emphasize the goal of crime prevention tend to identify specific types of criminal activity that trouble a community and then seek to resolve problems that make that crime occur. When community justice initiatives work at this end of the continuum, they may target serious crimes (such as burglaries or robberies) or broken windows offenses (such as prostitution or open drug markets) or even try to break up gangs. Still, their aim

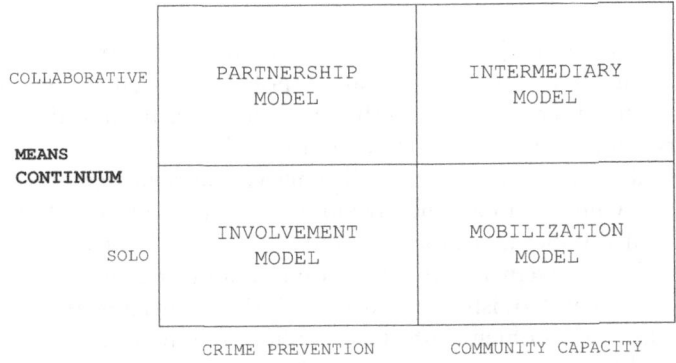

Figure 6.1 A Conceptual Model of Community Justice Strategies.

is always to eradicate criminal activity. At the other end of the continuum, the concern for community capacity aims to create a better community life by improving some aspects of the community's functioning. A prime example is the desire to promote collective efficacy, which makes some communities safer.

Means Continuum

Most governmental organizations work solo in that they attend to their responsibilities with little direct concern about the way other organizations affect and are affected by their work. Criminal justice is no exception. Working solo has its advantages. An agency working this way can quickly implement its policies and procedures without consulting other organizations, and it is easy to hold staff accountable for their obligations when no other organization is around to be blamed for things not going well. These advantages explain why most organizations seek to do much of their work solo without dealing with the involvement of other, potentially complicating, organizations. When complicated issues such as public safety are involved, there is a recognition that one organization, working alone, can have only limited success. This has led to an increasing interest in various forms of collaborative efforts to achieve community justice, where agencies form some partnership or coalition that spans organizational boundaries so that organizations trying to deal with similar (or related) problems can work together more efficiently.

Four Prototypes of Community Justice Programs: The Models of Community Justice

Figure 6.1, which arrays the two continua of goals and means, identifies four prototypical strategies of community justice. These can best be seen not as actual examples of existing programs but as ideal types of community justice approaches that help us develop a critical understanding of some variations in community justice activity. In the following discussion, the underlying importance of each of the prototypes is described, and the pros and cons of each are presented.

Involvement Model

The initial form of community justice was to seek greater citizen involvement in the work of public safety. From its first days, the community policing movement was a call for citizens and police to work together to deal with the problems of crime and disorder in urban settings. Community policing developed from an interest in having community members meet with the police to develop priorities for police activity in their neighborhoods. The belief was that the police would be more effective and the community would be better served if the people who needed police assistance worked together with the police.

A prototype of the Involvement Model of community justice is problem-oriented policing, developed by Herman Goldstein (Goldstein 1991). In this approach, police work with citizen groups to identify problems affecting public safety in a particular location, gather data about that problem, design a strategy to solve the problem, and implement that strategy. At each stage of the problem-solving approach, there is a role for citizen involvement, ranging from consultation regarding local priorities to providing feedback about the effectiveness of the implementation of solutions.

Since the development of problem-oriented policing in the late 1980s, a body of knowledge has been created to assist police agencies and citizens in addressing issues confronting communities. The Center for Problem-Oriented Policing has compiled case studies of problems that police agencies have managed throughout the United States. These case studies have been published as reference guides for police agencies that may encounter problems other agencies have already addressed. The Problem-Specific Guides for Police summarize knowledge about how police can reduce the harm caused by specific crime and disorder problems. Response Guides summarize the collective knowledge from research and practice about how and under what conditions specific common police responses to crime and disorder do and do not work. Problem-solving Tool Guides explain how various analytical methods and techniques can be applied to better understand crime and disorder problems. The availability of these guides allows police and neighborhoods to work more closely together to solve problems. The guides have also helped move police agencies toward the Intermediary Model, which takes a macro look at community issues and increases the number of stakeholders working on the issue.

As a community justice approach, the Involvement Model has several advantages for police and citizens. For police, the model provides another source of information about local public safety problems, and it is a superior way to gather information about policing priorities. It also gives the police a support system in the community for police practices. Citizens who have been consulted about the priorities for police activity are more likely to understand why the police do what they do and to support the police when inevitable problems arise. Working with a closer connection to the community, police are more likely to feel community encouragement for their work, and there is a direct sense of satisfaction for police officers who are engaged with, instead of estranged from, members of the community they serve.

Inherent within this strategy is a bilateral orientation involving the community – usually represented by some leaders and spokespersons – and the justice agency, working in tandem. The fact that the justice agency works independently of other agencies can also strengthen this approach. There are no boundary concerns or turf battles; one person can speak for the interests of the justice agency, and changes in justice practices or procedures can be relatively quickly achieved.

The Involvement Model is not solely a policing strategy, although that is where it has its most apparent expression. Probation departments have established community advisory boards, and community courts often work closely with citizen leadership groups. In many states, Reparative Justice Boards are relatively pure forms of involvement in which the citizens themselves determine the sanctions to be implemented by the corrections system. In each of these involvement strategies, the community justice managers experience a flow of information from the community to the justice process guiding their efforts, and there is a strong sense of support from the community for the actions of community justice.

However, the Involvement Model has weaknesses. Indeed, one of its strengths – that a single agency can act unilaterally with citizen groups – is also a weakness. Often, a neighborhood suffering from deficient public safety faces complex problems, and other agencies – social services, child protection, the courts, and so forth – have responsibilities that bear on the issue. Moreover, the residents may only sometimes speak for all the groups affected by public safety concerns in those areas. For instance, businesses, churches, and schools typically have important interests to consider in any public safety agenda facing a troubled neighborhood. For a single agency, such as the police or probation, to try to confront those problems without considering the interests of the other groups involved can reduce the impact of the community justice work and lead to frustration for the justice agency and disappointment for the citizens. Recognizing that public safety problems extend to relationships beyond those between community residents and a single justice agency has increased interest in partnership strategies. In addition, methods such as problem-oriented policing can be implemented with little community involvement and consultation, especially in the case of traffic accidents. Police organizations may be tempted to plan and do much of the work in addressing a problem if they perceive that consultation with the community may be problematic or time-consuming in addressing the problem.

Partnership Model

Under the Partnership Model, justice agencies such as the police collaborate with citizens and other public- and private-sector interests to identify problem priorities and generate strategic solutions to prevent crime. This approach recognizes that almost any crime or disorder problem facing a community raises the practical concerns of groups other than justice agencies and residents. If there is a problem of homelessness, for example, the local shelters will be involved, as will welfare agencies and religious groups. If there is a problem involving gangs, there is a need to consult with schools, family services, and juvenile probation. In both cases, unemployment and inadequate job skills raise the possibility that businesses (as employers) and job development services will need to be a part of the solution.

There are four layers of partnerships that justice agencies engage in. The first is the most obvious: the resident groups. Justice agencies may align their efforts with neighborhood councils, neighborhood development corporations, or citizen volunteer groups and use these partnerships to gain credibility with the community. This collaboration layer is essential to community justice; without the community's involvement, any new initiative will not likely represent community justice.

A second level of partnership occurs when one criminal justice agency aligns with another to try to increase the effectiveness of public safety efforts. A typical example is police/probation partnerships to work with offenders under supervision in the community. A community court can also form a centerpiece for a collaborative effort between probation and police to improve the services to a neighborhood. Police–prosecution partnerships are also common.

A third level of partnership involves nonjustice governmental agencies in public safety collaborations. Probation will often work with mental health agencies in a particular neighborhood, police will become aligned with child-protective services in a specific housing project, or the domestic violence prevention services will partner with police and probation in a troubled section of a city. Community schools are another joint partner for police, probation, and the courts. In these collaborations, agencies that share some responsibility for a given problem in a particular neighborhood or local setting will coordinate efforts through a cross-agency management team or a local coalition instead of working independently.

The final level of partnership involves the private sector. Businesses are natural public safety partners because they have a strong interest in safe environments for commerce. Moreover, community foundations and other philanthropies can also become active in supporting innovative community justice practices that require new funding for start-ups. It is also possible to have private volunteer groups, such as the Chamber of Commerce or the Kiwanis Club, become active sponsors in this kind of effort.

An excellent example of a collaborative public safety effort is the Ten Points Coalition in Boston, Massachusetts. Led by a group of ministers, the coalition brings criminal justice representatives from all parts of the criminal justice system (police, courts, and corrections, including local, state, and federal) together with an array of social services, local citizen leaders, and private-sector representatives to work to combat youth and family issues that can often lead to youth delinquency, especially violent behavior. The group focuses on the "troubled youth," those whom agencies are often unable to serve. The criminal justice involvement was originally to target gang gun violence by focusing efforts to investigate, prosecute, and punish those gang members who used guns. Social service agencies provided gang members with viable alternatives to gang membership and involvement so that when pressured, they could see ways out of their gang memberships. Citizens, led by ministers, supported the families whose children were involved in gangs and mobilized community understanding and support for the initiative. The private sector lent financial assistance to the effort (Beiman 1998). The Coalition has understood that the criminal justice system cannot solely address the issue of youth violence, and they have developed programs that form relationships with high-risk youth, create mentoring opportunities, address the trauma aspect of living in neighborhoods where violence is prevalent, and reconnecting with youth who have been incarcerated or stigmatized by mainstream society. They have also worked to create community-based economic development programs that enrich at-risk communities.

The results of the Ten Points Coalition in Boston demonstrate the cooperative advantage that the Partnership Model has over other models: it has a much more robust capacity for overcoming the public safety problem it is designed to reduce. In Boston, partly because of the work of the coalition, gang homicides declined significantly. The Coalition has partnered with seven schools/colleges, five community centers, eight green spaces, 47 faith institutions, and 54 organizations to address youth and family issues (btpc.org). Partnerships work because they bring to bear on a complex problem an array of resources, finding multiple avenues for addressing the full range of complex issues involved in public safety.

The great advantage of the Partnership Model is that it offers a far more sophisticated response to complicated and sometimes entrenched problems, which is now widely accepted. Most community justice initiatives today are not enterprises of single justice–citizen partnerships but employ multiple partnerships to achieve their ends. Police rarely work alone but typically work with one or more partners – probation, schools, businesses, or religious groups – to increase the scope and flexibility of what can be done.

Partnerships have proven successful, but they are not without problems. Many agencies trying to work together are funded by the same sources, and there is a natural rivalry among them for public support and funds. Moreover, years of isolation from one another may have created a history of conflict: police may distrust social services, and private businesses may distrust the justice system. Finally, there is a natural tension between organizations whose mission is to "help" and organizations set up to investigate, accuse, and punish, and this conflict in missions must be resolved.

The main difficulty, however, relates to the limited capacity of those neighborhoods with the most significant public safety problems. Places that suffer great deficits in public safety are also usually relatively poor. They lack an economic infrastructure because they have few businesses and are home to many unemployed people. Drugs are far easier to obtain than jobs. Few families are intact, and adults who work generally face severe demands for their time. They spend most of their time trying to make ends meet and engaging in childcare. There is little time available for voluntary participation in community projects, and there may also be minimal confidence in the ability of service agencies and justice to affect the neighborhood's problems. Morale is low.

In places with insufficient collective efficacy, there is little basis for collective action. People tend to mind their own business. There is often suspicion of the government and its agencies and widespread suspicion or indifference to their neighbors. People are frequently cynical about the motives of social services and justice, and they have plenty of experience to justify the cynicism. Obtaining participation in these locations is always hard work, and it takes time.

For these reasons, newer community justice initiatives have sought not simply to prevent crime but to strengthen the capacity of the communities within which they work. These approaches see public safety as a long-term issue of community functioning rather than a short-term issue of community circumstances.

Mobilization Model

Community mobilization was the earliest form of community action, which traces its roots to Saul Alinsky's Back of the Yards Project (Alinsky 1991) in poor Chicago neighborhoods. Mobilization seeks to counter the most prominent problem underlying poor neighborhoods: disorganization. The essence of the mobilization approach is to unite people to confront their problems and organize people concerning the quality of their lives. The idea is that people who live in poor places cannot rely on outsiders' altruism to improve their conditions. They must take their destiny into their own hands.

Concerning public safety, mobilization is an attractive idea. The image of residents of poor places coming together to make their neighborhoods safer is appealing, and numerous attempts to do so have occurred. The archetypal mobilization strategy is Neighborhood Watch. Here, citizens band together to keep an eye on one another's property and children, ensuring that strange people and "undesirables" cannot put them in danger. Usually, a Neighborhood Watch campaign is kindled by the work of a single authority – the police, a neighborhood citizen's group, or another governmental agency.

The theory underlying mobilization strategies is that these approaches create new capacity within neighborhoods. Neighborhood Watch, for example, builds new relationships among neighbors, even if that means no more than the occasional communication about an event in the area. Other Mobilization Model public safety programs have an impact on community capacity. The neighborhood probation centers in Phoenix, Arizona, offered literacy programs for residents not on probation. La Bodega de la Familia, a family drug treatment center that operated in the Lower East Side of Manhattan, provided drug rehabilitation services to children and partners in families with someone under the supervision of the criminal justice system.

Neighborhood organization strategies have a spotty history. For one thing, any attempt to improve a neighborhood's capacity must build upon something, and the places that most need improvement also have the least foundation to start with. It is an uphill battle to get residents of these places ready and able to come together to work on their area's problems. When the people who live or work in these places are struggling to make it from day to day, it is unrealistic to expect them to quickly make room in their lives for a whole new set of activities, especially when they do not see a likelihood for an immediate payoff to their community involvement.

Often, the way to get a poor community mobilized is to inflame a sense of anger about an event or the existing conditions and to use the anger to get a group to "march on City Hall" and demand changes. Such confrontational strategies can generate a lot of interest and action by residents initially. However, it takes much work to sustain interest or motivation after the first few public happenings. People work out their anger, and it subsides, or they see that the protest brings only resistance with little evidence of change and quickly become discouraged. The "protest" ends, and things return to how they were. In other cases, the group involved in confrontational tactics may become a target of lawmakers or the public. This was evidenced by the reaction to tactics the Association of Community Organizations for Reform Now (ACORN) utilized in 2009. Federal lawmakers targeted the group's actions and accused it of voter registration fraud. With the ensuing investigations swaying the general public opinion of the group and lawmakers threatening to cut off any federal funding being received by the organization, attention moved from the work ACORN was doing to defending the image of the organization.

This is why those seeking to produce public safety through improved community capacity today seek to build coalitions of efforts to improve multiple aspects of community life. In this strategy, a central group working on behalf of the neighborhood seeks to bring various interests together to help improve community life. It works to coordinate the activities of groups and resources already involved in the community. The role is a developmental intermediary, linking external resources to local interests.

Intermediary Model

The Intermediary Model operates under two assumptions. First, what troubled neighborhoods need most is an investment in capacity so that new strengths can be created and the natural base can be augmented. Second, ironically, what troubled neighborhoods have is a large contingent of uncoordinated, largely ineffective agencies and services involved in community life but not affecting it very much. From this point of view, what is needed most in any strategy to improve community capacity is not *new* services but instead *reinvestment* of existing resources to target the community's needs more directly.

For the most part, intermediaries comprise local groups with resident leaders, such as a neighborhood development corporation or a local development council, that have already been active in advancing other neighborhood interests, notably housing, health care, and economic development. The intermediaries now address the problem of public safety in the same way as previous problems by working with governmental and nonprofit groups to develop strategies for neighborhood improvement in specific priority areas. The intermediary group then turns its attention to the work of criminal justice agencies in its community. It builds collaborations with police, courts, and corrections representatives in the neighborhood, seeking ways to reorganize the efforts of those agencies to deal with specific public safety problems.

The Intermediary Model, therefore, does not spring up spontaneously, nor is it born in the planning of a particular criminal justice agency. Instead, this model represents a natural evolution of action for the neighborhood group and the criminal justice (and other) services working there. These approaches do not emanate from outside the neighborhood but come from a natural interest of the neighborhood in acting on public safety priorities.

Because intermediaries are not from the criminal justice system, they tend to develop public safety strategies that are different from typical crime-prevention approaches of criminal justice. They might initiate a new recreational program to occupy the free time of local youth, develop a drop-in center and a mentoring program for youth with insufficient parental supervision, provide educational daycare so single parents can work, create student internship opportunities, or support a police/probation partnership that provides employment to those in re-entry and makes sure they obtain decent housing under circumstances that will reintegrate them into community life. Local intermediaries can also work closely with local resources, such as businesses and religious institutions, to find places for ex-offenders to have positive community ties. Because the intermediary is operating in a neighborhood where ex-offenders are familiar to the residents and where they probably have family, the level of anti-offender sentiment in the community can often be lower, making it easier to generate support for reintegration programs. The intermediary aims to help criminal justice and other governmental agencies shift from a business-as-usual method of merely dealing with criminal events to a new way of working to strengthen the neighborhood. The Intermediary Model needs a more evaluative track record because it is the newest approach to community justice. Large-scale models such as the Omaha 360 project (Box 6.1) show success, but the evaluation of smaller initiatives needs to be studied. On the positive side, most community initiatives are moving toward this approach. Rather than making unilateral efforts, criminal justice agencies are increasingly working in partnership with existing community groups and important nonprofit and public collaborators. More and more, the orientation of justice innovation is to strengthen the capacity of the community to deal with its public safety issues and provide crime-prevention services. On the negative side, coordinating the agendas of the multiple agencies serving a single location is difficult. For a local neighborhood group to devote sufficient effort to the task requires more than just a handful of eager volunteers; it needs a core leadership for the long term and possibly support from appropriate entities outside the neighborhood. This implies a funding source, usually a governmental grant or subsidy. Once again, the problem arises that the neighborhoods most in need of this new capacity need to be more capable of securing the kind of funding that enables the capacity to be built.

Box 6.1 Omaha Empowerment Network and Omaha 360

In 2006, Willie Barney met with small groups in the African-American community in Omaha, Nebraska, to identify critical issues and solutions that affected African-American residents of Omaha, especially in North Omaha, where the problems were the most serious and pressing. At a meeting in September 2006, 70 leaders convened and agreed to work together to address the issues. Thus began the Empowerment Network, which hosted youth summits and small group meetings with teens, successful students, gang members, ex-offenders, parents, and grandparents. These meetings aimed to gain resident and stakeholder input on issues, solutions, and priorities (Empowerment Network, n.d.). The Network created a mission statement which states:

> Working together to TRANSFORM the ECONOMIC condition and QUALITY OF LIFE of African Americans, North Omaha residents, and citizens of the Greater Omaha area by implementing the Empowerment Covenant & 7 Step Empowerment Plan. The vision is complete with short-term and long-term goals,

strategies, activities, and measurable outcomes. We will close long-standing gaps in employment, entrepreneurship, education, housing, and other quality of life factors that have been traditionally based on race and geographic segregation.

(Empowerment Network, n.d.)

The plan focused not only on the economic needs of the African-American community in Omaha but also on public safety needs, especially gun violence. From the desire to reduce gun violence and homicides, the Omaha 360 project was formed. The project includes representatives of community, youth, faith, neighborhood, education, social service, gang intervention, and mentoring organizations that sit down with Omaha police leaders and work on defusing violence. The groups meet weekly to share information and receive questions and input from participants. The main focus of Omaha 360 is prevention, which is achieved by sharing information with the police about neighborhood gang hot spots and problem areas. The police, in turn, share information with the community about police activity and ways to keep their neighborhoods safer. Members of Omaha 360 conduct area canvassing to inform citizens about issues, provide information about the work being done, and encourage participation in the project.

The Omaha 360 project has proven its effectiveness in achieving its goals. It has significantly reduced gun violence in Omaha by 74% from 2008 to 2018 and has played a crucial role in boosting economic development in the 24th and Lake area in North Omaha. The project's emphasis on collaboration and transparent communication has been instrumental in its success, fostering trust among the participating groups. The relationship between the Omaha Police Department and the community has undergone a remarkable transformation, with officers now viewing the community as partners in their efforts to reduce gun violence. Chief Todd Schmaderer shared that in 2008, the Omaha Police's role was primarily enforcement, but it has since shifted to a more balanced 30-30-30 model, with 30% each dedicated to enforcement, intervention, and prevention (Washington Post, 2023).

The Omaha 360 differs from many other initiatives in an important way. It has been willing to share experiences and provide guidance to other cities looking to reduce gun violence. Members of the Omaha 360 staff and community members have hosted a yearly conference, provided tours of North Omaha, and shared strategies. Kansas City, Missouri, adopted the model in late 2022, and other future sites are New Orleans, LA; Tulsa, OK; Lansing, MI; Columbus, GA; and Davenport, Quad Cities.

References

The Empowerment Network (n.d.). https://empoweromaha.com
The Empowerment Network (n.d.). https://empoweromaha.com/omaha-360/
Washington Post (2023, April 27). *Omaha Police Chief on City's Decline in Gun Violence.* https://washingtonpost.com/washington-post-live.2023/04/27/omaha-police-chief-cities-decline-gun-violence/

Which Community Justice Model Is Best?

These four models serve as stereotypes for various community justice initiatives nationwide. Which is best? There is no correct answer to this question because there is no superior community justice approach. Each of these models has strengths and weaknesses. The "right" way for a community to do community justice depends upon several factors facing that community, including those related to the following questions:

- *How difficult is the public safety problem?* Long-term, complex problems require a considerable investment from more resources working in partnership to achieve change. Targeted, new problems may be overcome with more uncomplicated strategies developed by a single organization.
- *How ready are the justice agencies to collaborate?* Turf battles abound in local criminal justice activity: police distrust the courts (and probation), parole is at odds with treatment providers, and so on. At their most basic, these organizations often compete with one another for funding. Effective collaboration faces long odds unless these agencies share a vision for community justice.
- *Is active, effective community leadership available to address the problem?* In communities with strong community leaders, government agencies can rely on those leaders to effectively involve the community. When leaders (or their organizations) are absent, developing strong, reliable partners for public safety initiatives is much more difficult.
- *What natural private partners exist?* Are there local businesses in the neighborhood interested in promoting public safety? Is there a community foundation that can contribute to the effort?
- *What has been tried before? What are the untapped ideas?* In places with a history of failure, it can take time to generate an interest in new attempts to change the circumstances that cause problems in the community. Moreover, it is essential not to try ideas that have already failed; new ideas are at a premium, and new partnerships can help to seed them.

In the end, the key strategy for community justice is the one that best fits the needs and assets of the community. This means that any successful community justice effort will begin with a careful assessment of the needs and assets a community offers so that promising opportunities can be identified and probable dead ends avoided.

Leadership in Community Justice

Leadership will play an important role as community justice develops and gains momentum. Traditionally, leadership has been viewed as a process where a person or persons in a formal role organize and motivate group members to take action to achieve a stated goal. Informal leadership, performed by those in non-formal roles, has also been recognized as important and influential. In both formal and informal leadership settings, persuasion plays a crucial role. The primary goal is often to influence group or organization members to alter their behavior, thereby aiding the collective group in achieving their desired objective. Northouse (2021) offers this definition of leadership, "a process whereby an individual influences a group of individuals to achieve a common goal" (p. 6). Northouse also explains that leadership contains several concepts often recognized as an accurate reflection of what it means to be a leader. First, leadership can be considered a trait where individuals possess certain qualities that influence their leadership. Second, leadership can be viewed as an ability where individuals have the capacity to lead. Third, leadership can be seen as being skill-based, where people know the means and methods for carrying out leadership responsibilities. Fourth, leadership can be seen as a behavior, meaning it is what leaders do when they are in a leadership role. Finally, leadership can be seen as a relationship where a process of collaboration between leaders and followers occurs. None of these perspectives is incorrect, and each provides a different view of leadership practice. In truth, all are probably present where successful leadership is occurring.

Northouse also discusses leadership approaches that have emerged in the twenty-first century: *Authentic leadership*, which looks at the authenticity of leaders and their leadership; *Spiritual leadership*, which looks at how leaders use values and a sense of "calling" to motivate followers; *Servant leadership*, which focuses on the needs of the followers and helps them to become more autonomous and knowledgeable; *Gender-based leadership* which looks at how one's gender affects and differentiates a person's leadership; *Ethical leadership*, which addresses the character, duties, and decision-making and developed over concern about unethical behavior; *Connective leadership*, which addresses mutual concerns and needs of diverse communities and how they can be brought together to work toward common goals. While each of these approaches is important, the development of *Adaptive leadership* is the one that may be the most pertinent for growing the future of community justice.

Adaptive Leadership

Heifetz et al. (2009) write that adaptive leadership is the practice of mobilizing people to address complex challenges and thrive. They explain that the concept of thriving is drawn from evolutionary biology, where a successful adaptation has three characteristics:

> (1) It preserves DNA essential for the species' continual survival, (2) it discards (reregulates or rearranges) the DNA that currently no longer serves the species' current needs, and (3) it creates DNA arrangements that give the species the ability to flourish in new ways and in more challenging environments.
>
> (p. 14)

In essence, these successful adaptations enable a living system to take the best from its history into the future.

Leading adaptive change can be challenging because it involves leading people in the process of determining what is essential to preserve from their organization's or group's heritage and what should be eliminated. This process generates loss, and fear of loss often drives resistance to change. The challenge for adaptive leaders is to develop the ability to diagnose those losses and to identify patterns of response that may occur. An adaptive leader must also know how to counter those patterns. By leading people through adaptive challenges, the leader helps build the adaptive capacity that will enable them to better meet the adaptive challenges they will face in the future (Heifetz et al. 2009).

Introducing innovative or experimental processes will be required, but that is usually more painful to the dominant culture than just living with the current approach to addressing issues confronted by the organization or group. This is often seen in the actions of political figures at the state and federal levels of government. Heifetz et al. (2009) note that while it might feel embarrassing, the organization or group often opts to maintain the status quo rather than try something new or different where outcomes are uncertain and may result in setbacks for key stakeholders. They contend that the organization's resistance to change stems from a deliberate choice by those in positions of authority.

According to Heifetz et al. (2009), the most common failure in leadership is that adaptive challenges are treated as if they are technical problems. This observation meshes well with the discussion of clock and cloud problems in Chapter 1 of this volume. As we noted, many criminal justice problems are treated as technical, or clock, problems and can be addressed using a set prescription of actions. Heifetz et al. (2009) observe that while technical problems may be complex and critically important, they have known solutions that can be implemented using the organization's current structure and processes. On the other hand, adaptive challenges can only be addressed through changes in people's priorities, beliefs, habits, and loyalties. They argue that progressing in addressing adaptive challenges requires going beyond authoritative expertise "to mobilize discovery, shedding certain entrenched ways, tolerating losses, and generating new capacity to thrive anew" (p. 19).

The challenge in practicing adaptive leadership is helping people go through a time of disturbance as they determine what is essential and what is expendable. Helping them identify and experiment with solutions to the challenges they encounter while encountering feelings that may involve conflict, frustration, confusion, disorientation, and fear of losing something dear is vital, according to Heifetz et al. (2009). They add that adaptive leadership is a repetitive process that involves three key activities: observing patterns and events around you, interpreting what you are observing, and designing interventions based on the observations to address the adaptive challenges identified.

Heifetz et al. (2009) note that when two people observe the same event, they see different things depending on their previous experiences and unique perspectives. As a result, they will tend to have different interpretations regarding what occurred and why. The caution is that to practice adaptive leadership, a person needs to take time to think through their interpretation of what was observed before jumping into action. Another important point they make is that leading adaptive change is about something other than making a better argument or loading up people with more facts. The real challenge lies in addressing the reluctance of people who prefer the familiarity of the status quo over the uncertainties associated with change, even in the face of logical arguments and factual evidence. Adaptive leaders must demonstrate sincerity and work to reach these people in their hearts by aiming to understand and address the concerns that keep them entrenched in their current mindset. Establishing meaningful relationships becomes a significant step in effectively navigating this challenge and creating openness to new ideas.

Adaptive Leadership and Community Justice

Adaptive leadership techniques benefit community justice in several ways. They could provide a new approach to how communities and the criminal justice system address crime and disorder problems.

As the discussion in Chapter 1 noted, criminal behavior is often viewed as a technical issue that can be addressed by implementing a set of prescriptive actions. The most prevalent actions have been based on the Classical Criminology theory of pain versus pleasure to deter persons from behaving in an unacceptable manner. When criminal acts occur, often the response from politicians and members of the criminal justice system is to increase the sanctions, or pain, that is administered to the offender to prevent them from reoffending. This approach may be successful in some cases, but it tends to deter the focus from root causes to strictly dealing with the behavior displayed. This does not mean that appropriate sanctions are not utilized, but only utilizing this approach can lead to an ineffective loop in addressing long-term criminal behavior issues. Adaptive leadership could help criminal justice practitioners, communities, elected officials, and members of academia take a more comprehensive look at the root causes of criminal behavior using techniques and actions that are important to retain but also develop new innovative approaches to studying and addressing the issue.

The study of leadership has helped us understand that people want certainty and stability, and when those are missing, they look to leaders to step in and address the problems they face. Over the past few decades, members of the public have looked to the criminal justice system to address issues pertaining to criminal behavior, and they have expected that the system will respond appropriately to repair the problems. Members of the criminal justice system, especially law enforcement, have shouldered that responsibility and worked to address criminal behavior through investigation, apprehension, and incarceration. Unfortunately, the results have not been consistent, and when criminal behavior increases, the public becomes frustrated with the criminal justice system for not lowering the crime rate. Adaptive leadership could help criminal justice system members accept that, as the primary authoritative players in addressing criminal behavior, they do not have all of the answers and that using subject matter experts from the community is a sign of strength and not a sign of weakness.

Adaptive leadership techniques may also be helpful in addressing the Shifting the Burden archetype discussed in Chapter 1. Adaptive leadership calls for gathering as much information as possible from a wide-ranging group to help develop courses of action to address a problem. Including more input from persons outside the criminal justice system could provide momentum to look more at fundamental solutions and decrease the reliance on symptomatic solutions.

An additional benefit of including persons from outside the criminal justice system in developing fundamental solutions is that persons who "lived the life" or who work directly with an at-risk population may provide insights and information that can help develop effective long-term actions to address the issue at hand. The reality is that those working in the criminal justice system have not lived a life that involved committing serious criminal acts or spending time incarcerated in prison. Insights from these subject matter experts can be invaluable to those working in the criminal justice system. As a participant once said at a community meeting attended by one of the authors,

> You may have a Ph.D. in academics, but I have a Ph.D. in life. I committed crimes and did time in prison before I left that life. I understand the mindset and culture of those who are still in it.

Issues in Community Justice

Community justice is attractive but is only sometimes accepted as a solution. Critics of community justice raise the following questions:

Is it fair to have poor places take on their own crime-prevention issues? Some say that community justice puts too much of the public safety burden on the poorest places, with the least capacity to tackle the problems that lead to crime. Instead of the traditional approach, they say the community justice approach turns some of the responsibility over to the people who live there, asking that they assist various agencies that engage in public safety activity.

To some people, this seems like "blaming the victim." In those areas where the public safety needs are the greatest and where the formal criminal justice system has most failed in its community mandate, it seems somewhat unfair to expect people to promote their own safety. This is especially problematic because, as we have repeatedly noted, these are precisely the locations that have the fewest social resources and where residents are most challenged to make it from one day to the next. Placing some of the responsibility for public safety on these citizens will, some say, inevitably set the stage for the criminal justice system to point the finger at them when crime rates fail to drop. When the crime rates stay high because the community lacks the capacity to eradicate the social problems that produce crime, they suffer a cycle of crime and get the blame for it.

Community justice approaches cannot be used as an excuse for abandoning an interest in these troubled neighborhoods. The reverse must be true. The current criminal justice approach is not working, so a more significant investment is needed. What is required is a redoubling of traditional justice system efforts, not a divestment of them to community members.

Can there be equality across places? The essence of community justice is to deal with different neighborhoods in a specific jurisdiction differently, depending upon each location's problems. It is dangerous to start making distinctions across communities that are covered by the same laws, especially when one of the main characteristics distinguishing some communities from others is the level of concentration of minority groups and people experiencing poverty. Critics of community justice wonder if "different" treatment will eventually lead to "lesser treatment" for these places.

This is a realistic concern. The places targeted for community justice initiatives need more political and social resources. Compared to more advantaged locations, these areas need help getting their fiscal and programmatic priorities at the front line for resources. There are often few strong advocates for these locations, and other areas are typically more easily able to influence the policies that affect their lives. The nature of advantages in social capital is that some places can influence their critical environment more than others. Without social capital, poor places infused with disadvantage have trouble competing for public resources.

This means that community justice initiatives could quickly become standard in less troubled areas, where citizens are organized enough to demand responsiveness from the criminal justice system. Because community justice embraces the need for criminal justice to operate differently from one place to another, the fear is reasonable that for poor places, these differences will not work out to their advantage.

The criticism based on inequality raises an important, indeed a central, issue: inequality causes crime, so public safety cannot be promoted by policies that further exacerbate the consequences of inequality. Suppose community justice stands not just for different attention to some troubled areas but also means more resources for those locations. In that case, it can provide hope for a better justice system response to public safety concerns. Otherwise, areas suffering from reduced official impact will likely receive different and below-standard services.

Can there be impartiality in cases? One of the most important values that underlies our contemporary criminal justice system is impartiality. This is the most democratic of our fundamental values because it requires everyone to be treated equally without regard for their status: rich or poor, famous or ordinary. An impartial justice system will have no social axe to grind and no political agenda to advance. It will merely enforce the law. The right to impartiality gives every citizen a guarantee of fairness and the expectation that no one's status will be elevated above anyone else's.

Some wonder if community justice can be impartial, considering the target at which it aims. Because the target is the quality of life in a particular location, it must be, say some, partial to the people who live in that location. It must place the needs and interests of the people who live and work in the community justice area as superior to those of others living or working elsewhere. In this way, community justice faces an impartiality challenge. In cases where a community justice area resident faces a conflict with a person from somewhere else, the community justice approach will, it is said, naturally tend to grant higher consideration to the resident.

If this were true, the loss of impartiality would be a severe price to pay for community justice. Nobody wants a criminal justice system that gives one person an advantage over another merely because of where the person resides or who the person's neighbors are. Community justice initiatives must find ways to advance the community's interests without giving some people privileges. The paradox is that community justice seeks to give the residents of some communities a head start in achieving public safety, but this cannot be done at the expense of some other areas. There is no obvious way to prove that community justice does not advantage some places at the expense of others, but any other situation would also raise fairness problems.

How do you protect the rights and interests of individuals and community minorities? We all live in communities and live better lives when our communities are strong. However, few of us want to subjugate our personal dreams and aspirations to the community's quality of life. Community justice seeks to establish a stronger foundation of collective life so that individuals may prosper. Critics wonder if systems of government that emphasize the interests of the collective are likely to undermine the purposes of individuals to achieve the broader focuses of community life.

Trying to advance the interests of communities always raises the possibility of affecting the rights of individuals, especially when those individuals are somehow "different." Should a community be allowed to come together to stop some individuals from engaging in activities that are entirely legal but are upsetting to the dominant majority of the community? This issue continuously arises in America, where personal freedom is so important. If the neighbors generally like peace and quiet, should they be able to prevent young people from getting together on a street corner? If residents do not like activity late at night, can they prevent businesses from staying open past a particular "reasonable" hour? Moreover, suppose the residents can band together to enforce these preferences. What happens if the majority do not want some specific religious group to establish its temple, or if they resent the presence of some ethnic group's social club?

Community justice is about public safety through community capacity, but it cannot be a way for a community to act out its prejudices and bigotry. Community justice can always uphold the basic protections of the Constitution and the Bill of Rights. After all, a community that does not allow <u>all</u> its residents' fundamental rights to be protected can never be considered "just." The ultimate aim of community justice is not merely safer places but places where justice prevails. Safety is an essential element of justice, but achieving a safer environment at the expense of justice is no bargain.

Are there significant problems in reinvestment strategies? Community justice seeks to reallocate public safety investments from traditional criminal justice activity toward community-focused activity. This is easier to accomplish with some justice functions than with others. For example, police already expend their resources at the community level. Hence, the community justice movement is primarily a matter of shifting from traditional paramilitary policing models toward more community-oriented ones, which has been occurring broadly. The shift to community can increase court costs when new courtrooms are opened to serve community and neighborhood interests. However, these costs are reduced because the new courts handle their fair share of cases and reduce the caseloads of other courts.

The most challenging resource-redistribution problem arises regarding corrections. The most considerable correctional costs apply to prisons; by comparison, probation and parole – the obvious community options – are as little as one-twentieth the cost per case. As the preceding chapter showed, most correctional dollars, by far, support incarceration. This means that the only way to reinvest this money into community settings is to move offenders who would otherwise have been in prison to the community. Without this, community justice correctional programs require new funding.

Moving offenders from prison to the community happens every time an offender completes the prison sentence, and this will apply to at least 95% of sentenced offenders. The problem comes when trying to change the sentence by keeping the offender in the community instead of going to prison or getting released earlier. There are two reasons why this is challenging to do. First, community pressures often make it harder to choose community sanctions in place of incarceration. Second, there are powerful financial interests that want to maintain a large prison population: the "prison/industrial complex" that constructs and staffs the prison. As long as prisons remain a booming industry, these interests remain strong.

To overcome these impediments, community justice leaders must deal with each one directly. Residents must be involved in planning community justice correctional strategies to confront community attitudes. This will reduce the impact of fear and give residents confidence that they can build community justice programs that enhance community safety rather than endanger it. Second, the resources that go to incarceration need to be thought of as being shifted to new investment opportunities with financial interests at stake in the community context. This incentivizes an interest group coalition to push for community justice reinvestment.

Will it work, or will it backfire? The point of all these criticisms is that community justice represents a change in and a challenge to the status quo. Some of these criticisms are less compelling as long as we know the status quo. For example, it is easy to wonder if disadvantaged areas will suffer if the new approaches allow them to be treated differently from the more advantaged places. However, the truth is that they are *already* treated differently than those areas. People who live in those places know they are treated less well than elsewhere: they get less enthusiastic, less effective service from the justice system; they need more help meeting their individual needs; they get less consideration in political circles than in other places. Community justice can backfire, but the current system, it must be admitted, already leaves these places at a disadvantage in terms of services and safety. This can only be changed by upsetting the status quo.

Nevertheless, there remains an all-too-common theme in justice reform: highly touted reform efforts often need to catch up to their promise. This, too, could be the fate of community justice. Surface changes in criminal justice are common but purposeful; fundamental changes are much harder to achieve. The criminal justice system tends to respond more readily to external forces, such as Supreme Court decisions or shifts in public opinion, than it does to the decisions of criminal justice planners and managers. To the extent that community justice remains an initiative of the criminal justice system, it risks being reconciled to this pattern of failed promises. Fundamental change in criminal justice may occur if community justice can manifest the interests and influences of the community movement that is so prominent in other arenas.

How will community justice initiatives be measured to ensure funding is received? To make decisions about funding for programs and staff, government and nonprofit sources will examine the effectiveness of proposed and existing programs to justify funding. Criminal justice organizations have traditionally utilized numerically based evaluation systems to measure achievement. Using an evaluation system solely based on numbers can only provide a partial picture of the success of community justice. Methods of evaluation will need to be arrived at through collaboration between criminal justice elements, academics, governmental agencies, and nonprofit groups. This collaboration will be essential because what one element utilizes may not be acceptable to others involved in the collaborative effort. Goals and objectives must be set, and knowing if the partners are meeting those goals and objectives is vital.

As previously discussed, evaluators examine outputs, outcomes, impacts, and processes in most evaluation practices. Outputs are the goods or services produced by the program or project. They are usually easily measured but do not address the effect of the program or project. Outcomes are the effects of the interventions and can be measured. Measurements can inform the evaluator what events or actions resulted from implementing the program or project. Impacts are longer-term effects and address broader issues beyond the specific program or project. Because impact evaluation depends more on longitudinal methods, they do not tend to provide the immediate feedback that outcome and output evaluation can provide. Processes are the methods or mechanics used to implement and carry out the program or project. Evaluation of processes focuses on the efficiency issues relating to the program or project. All four evaluation methods should be utilized to comprehensively evaluate a program or project. It will also be essential to continue to utilize evidence-based practice in gathering and analyzing data. Ensuring the inclusion of academic partners will be essential since they can approach the evaluation process independently and not with a bias toward a program or process.

Since the United States is encountering continuing financial crises, it will be essential to have agreed-upon standards of measurement that can allow community justice initiatives to draw funding from all levels of government and the nonprofit sector. There will be much competition for scarce funds, and if the funding sources see little value in programs requesting funding, they will put their money elsewhere. After diverting money from policing programs funded through the Office of Community Oriented Policing (COPS Office) to Homeland Security projects due to September 11, 2001, the federal government has been working to increase funding to the COPS Office and Bureau of Justice Assistance. While competition for these funds will be keen, creative projects involving collaboration with multiple stakeholders will be positioned to be more likely to be awarded the necessary funding. The same process should play out in competition for funding from private grants and nonprofit sources.

The Future of Community Justice

There is no question that community justice is no longer an emerging idea but a prominent new conceptualization of how criminal justice should be delivered. Community justice has developed deep roots in police practice, informs most of the current innovation in courts, and has become an important new force in correctional practice. Almost all the new ideas in criminal justice contain some aspect of community justice thinking: place, problem-solving, partnerships, restoration, and so forth. Overall, the underlying value of community justice has developed salience in criminal justice thinking.

Nevertheless, the appeal of traditional criminal justice remains very strong. Television offers another cop chase-and-capture show every night, punitive sentencing strategies are prevalent in the public mind, and the idea is widely held that public safety comes from no-holds-barred criminal justice. Criminal justice insiders know that traditional methods have significant limitations, and their growing interest in community justice stems from a sense that the practices of community justice can overcome some of those limitations. There is also a prevailing desire to work in closer cooperation with the community rather than in isolation. These beliefs within the system have made the formerly cautious and even defensive criminal justice establishment increasingly interested in the possibilities that arise when community justice approaches are employed.

Community leaders have also started to recognize the potential of the underlying principles of community justice. Leaders seek locally relevant justice practices in which citizens have a role and for which the quality of community life is an aim. As new initiatives develop that offer this as a way of providing justice services, many community leaders see the advantages and seek even broader applications of these principles. With each success in community justice, resident resistance to innovation fades, and mutual support for more of these new ideas grows. The community justice movement has been strong partly because it meets the various needs of a changing justice system and an insistent public.

Community justice has been a popular idea, even though evaluative evidence supporting it must be more precise. As the previous chapters have shown, community justice makes sense from what we know about public safety and strong communities. There are a few significant evaluation studies that confirm the wisdom of some of the community justice conceptual foundations: community policing has paid dividends in law enforcement; community courts and special courts (such as drug courts) have developed impressive track records; restorative justice offers sufficient benefits to encourage expansion of the idea. However, the empirical foundation for a community justice movement is not as strong as any of these parts.

A core aspect of the future of community justice, then, is evidence. New initiatives must be studied, and their results must be fully understood. The relative benefits of different strategies of community justice need to be documented so that an informed conception of community justice priorities can be developed. This will happen slowly but requires sustained attention to the benefits and costs of community justice activities.

A second aspect of the future of community justice is political. A great deal will depend upon whether the current coalescence of opinion favoring community justice concepts will continue. Today, there is a broad consensus among criminal justice leaders, researchers, and community leaders that the potential of community justice justifies continued interest and experimentation. New programs have solid support among the key constituencies needed to sustain community justice action. However, the criminal justice system has a way of shifting its attention from time to time, and when the inevitable shift occurs, the momentum of community justice will be tested. If the primary support for community justice continues, this shift in interest will be fine; if the support evaporates when the attention shifts, community justice will struggle to survive.

Finally, there is the question of whether this community justice idea can retain its creativity and innovation quality. Central to the idea of community justice is a challenge to the inventive capacities of collaborative partnerships of citizens and justice officials working together on the problems that face a particular geographic area. The idea is to avoid the routine response to crime and instead invent new ways of responding to the challenge of public safety. It is easy to develop a copycat version of community justice, where local partnerships try to re-create the experiences of other areas rather than produce their own. Community justice will endure so long as the innovative and inventive spirit that fueled its inception supports its continuation.

In many ways, this book has been about the future of community justice in the United States. Every idea presented in this book is a conception of how a commitment to the values and vision of community justice could change the future of criminal justice here in America. However, crime is a worldwide phenomenon, and the next chapter briefly examines how community justice might fare in international settings.

References

Alinsky, S. [1946] (1991). *Reveille for radicals, reissue*. Random House.
Goldstein, H. (1991). *Problem oriented policing*. McGraw Hill.
Heifetz, R.A., Linsky, M., & Grashow, A. (2009). *The practice of adaptive leadership: Tools and tactics for changing your organization and the world*. Harvard Business Review Press.
Northouse, P.G. (2021). *Introduction to leadership: Concepts and practices*, 5th ed. Sage.
Van Beiman, D. (1998). In search of Moses. *Time Magazine*, 152 (December 14).

For Further Reading

Bazemore, G. (1995). Rethinking the sanctioning function in juvenile court: Retributive or restorative responses to youth crime. *Crime and Delinquency, 41*, 296–316.
Clear, T.R., & Karp, D.R. (1999). *The community justice ideal: Preventing crime and achieving justice*. Westview Press.
Clear, T.R., & Rose, D. (1999). *When neighbors go to jail: Impact on attitudes about formal and informal social control. Perspectives in justice*. U.S. Department of Justice, Office of Justice Programs, National Institute of Justice.
Decker, S.H., & Van Winkle, B. (1996). *Life in the gang: Family, friends and violence*. Cambridge University Press.
Karp, D.R. (ed.) (1998). *Community justice: An emerging field*. Rowman and Littlefield.
Rose, D.R. & Clear, T.R. (1998). Incarceration, social capital and crime: Examining the unintended consequences of incarceration. *Criminology, 36*(3), 441–479.
Sampson, R.J., Morenoff, J.D., & Earls, F. (1999). Beyond social capital: Spatial dynamics of collective efficacy for children. *American Sociological Review, 64*, 633–660.
Smith, M.E., & Clear, T.R. (1997). *Fathers in prison: Interim report*. Draft report to the Edna McConnell Clark Foundation by the Rutgers University School of Criminal Justice.
Smith, M.E., & Dickey, W.J. (1998). What if corrections were serious about public safety? *Corrections Management Quarterly, 2*(3), 12–30.

Mobilization

Merry, S.E., & Milner, N. (1993). *The possibility of popular justice: A case study of community mediation in the United States*. University of Michigan Press. Investigates the circumstances leading to and consequences of a community-based alternative to the formal legal system for solving local conflicts.

Podolefsy, A. (1983). *Case studies in community crime prevention*. Charles C. Thomas. Demonstrates a series of ways that communities can systematical come together to prevent crime.

Partnerships

Crawford, A. (1997). *The local governance of crime: Appeals to community and partnerships*. Clarendon. Describes the conceptual and practical limits of community-based crime-prevention partnerships.

Politics of Crime Prevention

Chambliss, W.J. (2001). *Power, politics, and crime*. Westview. A critical analysis of the way political interests affect the formulation of crime policy.

Miller, L.L. (2001). *The politics of community crime prevention*. Ashgate Dartmouth. Description of the politics of the Federal Government's Weed and Seed program, in which law enforcement (Weed) is coupled with community services (Seed).

7
Community Justice in International Settings

As we complete our discussion on community justice, one question often arises: Is this a concept only workable in the United States, or is it possible to use it internationally? We noted in previous chapters that this broad concept encompasses more than just criminal justice system issues. However, since this book focuses on the use of community justice in the criminal justice system, we will stay with that line of thought to consider how well it might work in international settings.

The field of comparative criminal justice can help us begin this discussion. We have chosen to look at international dimensions of community justice through Reichel's (2018) method of comparative criminal justice. In this model, we will examine four basic forms of law worldwide and then see how the concept of community justice may fit within any of those types of law.

The Four Legal Traditions

Reichel (2018) identifies the four legal traditions as Common, Civil, Islamic, and Eastern Asia. The following brief descriptions of each tradition are taken from the work of Reichel (2018).

Common Legal Tradition

The common legal tradition between 500 and 1450 AD was feudal practice. In the feudal system, the Lord provided vassals with land and exchanged it for military and other services. Disputes often arose between the vassals, which were addressed by the Lord. Prior to the Norman conquest of England, disputes were settled through assemblies of freemen in both shire and 100 courts. Shires were similar to the present-day counties in the United States, while hundreds were divisions within a shire and fulfilled administrative, military, and judicial functions. Each 100 had a court where customary law was used to settle private disputes and criminal matters. Customary laws were based on a local community's traditions, customs, or norms. Because customs could vary, the jury system was one way to determine if a custom met the criteria for being a good legal custom. Citizens became. Citizens, frustrated with some of the decisions that came from the juries, asked for a sense of fairness to be used in the decisions. That led to the addition of equity as one of the elements of the common legal tradition. Equity was created by the meshing of common law courts, which dealt with technical law, and Chancery courts, which dealt with moral issues.

DOI: 10.4324/9781003393818-7

Civil Legal Tradition

Reichel (2018) explains that the civil legal tradition is based on the code of laws that was collected by the Roman Emperor Justinian. The Twelve Tables provided basic rights of Roman citizens and consisted mainly of ancient customs. They are concerned with procedure more than substantive law. Roman law was the result of interpretation by jurists who were statesmen knowledgeable about the law rather than lawyers as we think of them today. A key element of civil tradition was Canon law. Canon law primarily originated from decretal letters, which comprised authoritative papal statements that addressed controversial points in the doctrine or ecclesiastical law, according to Reichel (2018). Another major element of the civil legal tradition is codification. The civil legal tradition has relied on written, or codified, laws. The importance of codified laws is that they are recognized as having been enacted by a recognized authority, such as a monarch or legislature, following formal procedures. In the civil legal tradition, civil law codes can replace prior law rather than extending or "fine-tuning" it. This differs from codes in the common law tradition where codes do not abolish all prior law in the field but, instead, perfect and supplement it.

Islamic Legal Tradition

Those who follow the tenets of Islam are called Muslims, and they believe in one God called Allah. According to Muslims, Allah's messenger was the Prophet Muhammad, who had been preceded by Jesus and Old Testament prophets. Islam recognizes no distinction between a legal system and other controls on a person's behavior. In fact, Islam is said to provide all answers to questions about behavior in any sphere of life. While the other legal traditions took some principles and techniques from religion, the traditions remained distinct and separate from religion. At the same time, Islamic law is intrinsic to the Islamic faith and life in Islamic countries.

The primary sub-traditions of Islamic law, or Shari'a, are the Qur'an and the Sunna. The Qur'an is the holy book, and Sunna is how the Prophet Mohammed lived his life, which is reported as *hadiths*. Hadiths are statements providing narration about the Prophet's life regarding what he said, did, or approved. Both the Qur'an and the Sunna are indispensable, and both must be consulted by practicing Muslims. The Sunna helps to explain, clarify, and amplify the Qur'an. Cases that are not seemingly answered by the Qur'an or Sunna are to be handled through a consensus of legal authorities called *ijma* and a process of reasoning by analogy called *qiyas*.

When Muslims differ on how Islam is interpreted and applied, they are linked first to one of the two sects of Islam, the Sunni or the Shi'a, and then to the school of law to which particular Muslims adhere. Originally, there were over 100 schools of law, but recently, they have been narrowed down to five. Determining the appropriate school of law can be complicated.

Eastern Asian Legal Tradition

In defining Eastern Asia, Reichel (2018) includes the following countries: China, Japan, Mongolia, North Korea, and South Korea. Eastern Asian legal tradition can be seen as more of a hybrid containing elements from the common and civil legal traditions.

Confucianism is the most important single source of Eastern Asian legal tradition. It is a moral and ethical system that was developed from the teachings of Confucius.

In Confucianism, there is an emphasis on family or group based on collectivism, hierarchy, harmony, and informal control mechanisms.

There are two essential principles of Confucianism: *li* and *fa*. *Li* is the moral and social rules of conduct that individuals share and internalize. *Fa* is the process of criminal law and punishment. It is believed that when *li* is successfully implemented in society there is no need to use *fa*. However, if *li* is not able to prevent misbehavior, *fa* can be used to maintain social order. Confucius did not deny the utility of formal law and punishment, but he did stress the superiority and effectiveness of *li*.

Another element of the Eastern Asian legal tradition is collectivism. In collectivism, the emphasis is on the importance of groups versus individuals. This contrasts with the Western view of a person as an individual and not part of a group. As socialization occurs, Eastern Asian children learn the importance of being a part of a group and the negatives of acting as individuals. In the Western world, one tends to see the opposite.

The Eastern Asian legal tradition does have legal institutions, but they are mostly non-bureaucratic. Reichel (2018) explains that legal informalism is preferred where there is less reliance on bureaucratic legal institutions containing professionals. The preference is for reconciliation, restitution, and reintegration, which fits well with the collectivist societal approach.

Cultural Components of the Legal Traditions

Reichel (2018) suggests that comparing the four traditions is best handled by considering cultural, substantive, and procedural components. One cultural component Reichel (2018) discussed is private versus public law, which refers to where legal rights and obligations lie. Private law refers to whether legal rights and obligations lie with the individual versus public law, where they lie with the state. In the common tradition, it is public law because both the individual and the state have a legal personality. The concept of legal personality refers to any person or entity that can undertake legal actions. In the civil tradition, it lies with public law when concern is with the state's legal personality and with private law when concern is with the individual's legal personality. In Islamic tradition, it is private law because the concern is always with the individual's legal personality. In Eastern Asia, tradition, legal rights, and obligations simultaneously have both public and private aspects.

Reichel (2018) discusses a second cultural aspect: substantive law. In this discussion, substantive law concerns where laws come from. In the common tradition, the primary source of law is custom, where the law expresses entrenched visions of what is seen as right and wrong. In the civil tradition, codification is the primary source of law. Codification is the written code that is provided by rulers or legislators. In the Islamic tradition, the primary source of law is divine revelation, which has God's authority rather than tradition or written code. In the Eastern Asia tradition, the primary source of law is drawn from the principles of Confucianism, where the source of law is seen as within each individual.

Reichel (2018) identified the final component as procedural law, where laws come from. The important issue in this area is how flexibility is provided to keep up with an ever-changing society. In the common tradition, flexibility occurs through judge-made law and the case's particulars. In the civil tradition, we see variation in reasoning and definition and identify issues as either questions of law or fact. In the Islamic tradition, it is the Fatwa (legal opinion) and the process of ijtihad (independent reasoning). In Eastern Asian tradition, it is the reliance on informal procedure and, in some cases, on vagueness in how the law is written.

There do not appear to be areas in each of the four legal traditions that would overtly prevent the application of community justice principles. Some traditions would be more open to community justice than others, but none of the traditions appear to oppose prevention activities or rehabilitation. One major issue could be how the use of non-justice-related persons, such as community members, nonprofit organizations, and private sector organizations, fits into the application of the law. It is also important to remember that countries following a particular legal tradition do not necessarily interpret the traditions similarly. That can lead to a variation of how a legal tradition is applied in each country or jurisdiction.

International Policing and Community Justice

As discussed in Chapter 3, policing organizations in the United States have great latitude in establishing operational guidelines and guiding principles. Often, we see police agencies adapt their policing styles to the community's personality. For example, a community that values law and order will tend to have a police department that enforces laws and ordinances more rigidly. In the United States, local communities have the ability to enact ordinance-level laws that are less serious than misdemeanors and felonies. Local police agencies have more latitude in how they enforce ordinances, and that can be helpful in implementing actions such as restorative policing, where an officer can choose not to enforce the ordinance if the community member changes behavior and/or makes restitution for any harm they may have created by their actions.

In international policing, various policing structures can be identified, and the different structures can affect the latitude police officers may have in enforcing the law. Bayley (1985) recommends using a categorization of policing based on the number of forces and the dispersal of command. He identifies three categories under the number of forces category: Single (one national police force), Multiple coordinated (a central government head with multiple agencies reporting to it), and Multiple uncoordinated (many agencies that operate independently of each other). In addition, he identifies two categories under the dispersal of command category: Centralized (meaning there is one command over all operations) and Decentralized (meaning there can be multiple commands for multiple agencies). In decentralized organizations such as those in Mexico and the United States, multiple levels of policing can be found. In many cases, the levels do not work together on a regular basis. For example, a municipal police agency may work with the state police or other state agency irregularly and a federal agency on rare occasions or never.

The different police structures could affect police agencies' ability to have the latitude to make decisions about partnering with community members to address a crime problem or taking a proactive approach to prevent an incident from occurring. Countries with one police agency that has oversight over policing may not be able to operate as effectively on a micro level with individual communities. They may tend to follow guidelines that are uniform for all areas of the country.

International Court Operations and Community Justice

Court operations also differ in the four legal traditions. One commonality is that the three major actors, judges, prosecutors, and defense lawyers, appear to be present in each tradition. One major difference is the amount and type of education and training a person may be required to have to serve in the roles. Reichel (2018) identifies two different types of the legal profession: unified or specialized. In a unified profession, all legal professionals have the requisite knowledge and training to participate in any legal field. In a specialized profession, each field has specific entrance requirements that restrict horizontal movement by legal professionals.

Prosecution of cases can be done through either private or public prosecutors. Private prosecution allows the victim or the victim's relatives to initiate action against the offender, while public prosecution is initiated by a government representative. While private prosecution is not widespread, it can be helpful in areas where a public prosecutor declines to file charges.

Regarding defense, the accused is usually represented by a trained professional, whether appointed by the court or secured privately by the accused. However, in an Islamic system, the accused may be defended by a layperson such as a friend, family member, or self. The interesting aspect of having a layperson provide a defense is that more personal information can be presented about the accused. In contrast, professional lawyers may know little personal information about their clients and rely mainly on the specifics of the law for the defense.

In the area of the judiciary, Reichel (2018) notes that in the international arena some courts rely only on professional judges, while others may provide for input from laypersons. He also observes that in civil tradition, there appears to be more preference for codes that set forth general principles for judges to follow, which may limit the latitude they have in how they adjudicate cases. In the common tradition, judges follow case law established from previous decisions handled by the same or different judges. This concept, called *stare decisis*, allows for more flexibility in adjudication since case law is always changing.

International Corrections and Community Justice

Of the three branches of the criminal justice system, corrections stand out as the one where abuse against the accused and convicted is most likely to occur. A number of international agreements on corrections have been developed aimed at addressing the treatment of those who have been incarcerated.

The most prominent topic faced by corrections is that of punishment. People everywhere tend to expect that behaviors that deviate from social norms should be punished. The use of punishment is justified through the principles of retribution, deterrence, rehabilitation, and incapacitation. Reichel (2018) notes Retribution is most often seen as the justification for punishment, with the argument being that punishment is a necessary and natural response to those who violate social norms.

It is not uncommon to find countries shifting between rehabilitation and incapacitation approaches. Reichel (2018) suggests that this fluctuation is influenced by factors such as public opinion, media attention, the seriousness of the crime, political ideologies, and the offenders' characteristics. Additionally, he notes that there are numerous possible combinations of sentences and justifications, making it unlikely for any single approach to be used.

When it comes to penalties, many countries assess financial penalties to those convicted of wrongdoing. In most cases, these financial penalties are assessed in the form of fines. Some countries have adopted "day fines." These fines are based on the belief that fines should be proportionate to the seriousness of the crime and have roughly the same financial sting on persons with differing financial resources. For example, in the United States, assessing the same fine of $100.00 to offenders earning minimum wage and those making over

$100,000.00 is disproportionate because it can create a hardship for the minimum wage earner while the wealthier offender feels little, if any, financial harm.

Also popular in many countries is compensation to victims and communities. This concept has been present in many countries for hundreds of years. In the Islamic tradition, *diyya* is used as a possible punishment for *qisas*, lower level, offenses. The goal is to obtain appropriate compensation but also a way to rid grudges over the offense. It works to make the victim and community whole.

Other topics of concern in corrections are corporal punishment and capital punishment, custodial issues regarding women and minorities, and non-custodial sanctions such as community corrections. Non-custodial sanctions, such as community corrections and probation, are used successfully in many countries throughout the world, according to Reichel (2018).

This brief discussion of policing, courts, and corrections in international contexts highlights the presence of certain aspects of community justice within these institutions. While the use of discretion varies, it is evident across all elements. Moreover, in many countries, courts have welcomed input from non-professional actors such as community members, while non-custodial sanctions are often utilized in correctional practices.

Can Community Justice Be Effective in International Settings?

This chapter aims to generate a deeper discussion regarding the effectiveness of community justice outside the context of the United States criminal justice system. Experts who work in the fields of comparative criminal justice, comparative political science, policing, courts, corrections, and community organizing are essential in examining this question in greater depth.

As discussed earlier in the chapter, elements of community justice do seem to be present in policing, courts, and corrections internationally. The brief overviews of legal traditions did not find that these elements were prohibited or discouraged. Because the specifics of the legal traditions can be complex, more analysis needs to be completed to determine if that is correct.

In Chapter 1, we noted that Community Justice entailed much more than just the criminal justice system. Social justice and economic development are important parts of the concept. It is vital that nonprofit organizations, governments, and the private sector are active contributors to the creation of healthy communities. Discussion of those roles is outside of the scope of this book, but must be considered by any jurisdiction that wants to adopt the philosophy of community justice.

There are many factors that may affect the implementation of community justice in an international setting. One of the most significant factors is the political climate. The increasing discussion regarding populism and its effect on democracy concerns not only the United States but also countries and nations throughout the world that adhere to the principles of democracy. In many locations, far-right populism has grown, and it remains to be seen how the growth of that viewpoint would affect community justice. Sentiments about law and order versus rehabilitation and forgiveness may also affect the adoption of community justice. While community justice recognizes the need for law and order, it also calls for appropriate sanctions to assist the victim, correct the offender's behavior, and involve the community in the sanctioning process. Those who subscribe more to Classical Criminology may not feel that there is a need for philosophies such as restorative justice. Economic conditions also play a role in implementing community justice. Long-term benefits may only be realized if funding sources are available to help communities or designated geographical areas build capacity that promotes growth and self-governance.

The best approach is to ask the question on a micro level. As the discussion in this chapter indicated, countries with a particular legal tradition may apply the basic elements differently. That makes it difficult to make a blanket observation that community justice might not be successful in a specific legal tradition. It might be more appropriate to identify a country or nation and examine the role of the criminal justice system, the political climate, the economic conditions, and the role of the government to determine better if community justice would be an effective strategy to adopt.

References

Bayley, D.H. (1985). *Patterns of policing*. The State University of New Jersey.

Reichel, P.L. (2018). *Comparative criminal justice systems: A topical approach*. 7th ed. Pearson.

Appendix A

Community Justice as a Strategy
How CASES Make It Work

Adapted from Clear, T.R. (2000). Community justice as a strategy: How CASES make it work. *Community Corrections Report*, 7(4), 49–50 and 60–62. Copyright 2000 by Civic Research Institute, Inc. Reprinted with permission from *Community Corrections Report*, 7(4), through www.copyright.com. All rights reserved.

A team of correctional professionals at CASES (Center for Alternative Sentencing and Employment Services) created a community justice project that begins by responding to the kinds of questions that community justice raises. Unlike other strategies, such as community court or community policing, the CASES approach is not linked to a particular criminal justice agency. Rather, it begins with "the problem" and "the place" and develops a comprehensive community justice strategy tailored to each community it serves.

The CASES philosophy is as follows:

The PURPOSE of community justice is to improve the long-term public safety of areas hard hit by crime through developmental approaches that increase the community capacity and well-being of people who live and work in those places.

The METHOD of community justice is reinvesting public resources in public safety strategies that build stronger community life.

The PRINCIPLES of community justice are as follows:

- Share decision-making between criminal justice
- professionals and community leaders.
- Coordinate cross-agency criminal justice responses to community priorities.
- Merge criminal justice investments and community resources locally.
- View offenders as untapped resources.

To implement this philosophy, the CASES team includes, in addition to a project manager, a community organizer, a program developer, and a data mapper. Using the skills this set of specializations represents, the CASES team addresses community justice from a unique perspective. Using the skills this set of specializations represents, the CASES team addresses community justice from a unique perspective. CASES designs community justice to work through partnerships between the criminal justice system and the residents and businesses in the community. These partnerships have two effects. First, they provide a vehicle for residents to make their neighborhood's priorities a part of the justice response at their location. Second, the participation of residents in the justice process enables the justice system to achieve a new level of credibility with the residents in the area it serves. The experience of just about every community justice initiative is this two-pronged result: a shift in justice priorities and a growth in the credibility of justice.

The new priorities typically involve a variety of programmatic emphases. A partial list of the kinds of new ideas promoted by citizen partnerships would include the following:

- An emphasis on *prevention* that provides programs and support for at-risk youth and their families.
- Changes in the *physical aspects* of the neighborhood – graffiti, debris, dilapidated housing, abandoned lots, etc. – that so often contribute to a sense of diminished safety.
- Victim restoration strategies that enable the offender to make direct *reparation* to the victim and the community.
- Support systems for *returning offenders* whose successful adjustment to the community will do so much to improve community life.

Community justice initiatives are not arrest-focused. They are oriented toward problem-solving: They try to identify the conditions that contribute to diminished public safety and determine how to overcome them. Because citizens are involved in that process, a much richer, more comprehensive, and more promising set of answers can be developed.

In the end, community justice is a set of programs that operates at the community level. However, these programs are not simply the criminal justice agencies' brainchild, nor are they reproductions of strategies undertaken elsewhere. They are place-specific, designed to confront problems particular to the location for which they are designed. They use citizens as resources in implementation – they leverage resources by partnering with residents, businesses, and other governmental services to develop a broader, more complete program. Finally, the measure of success of these programs is not "more criminal justice," as is often the case in traditional programming, but "less need for criminal justice," as public safety problems begin to be resolved.

Community justice initiatives in the CASES model work through three independent strategies: partnership development, information analysis and mapping, and resource leveraging.

Partnership Development

There is usually a degree of mistrust and misunderstanding between the criminal justice system and the residents of the communities in which justice actions are concentrated. Community justice initiatives cannot be effectively undertaken until this distrust and misunderstanding are addressed.

CASES begins its work with an assessment phase that involves up to six months or more of intensive interviewing in the community and among justice officials. During this process, CASES officials get to know the key people in the community and the justice system and learn their points of view on the need for new approaches to justice in that area. This lengthy process may seem to delay the project, but it is an essential way to develop the foundation for effective partnerships. CASES seeks to understand the differences and commonalities in points of view, the potential areas of consensus, and the likely active individuals in the innovations that will be undertaken.

Among the people involved in this assessment process will be the resident leaders, whose opinions are seen as important in the neighborhood; financial partners, who might be willing to support some aspects of the new programs; and justice innovators, who will be willing to take an imaginative view of their investments in the neighborhood. From these three elements, an effective partnership strategy can be built that can bring a comprehensive community justice strategy to the neighborhood.

Only after this initial phase of assessment is completed will the first meetings of community members and justice officials occur. In this way, the CASES strategy differs from many community justice approaches that *begin* with a big meeting of the stakeholders. If such a meeting occurs too soon in the process, it can lead to unresolvable conflicts or a sense of frustration that impedes collaboration aims. The CASES approach, referred to as "consensus organizing," sees the meeting and planning phases of the community justice project as intermediate stages in the change process, only to be undertaken after the CASES team has established good, one-on-one working relationships with all major stakeholders.

Information Analysis

The community justice orientation to a particular place requires a significant shift in thinking for everyone concerned. Criminal justice officials and residents alike are used to thinking about criminal cases – offenders and crimes – but they find it hard to replace that emphasis with one on "location." The best way to help people develop a "place" frame of reference is through maps.

Like many a picture, a good map is better than 1,000 words. Maps showing offenders in concentration in a neighborhood demonstrate startlingly why merely arresting more residents cannot add much to community safety. A density map of crime can show why a given area deserves more attention in criminal justice investments.

However, the most important maps are "resource" maps. CASES do two types of maps. The first is a map of neighborhood resources, which shows churches, schools, and other services available in the community. More interesting, sometimes, are the maps of criminal justice resources devoted to the area. These maps show, block by block, how much money is currently being spent by criminal justice agencies across the neighborhood. The impressive number of dollars spent on current policy sets the stage for people to think somewhere along the lines, "Surely we can get more impact for these expenditures."

The final type of information is programmatic. After leading the community justice partners through analyzing information about crime and justice, a series of ideas emerge about new ways to deal with criminogenic problems in the neighborhood. These are folded into an understanding of "what works" based on various reviews of existing literature on crime prevention. The aim is to develop programs with a proven track record, not programs that fail.

Resource Leveraging

The final strategy is to find ways to expand resources for new programs. Four sources are tapped: reinvested justice resources, resident contributions, offender contributions, and private partners.

The most significant resources are those already invested in the area by the criminal justice system. In our earlier examples, it is clear that this can amount to millions of dollars, mostly in staffing. Because the bulk of these dollars is assigned to personnel, what this amounts to is reassigning the tasks of existing staff. For example, a probation agency may shift a probation officer or two from a caseload of an after-school project; a sheriff might shift a correctional officer from the cell range to an offender work project in the neighborhood.

Criminal justice agencies are, for obvious reasons, cautious about assigning staff to new tasks. Each staff member was already assigned to a mandated service, and most agencies feel hard-pressed to meet existing commitments, much less take on new ones. This is where resident and offender resources contribution can play a role. Resident volunteers can take responsibilities that make it possible to free staff for new assignments, and offender labor can help pay for the costs of those reassignments. One can imagine, for example, a youth center staffed by criminal justice professionals but has a heavy commitment of citizen volunteers who help round out the supervision. Several youth who might attend such a center are already on probation, thus making their "reports" to the probation officer with the caseload less critical. Offenders might perform some of the routine maintenance tasks to keep the center clean and open.

Even though it is possible to leverage these existing resources, it is necessary to have unencumbered dollars available for program start-ups and to support the development and organization of activities in the neighborhood. Thus, the final source of resources is a private partner who contributes financially to the innovative programming – typically a nonprofit organization or otherwise philanthropic venture. Identifying a financial partner is a crucial aspect of the CASES approach to community partnerships.

How Does Community Justice Look in the Long Term?

CASES helps the community establish an intermediary function to support community justice – a localized community justice center. The center has three capacities: citizen organizing, program development, and information analysis. The continuing function of the center is to "grow" community justice initiatives. They typically begin with a single-interest program, such as an after-school project, that will generate strong citizen support and good results for criminal justice and can be easily implemented. From these successful experiences, the center branches out to other problems based on an assessment of the information about the community and effective working relationships with the community and criminal justice partner.

Thus, what CASES is trying to build is a long-term capacity for community justice in the form of a community justice center that operates in the neighborhood and can generate ideas about reinvesting justice resources in new ways that promote community safety, working with citizens and justice officials to build confidence in those programs, and helping residents become more in control of the safety of the places where they live.

Appendix B

Focused Deterrence

Over the past ten years, the concept of Focused Deterrence has grown in popularity as a philosophy that can effectively address violent crime, especially violent crime that occurs in major urban areas. The philosophy is usually associated with law enforcement since they play a prominent role in implementing and managing the focused deterrence process. Focused deterrence has its roots in the Boston Gun Project, which eventually became Operation Ceasefire. Operation Ceasefire was seen as being very successful because it resulted in a 63% reduction in youth homicides and a 50% reduction overall (Abt, 2019). As mentioned in Chapter 3, a successful focused deterrence program includes law enforcement, courts, corrections, community members, nonprofits, and the private sector. Abt (2019) writes that to effectively address the issue of violent crime, action should be evidence-informed, meaning informed by the best evidence and data currently available, and community-informed, meaning voice is given to those most impacted by urban violence and including them in the decision-making process for addressing it. He also identifies three basic fundamentals to guide a focused deterrence program: focus, balance, and fairness.

The Rand Corporation provides a good overview of the philosophy and mechanics of focused deterrence. They describe it as a problem-solving strategy for intervening with high-risk groups and individuals to prevent future criminal behavior, especially violent behavior. The focused deterrence process consists of five steps that should be followed to ensure that the goal of crime prevention is achieved. The five steps are:

1 Identify those at risk of being involved with violence.
   - This is usually best done by police and local community members.
   - Selection of the individuals should be based on clear criteria that identify why the individuals might pose a threat to the community.
2 Hold an intervention meeting.
   - In the meeting, individuals are informed why they have been selected and what that means for them.
   - Meeting topics can include:
     - Review of the individuals' histories to explain why the intervention is occurring.
     - Providing a list of charges faced and other consequences if violence does not stop.
     - What the evidence is that authorities have to convict them.
     - Some examples of what happened to prior individuals who chose to continue violence.
     - A discussion among friends, family, and community members about the effects the violence is having on them.

- The consequences the individual will receive if the violence does not stop.
- A discussion of services and support that the individuals will receive if they choose to change.

3 Provide services to those who want to change
- Some examples of this might be:
  - Counseling
  - Substance abuse treatment
  - Housing
  - Education
  - Employment training and placement.
  - Help in obtaining identification cards (including state ID cards, driver's licenses, or social security cards).
  - Community corrections (if applicable).
  - Veterans Affairs benefits for those who are veterans.

4 Have community members provide ongoing support
- Ongoing support and mentoring of at-risk individuals from the community beyond the influence of law enforcement and social services.
  - Family and friends
  - Community organizations (churches, nonprofits, and schools)
  - Other criminally involved individuals or syndicate members who want to avoid trouble and can pressure their high-risk peers to desist from violence

5 Enhance enforcement for persons or groups that persist in crime.
- The actions taken are intended to sanction the offenders quickly with certainty and proportionality.
  - Airing unwanted publicity in the media
  - Prioritizing prosecution of the violent offender
  - Subjecting offenders to stricter pre-trial sanctions
  - Subjecting offenders to stricter sentencing
- Enhanced enforcements
  - Prioritizing services of any outstanding warrants to group members.
  - Making other law enforcement contacts with groups on a regular basis
  - Disrupting and sanctioning the group for committing low-level crimes
  - Prioritizing the collection of law enforcement intelligence against the group to gain evidence of additional crimes for prosecution
- The major purpose of the sanctions is future deterrence

Braga et al. (2018) conducted a comprehensive review of 24 sites using focused deterrence and found noteworthy crime declines. While they caution that more rigorous and consistent evaluations need to be undertaken in the analysis of these types of programs, the evidence does show that the focused deterrence approach is effective in crime reduction.

References

Abt, T. (2019). *Bleeding out*. Basic Books.
Braga, A., Weisburd, D., & Turchan, B. (2018). Focused deterrence strategies and crime control. *Criminology & Public Policy*, 17(1), 205–250.
Rand Corporation. (n.d.). *Focused deterrence*. Retrieved 3/9/2024 from www.rand.org/pubs/tools/TL261/better-policing-toolkit/all-strategies/focused-deterrence/in-depth.html

Index

Note: **Bold** page numbers refer to tables and *italic* page numbers refer to figures.

Abdel-Salam, S. 140
aboriginal peoples 98
accountability 3, 36, 101, 109, 120–121, 141, 143–144
actions, creation of 8
adaptive leadership 163–164; and community justice 164–165; techniques 165
adding value 151–152
adjudication: community-oriented 92–95; of complaints 83–84; flexibility in 177
African Americans 23–24, 28, 48, 52, 137, 161
age 47
Aim4Peace (A4P) Violence Prevention Program 136
Albany, Georgia Mental Health Court 102–104
Alinsky, Saul 28, 158
alternative dispute resolution (ADR) 98, 100
American Addiction Centers 107
American Prosecutors Research Institute (APRI) 93–94
American Psychiatric Association 101
Andrews, D.A. 141–142
Arbinger Institute 71–72
arbitration 64, 98
Arnold, K. 95
arrests 9, 12–13, 15, 50, 61–62, 90, 100–103, 145
assessment 182–183
Association of Chief Police Officers 67
Association of Community Organizations for Reform Now (ACORN) 159
authentic leadership 163
authority 49–51; hierarchical 35

Back of the Yards Project 28, 158
Barajas, E. 3
Barnum, J.D. 61
Bayley, D.H. 176
Bentham, J. 6

blaming 35
Bordin, E.S. 141
Boston 32, 157, 185
Boston Gun Project 185
Bowman, J. 94–95
Braga 186
Braithwaite, J. 66
Bratton, W. 27
broken windows theory 27, 41; policing strategies 61–62
Brooklyn: community policing 56; crime rate 25, 138; domestic violence courts 100–101
Brown, M. 75

California Department of Corrections and Rehabilitation (CDCR) 139
Canon law 174
Caplan, J.M. 61
Carey, S.M. 106
caseload pressure 85–86
Center for Alternative Sentencing and Employment Services (CASES): approach to community partnerships 184; designs community 181; model 182; strategy 183; types of maps 183
Center for Conflict Resolution (CCR) 143–144
Center for Court Innovation 91
Center for Justice Innovation (CCI) 91–92
Chicago 28–29, 57, 158
chronic social problems 11
circle sentencing 98
citizen partnerships 182
civil legal tradition 174–175
Clamp, K. 66–67
Clarke, R.V. 60
classical criminology 6, 13, 164–165, 178
Clear, T.R. 2–3, 181
cloud problems 7, 164
Coaching Model for Change (CMC) 129

codification 174–175
Coles, C. 61
collaboration 2, 41, 100, 101, 114, 117, 143, 156, 159, 163, 169
collective efficacy 28–29, 41, 117, 154, 158
collectivism 175
Colwell, J.L. 72
common legal tradition 173
communitarianism 19, 52
community 21–23, 81–82, 151: building 5, 57; capacity 152; community life 24–33; compensation to 178; comprehensive community change (CCC) 36–38; corrections 126, 144–145; definition of 3; groups 132; intermediary model 153, 159–160; involvement 4; life, enhancement of 2; mediation centers 135–136; members 2, 9; mobilization model 153, 158–159; reparative boards 97; safety 3; well-being 2; *see also* neighborhoods
Community Alternative with Restorative and Educational Services (CARES) 121–122
community-based restorative program 145
community courts 88–90; contemporary community court movement 90–92; historical look at 89–90; judiciary 95; Midtown 90–92
community justice 3, 12, 14–16; adoption of 178; authority 3; characteristics 4–5; and the community 17–41; concept of 2; conceptual foundations 170; copycat version of 171; and correction 113–148; and courts 81–109; critics of 166; definition of 1–2; development of 2; elements of 2–5; form of 184; framework 122–124; fundamental principles of 2–3; future of 151–171; implementation of 178; information analysis 183–184; initiatives 14, 167, 169, 182, 184; international corrections and 177–178; international dimensions of 173; international policing and 176; issues in 165–169; leadership in 162–165; in long term 184; long-term capacity for 184; method, principles and purpose 181–184; multicultural 109; orientation 183; partnership development 182–183; and policing 44–77; principles of 176, 181; probation and parole 126–127; purpose of 181; resource leveraging 183–184; Shifting the Burden 13; as strategy 15, 163, 181–182; supervision 127; within traditional criminal justice functions 40–41; values of 125–126; varieties 151
community-oriented defender (COD) network 94
community-oriented policing services (COPS) 54, 64, 64–65, 169
community-oriented strategies 82
community patrol officers (CPOs) 56
community policing 3, 5, 39–40, 54–64, 73, 154; Brooklyn 56; community-building strategies 57–59; and community justice 64–66; community relations rationale 46–57; criminal justice rationale 54–56; dual-track rationale 45–46; history of 44–45; levels of 73–74; movement 44; National Center for 56–57; problem-oriented strategies 59–61; SARA method 59
complaints 34–35; and courts 83–84; and police 67–68
complex systems, operation of 9
comprehensive interactive management strategy 60
CompStat process 60–61
computerized information systems 114–115
Confucianism 174–175
connective leadership 163
Connell, N.M. 59
constitutional right 82, 85–86
contemporary policing 47
control 123; of offenders 116, 123; police 50–52, 64; social 3, 19, 28–29
Cooper, C. 64–65
core correctional practices (CCP) 129, 141
Cornish, D. 60
corporal punishment 178
correctional/corrections 40–41, 81, 113–148, 168, 178; institutions, partnerships 118–119; leaders 115; pillars 114–117; work, stages of 115
correctional officers (COs) 114, 124, 129, 140, 148
corrections workers (CW) 114–116, 123, 127–128; internal commitment 142–143; well-being and job satisfaction of 142
courts 81–109, 168, 178; caseload pressure 85; Center for Court Innovation 91; community courts *see* community courts; community-oriented 92–98, 95–98; courtroom 85; decision-making, stages 86; defender services 94–95; functions 82–85; negotiated settlements 86; prosecution 92–94; re-entry 106–107; sentencing and sanctions 84–85, 95–96; for specialized communities 98–109; victims 84–85, 87–88
Crank, J. 51–52
crime: concentration 25; fear of 55, 118; high-impact areas 14–15, 18–19, 26; hot spots 25, 60; mapping 25–26, 61; problem of 2
crime prevention 5, 45, 57, 152, 165–166; goal of 185–186; hardware 54–55; involvement model 153, 154–156; partnership model 153, 156–158; situational 60

Crime Prevention through Environmental Design (CPTED) 58
criminal: accusations 82; behavior 2, 8, 185; cases 81–82
criminal courts, functions of 82–83; rights and justice issues 83, **83**
criminal justice 1, 3, 5, 8–9, 14–15, 15–16, 165; agencies 3, 182–183; approaches 14; branches of 177; changes 151, 168; community-oriented strategies 34–36; description of 2; elements of 4–5; fundamental change in 169; operation of 8; philosophies 6; professionals 184; rationale for community policing 54–56; surface changes in 168–169; system 183; value of 8
criminogenic problems 183
cultural deviation 52–53
customary laws 173

Dean, R. 102
decentralized organizations 176
dependency 13
deterrence: focused 67; theory 6
disadvantage 17–18, 24, 48, 168
disorder, public 26–27, 61–62
domestic violence courts 100–101
dominion, police 49–52
Dowden, C. 141–142
drug: courts 99–100; dealing 60; treatment 99, 158
DUI Courts 107–109
Dykstra, G. 90

Eastern Asian legal tradition 174–175
Eck, J. 8
economic development 31, 33, 37–38, 40, 157–158, 161, 178
Emerson, B. 70
empowerment 37–38
equality 89, 96, 166
equal justice 82, 89
equity 173
ethical leadership 163
ethnic: diversity 19, 23; heterogeneity 28; integration 23
evaluation 38–40, 169–170
evolutionary biology 163
exchange, reality of 86
Executive Office of Public Safety and Security (EOPSS) 119

facilitation 135, 143
families: control 29; group conferencing 97; Rhode Island 88; structure 11
fa, principle of Confucianism 175
far-right populism 178

Fatwa (legal opinion) 175
feedback: loop, definition of 10; processes 10
feudal system 173
financial partners 182, 184
Fixes That Backfire and Shifting the Burden 13–14
flexibility 35, 65, 86, 91, 175, 177
Floyd, G. 48
focused deterrence 67, 185–186; concept of 185; philosophy and mechanics of 185
foot patrol 55–56, 59
forces category 176
funding 29, 38, 101, 156, 159–160, 169, 178

Gallup poll 2022 47
Gase, L.N. 105
gender-based leadership 163
ghettos 23
goals 18, 152, 169
Goldstein, H. 59, 62, 154
Gordon, A. 146
Goss, S. 102–103, 102–104
Gottlieb, A. 95
Gover, A. 100
Grand Prairie, Texas 104
Gray, K.B. 93–94
Greene, J.R. 73
gun crime 30–31

Haas, S.M. 141
hadiths 174
Hamer, E. 95
Harlem Community Justice Center 91–92
harm, preventing 2
Harpold, J.A. 57–59, 58–59
Harron, A. 108
health care 2, 17, 36, 38, 41, 142, 159
hedonism 6
Heifetz, R.A. 163–164
helplessness 13
Herman, S. 97
high-impact crime areas 14–15, 18–19, 26
Hispanic 23, 52, 102, 137
Holsinger, A.M. 113, 128
homelessness 11–12, 134
homicide 92, 136, 185
hospitals 1, 46, 134, 136
hot spots 25–26, 60
Houses of Healing Program (HOH) 138–140
housing 17, 23, 26, 31, 37–39, 102, 104, 128, 132, 156, 159
Houston 55
hunkering down 19
Hurricane Katrina 22
Huth, C. 72

ijma 174
ijtihad (independent reasoning) 175
immigrants 19, 23, 32–33
impartiality 81, 95, 166–167
incapacitation 96, 177
incarceration 15, 132–133, 137–138, 168; rates of 138; women 145–146
Indiana 89
individuals 19–20, 167; communities 176; rights 108–109
informality 85–87
informal social controls 3–4, 14–15, 19, 26–29, 117, 126, 132–133
information 57, 60; analysis 28, 183–184; mapping 25–26, 60; programmatic 183
institutional/institutionalization 35, 52–53, 113–114, 116–118, 123
interconnectedness 8–9
international: court operations 176–177; policing 176–177
international settings, community justice in 178–179; civil legal tradition 174; common legal tradition 173; cultural components of legal traditions 175–176; description of 173; Eastern Asian legal tradition 174–175; Islamic legal tradition 174
investigation technologies 54–55
Islamic legal tradition 174
isolation 19, 23, 118, 121, 138–139, 157, 170
Ivanhoe Neighborhood 29–31

jail *see* prison
Jean's Relational Model 147
Johnson, B. 68–70
Jones, K. 120
judges 34, 39, 50, 81, 85, 89, 95, 105, 176–177
jury trials 85–86
justice 63, 84, 106; parallel 97; social 17–20; traditional 40–41; *see also* community justice; criminal justice, restorative/restoration, justice
juvenile delinquents 28, 99

Kajstura, A. 145
Kansas City: Office of Community Complaints 67–68; Preventive Patrol Study 55; Problem-Oriented Policing 30
Karmen, A. 98
Karp, D. 2–3
Kauffman Foundation 31
Kavanaugh, J.M. 108
Keith, P. 76
Kelling, G.L. 61
Kennedy, L.W. 61
Ku'ikahi Mediation Center 135
Kurki, L. 5

larcenies 7–8
law enforcement 2, 12, 27, 35, 44–45, 49, 58–59, 74, 113, 133, 165, 170; community 3; officers 12–13; proponents 2
Lawson, S.G. 106
leadership: adaptive 163–164; authentic 163; in community justice 162–165; connective 163; definition of 162–163; ethical 163; formal and informal 162–163; gender-based 163; servant 163; skill-based 163; spiritual 163; study of 165
legal: personality 175; profession 176–177; rights 175; traditions 175–176, 179
Lewis, K. 70
Lexington County domestic violence court 100
life chances 22, 24
Lionheart Foundation 139
li, principle of Confucianism 175
litigation 82
local police agencies 176
Lofty, M. 143
Lovins, B.K. 129
Lucas, Q. 137

maps/mapping 25–26, 60–61, 183
Martinson, R. 115
Massachusetts Parole Board 119
Massachusetts Parole Preparation Partnership (MPPP) 118
McKay, H.D. 28
McLeod, C. 65
Meadows, D. 8–10
mediation 67–68, 97–98
mental health courts 101–104
Methods of Alternative Dispute Resolution 98
Midtown Community Court, NYC 90–92
migrants 23
Mika, H. 4
Miller, J.B. 147
Miller, P.G. 108
Minneapolis Police Department 48
minority/minorities 167; groups 166; owned businesses 15–16
Missouri 88; Department of Corrections (DOC) 114; Police Department 29–31, 67–68
mobility 28
mobilization, community 153, 158–159
Moore, M. 57
morality 19–20
multicultural community justice 109
municipal police agency 176

National Center for Community Policing 56–57
National Center for Victims of Crime 97
National Crime Victimization Survey 100
Neighborhood Defender Service, Harlem 91–92

Neighborhood Opportunity Network (NeON) Initiative 129–131
neighborhoods 3, 14–15, 21–28, 182; activities in 184; comprehensive community change 36; and corrections 117–118; defenders 94; effect on community life 24–33; least safe 14–15, 158, 158–159, 165–166; living conditions in 3; maps 183; Maricopa County probation centers renters 26; organization strategies 158; resources 183; social relationships 29; types 58
Neighborhood Watch 2, 57–58, 158
Nelson A. Rockefeller Center for Public Policy 99–100
neoclassical theories 6–8
networks, social 18, 20, 29, 117
New Orleans 22, 161
New York City 27–28, 30; Brooklyn *see* Brooklyn; Model of Probation 129–130; State Unified Court System 91–92
New Zealand Model 66
Nicholl, C. 3
non-criminal justice agencies 118
non-custodial sanctions 178
non-jail crisis response 133–134
nonprofit organizations 38, 40, 67, 130, 133, 135, 176, 178, 184
Northouse, P.G. 162–163
North Shore Community Development Coalition (NSCDC) 32–33

Obama, B. 74
offenders: hunkering down 19; management 114–115, 120, 122–123; re-entry *see* prison; resources contribution 183–184; surveillance 116
Office of Community Complaints for the Kansas City 67–68
Office of Community Oriented Policing (COPS Office) 169
Office of Justice Programs initiative 106
Officer Program 56; CompStat 60–61; drug-treatment center 158; Harlem Neighborhood Defender Service 91–92; Midtown Community Court 90–92; release from prison 132; zero-tolerance 62
O'Hara, P. 52–53
Omaha 360 project 160–161
Omaha Empowerment Network 160–161
Operation Ceasefire 185
organizations, criminal justice 36, 41, 169; partnerships 118–119; *see also* corrections; courts; police
Ostrom, B.J. 94–95
outward mindset 71–77
oversight failure 52–53

"pain-pleasure" principle 13
PANDA model 63–64
parallel justice 97
parole: description of 124–125; relationship building in 125–127; transformative power of relationships in 127–129; *see also* prison
partnerings 182; with community members 176
partnerships 3, 12, 15, 18, 170, 182–183, 184; correctional 118; criminal justice organizations 118–119; development 182–183; model of crime prevention 153, 156–158; relationships and 114; Ten Points Coalition 157
Paternoster, R. 100
Patterson, C. 66–67
penal sanction 84, 87
penalties 7, 62, 84–86, 96–97, 177; *see also* punishment; sanctioning/sanctions
perpetrator displacement 8
personal information 177
persons who are incarcerated (PWAI) 142
Phoenix, Arizona 158
physical security modifications 8
physical systems 6–7
Piza, E.L. 61
place 20–21, 150–151, 166; improvement 37; and life chances 23–24; and public safety 25–28; *see also* neighborhoods
Plumb 108
Point neighborhood in Salem, Massachusetts 32–33
polarity management 68–71, 71
police 44–45, 81, 168; agency 7; Brooklyn 25, 56; culture 50–51, 50–52; essential services 46–47; as function of legal system 49; as function of power in society 49–54; Missouri 29–31, 67–68; in partnerships 118–119; performance 55; as symbol of modern culture 48; training 54, 64
Police Executive Research Forum (PERF) 39–40, 57
Police Task Force 75–77
policing 44–77, 178; community policing *see* community policing; hot spots 25–26; Problem-Oriented 30, 59, 154–155; traditional model 54
political empowerment 37
Popper, K. 6–7, 11
Portland 92–93
positive social elements 140
post-traumatic stress disorder (PTSD) 107
poverty 11, 28–29
power 49–54; empowerment 37; *see also* authority; control; dominion
President's Commission on Law Enforcement 55

prison 106, 132–133, 132–137, 168; community-based alternatives to 132–137; community justice and 137–138; re-entry courts 106–107; re-entry/parole/release from 119–120, 132, 168; relationship building in 140–143; women in 145–147
private: disputes 173; law 175; partners 183; prosecution 177; sector 117, 156–157, 176, 178
probation 105–106, 113–114, 124–129; partnerships, officers 118–119; Phoenix 158
problem-based learning (PBL) 54
problem-oriented policing 3, 30, 59, 154–155, 155
problem solving 3, 5, 35–36, 40, 109, 120–121, 123, 182
procedural law 175
property crime prevention 6
property-oriented crimes 98
Prophet Muhammad 174
prosecution of cases 177
prosecutors 88; community 93; neighborhood-based 95
public: defenders 85, 94–95, 118; health-based violence prevention 136–137; order violations 62, 133
public safety 2–3, 8, 14, 35–36, 152–153, 154–155, 157–159, 160–162, 165–166; co-production of 3; and courts' sentencing 84–85; creating 5; functions 118; and place 25–28; strategies 159–160
punishment 6, 17, 83, 87, 96, 116–117, 123, 177
Punto Urban Art Museum (PUAM) 33
Putnam, R. 18–19

qiyas 174
quality of life 1–3, 15, 24, 60, 73, 94, 118, 124, 152, 161, 167

race issues 47; ethnic diversity 19, 23; ethnic heterogeneity 28; ethnic integration 23
Ramsey, C. 75
Rand Corporation 185
Ratcliffe, J. 63
rational choice theory 6
rational thinking 7
recidivism 101–102, 105–106, 108, 120–121, 128
reciprocity 18–19
reconciliation 98, 135
Red Hook Community Justice Center 91–92
Red Hook Youth Court 106
re-entry courts 106–107, 106–107
rehabilitation 84, 96, 98, 115–116; approaches 177; programs 138–140
Reichel, P.L. 173–178

reintegration 123–124, 160
reinvestment: justice resources 183; strategies 167–168
relationships 8–9, 11; building 128; changing 9
reparation 95, 119–120
Reparative Justice Boards 155
residents: contributions 183; volunteers 183–184
resources 168; leveraging 183–184; source of 184
restitution 127, 132–133
restorative/restoration 97, 121, 132–133, 144–145; cautions 66–67; community 145; justice 5, 67, 97–98, 122; policing 65–67, 176
retribution 177
Ricciardelli, R. 142
rights 82–83, **83**, 89, 108, 167
risk 115, 123
risk terrain modeling (RTM) 61
Rohr, R. 69
Roman law 174

safety *see* public safety
Safir, H. 27–28
Sampson, R. 29
sanctioning/sanctions 84–85, 106–108; community–oriented 95–98; drug treatment 99; models 95–96; process 178
San Diego 55
SARA (Scan, Analyze, Respond, Assess) method 59, 63–64
Sawyer, W. 145
self-governance 178
Senge, P. 13
sense/sensemaking 69; development and use of 70; of right and wrong 7; of stock change rates 9
sentencing 84–87, 94, 96, 98, 100, 113, 128, 138
servant leadership 163
service sector 38
Shaw, Clifford 28
Sherman, Lawrence 25, 30
Shifting the Burden 12–14, 165
Shrunk, Michael 74
Skogan, W. 57
Smith, J. 141
social: capital 18–19, 20, 166; controls 13–14, 19, 29; disorganization theory 28; issues 11; justice 17–20, 24; norms 177; services 36, 118, 133, 155, 157–158, 161
Social Impact Bond Initiative (SIB) 134
socialization 175
Social Sciences at Dartmouth University 99–100
Sparrow, M. 63–64
spiritual leadership 163

stakeholders 11, 39, 66–67, 95–96, 114, 117, 135, 155, 164, 169, 183
standards of behavior 20
state prosecutors 85, 88
Still, W. 126
stocks 9; change rates 9; collection of 10
Stroh, P. 11–12, 14
structural failure 52–53
substance abuse disorders (SUDs) 107
substantive law 174–175
surveillance 6, 60, 116, 122–123, 125, 147
systems thinking 8, 10; approaches 11; archetypes in 12–14; elements of 9–12

technological innovations 45
teen courts 104–106
Ten Points Coalition 157
territoriality 51–52
Thames Valley approach 66
therapeutic alliance 141–142
Therapeutic Communities (TCs) 138–141
Thielo, A.J. 109
Third Way 69–70
Thomson, Douglas 96
Thurman, Q. 39
traditional: corrections 114, 116, 147–148; criminal justice 170
Transition Center of Kansas City (TCKC) 143–144
transition planning 132
Treatment Alternatives to Street Crime (TASC) 99
treatment programs 116–118, 123, 138; drug 99, 158; strategies of 123
Trojanowicz, R. 56–57
Trump, D. 74, 76

Urban Institute 134
urban violence 185
U.S. Department of Justice Working Group 2–3

vandalism 105–107
Veterans Administration (VA) 107
veterans courts 107, 122
victims 84, 87–88, 96–97, 132–133, 144–145, 166; advocates for 88, 100; and communities 120; compensation to 178; of crime 87–88, 121; domestic violence 100–101; families 88; National Center for Victims of Crime 97; National Crime Victimization Survey 100; offender mediation 97; popular image o 87–88; rehabilitation and treatment 100; restitution to 132–133; role of 96–97; studies of 96
violence, addressing cycles of 135
violent crime 7, 13, 185
Von Hirsch, A. 35

Wagga Wagga Model 66
Weed and Seed program 29–30
well-being, community 2, 113
Whatcom County Teen Court Program 105
Wilson, J.Q. 27
Wilson, W. 23
women: incarcerated 145–146; in prison 145–147
wrongdoing 177

YouGov America, Inc. 109
youth courts 91–92, 105–106

Zahnd, E. 121–122
Zehr, H. 4, 121, 144
zero-tolerance 62, 151

9781032488578